THE BIG 50
CHICAGO BLACKHAWKS

The Men and Moments That Made the Chicago Blackhawks

Jay Zawaski

Library of Congress Cataloging-in-Publication Data

Names: Zawaski, Jay, author.
Title: The big 50 : Chicago Blackhawks : the men and moments that made the Chicago Blackhawks / Jay Zawaski.
Other titles: Big fifty
Description: Chicago, Illinois : Triumph Books LLC, [2020] | Includes bibliographical references. | Summary: "Exploring the living history of the team, this dynamic and comprehensive book brings to life the iconic franchise's remarkable story, including greats like Toews, Kane, Mikita, Chelios, and more"— Provided by publisher.
Identifiers: LCCN 2020032936 (print) | LCCN 2020032937 (ebook) | ISBN 9781629377728 (paperback) | ISBN 9781641255387 (epub) | ISBN 9781641255394 (kindle edition) | ISBN 9781641255400 (pdf)
Subjects: LCSH: Chicago Blackhawks (Hockey team)—History.
Classification: LCC GV848.C48 Z39 2020 (print) | LCC GV848.C48 (ebook) | DDC 796.962/640977311—dc23
LC record available at https://lccn.loc.gov/2020032936
LC ebook record available at https://lccn.loc.gov/2020032937

This book is available in quantity at special discounts for your group or organization. For further information, contact:

Triumph Books LLC
814 North Franklin Street
Chicago, Illinois 60610
(312) 337-0747
www.triumphbooks.com

Printed in U.S.A.
ISBN: 978-1-62937-772-8

Design by Andy Hansen

In memory of Anne Lorayne Zawaski

This book would not be possible without the support of my wife, Hope, and daughter, Addie, whose patience, support, and encouragement throughout the process pushed me across the finish line and helped me believe I could accomplish something I never imagined possible.

To my dad…my love of hockey wouldn't be what it is without him taking me to Blackhawks game after Blackhawks game after late nights on his job. I know the last thing he wanted to do was drive back downtown after a long day, but I always appreciated it, even though I may not have said it out loud.

And to my mom…who has always been my number one fan.

[Contents]

[Foreword]

I started playing hockey when I was five or six years old. My parents immigrated to Mimico, Ontario, a suburb of Toronto, from Scotland. My dad didn't know anything about hockey, but my uncle loved the game, so my older brother started to play. I wanted in. I got my first pair of skates and that was the end. I was hooked.

It wasn't until my second year with the London Knights of the Ontario Hockey League that I had a suspicion I might be NHL-worthy. My first season in the OHL wasn't great; I only had 17 points. After that, I thought I might have to find another job, but the next year (2003–04), I put up some big points and Chicago drafted me 32nd overall.

I was ecstatic. Yes, the Hawks weren't doing too well, but teams that picked ahead of them in that draft were older, winning teams. I knew in Chicago I'd get an opportunity to play. I was also happy going to an Original Six team. As a fan of the Maple Leafs growing up, that was a dream. Seeing those Hawks jerseys when they'd come to town was always cool too.

My first full season with the Hawks was in 2007–08. I was excited to get to play in the NHL and really be up there. We had Tazer, Kaner, Marty Havlat—we knew that something was around the corner. We knew we were getting better. It was a turning point. After that season, we knew we were going to be a contender soon.

The next season, we made the playoffs and beat the Calgary Flames in the first round. Then we squared off with the Vancouver Canucks in the semifinal. I always got up for these games. I hated them. They hated us. Later, I got to play with former Canucks defenseman Shane O'Brien in Florida and we became good buddies, but we used to chat on the plane and talk about those games. He'd say, "We hated you guys," and I'd say, "We hated you too!" It was always a blast playing against Vancouver. In 2009, we beat them in six games, advancing to the conference final against Detroit, a series we lost in five games.

The Wings were a great team that year. I remember checking against Pavel Datsyuk and Henrik Zetterberg. I learned a lot from playing against those guys and that team. That was the year that we knew we were just missing one piece.

Who comes in that summer but Marian Hossa? He was the missing piece and we won the 2010 Stanley Cup.

While I'll obviously never forget that first Stanley Cup win, I scored the Cup-winning goal in Game 6 in 2013. It was unbelievable. It was one of the best moments in my life. Every kid dreams of scoring that goal. I had that chance, and I got to do it for Chicago.

If there's one thing I miss about playing, it's being around the Chicago fans. It was always fun hearing stories about how fans watched us win, be it on TV or at the bar or at the United Center. It's a great memory.

I didn't know much about Chicago when I got drafted. I didn't know much about the Blackhawks. When I got there, I fell in love. To win two Cups as a Blackhawk, to do it for Chicago fans, I'm so grateful for what they did for us and for me. The fans were always great to me. It was special to play in front of Chicago fans. They're the best in the league.

Dave Bolland played 10 seasons in the NHL, including seven as a Chicago Blackhawk. He is a two-time Stanley Cup champion and scored the winning goal against the Boston Bruins in 2013.

THE BIG 50
CHICAGO BLACKHAWKS

1

A KINDER, GENTLER STAN

Stan Mikita is the best all-around player in Blackhawks history. He spent his entire 22-year NHL career in Chicago. He won the Calder Trophy as the league's best rookie. He was a member of the 1961 Stanley Cup championship team. He was named an All-Star nine times. He won the Art Ross Trophy, awarded to the league's top scorer, four times. He won the Hart Memorial Trophy, presented to the NHL's most valuable player, twice. Then there's the Lady Byng.

The Lady Byng Memorial Trophy is the award given to the "player adjudged to have exhibited the best type of sportsmanship and gentlemanly conduct combined with a high standard of playing ability." Recent winners like Detroit's Pavel Datsyuk, Tampa Bay's Martin St. Louis, and former Blackhawk Brian Campbell exemplified the award throughout their careers. Mikita won the trophy twice, but there was a period where he would have been considered one of the least likely players to win the honor.

In his first six NHL seasons, Mikita picked up 679 penalty minutes, including 119 in his first full year. "I was a hellion as a rookie," Mikita recalled. Mikita, who stood only 5-foot-9, would often get run by the opposition. "I didn't take kindly to that kind of treatment. I think Glenn Hall was the guy who took me aside early in that season and suggested that I didn't have to get back at guys five minutes after they've beaten the crap out of me."

Hall's message didn't exactly get through to the Blackhawks legend. Instead, it was a comment from his daughter that transformed Mikita from an irritant into a model citizen.

Mikita was playing in New York against the Rangers in 1965. His young daughter Meg was watching her father play on television. During the game, Mikita committed another penalty.

"Why does Daddy always sit by himself?" Meg asked her mother, Jill. "Why doesn't he sit with his friends like Uncle Kenny [Wharram] and Uncle Bobby [Hull]?"

When Mikita returned home, Meg asked him a similar question.

"When that guy with the stripes on his shirt blew his whistle, why did you have to skate all the way on the other side of your friends to sit alone? Why did you do that, Daddy? Didn't you like those players?"

Mikita, forced to explain, responded, "Well, honey, that meant Daddy did something bad and he had to go sit out for two minutes."

"Her reaction made me stop and think," Mikita said. "If our baby daughter sees this and feels something is wrong, why can't I?"

From that day forward, Mikita made a concerted effort to stop yapping at referees and to avoid taking lazy penalties. High-sticks, slashes, spears, trips, and hooks all fell under the "lazy" category for Mikita.

"I looked at my statistics and I jotted down the two-minute penalties and what they were for," Mikita explained. "The majority were what I call lazy penalties—hooking, holding, tripping. With an extra stride or two, I could have caught the guy and done it cleanly. Then I looked at the misconducts. One year, I must have had five or more. That's 50 minutes right there. So, I said, 'Keep your mouth shut. Don't change your style of play but don't take those lazy penalties and let's see what happens.' The next season, in the first 20 games, I only had one penalty. It was unbelievable."

The changes worked for Mikita. After taking those 679 penalty minutes in his first six seasons, he only picked up 581 more over the next 15 campaigns. But he can't give all the credit to his daughter. Jill's influence set Mikita straight as well. In those days, a 10-minute misconduct would cost the player $25, and a game misconduct was $100. Those fines were automatically removed from the players' checks.

"I was throwing away a lot of cash, often by trying to referee a game in addition to playing it," Mikita said.

The next two seasons, 1966–67 and 1967–68, Mikita was whistled for just 26 combined penalty minutes. He won the Lady Byng Trophy both of those years. "I guarantee you, if you had placed a wager during my first few seasons in the NHL that I would someday be hailed for sportsmanship and gentlemanly conduct, you would have gotten some really long odds," he said.

Mikita's overnight transformation came as a surprise to many around the league, including some of the referees he used to abuse. "John Ashley, a referee you could talk to, even came up to me one night and felt my forehead as if to take my temperature," he said.

If Mikita needed any proof that changing his style was a good idea, he posted a career-high 97 points in 1966–67. Ninety-seven points and just 12 penalty minutes; apparently having one of the all-time greats on the ice instead of in the penalty box is a sound strategy. Mikita never exceeded 85 points in penalties at any point in his career after the change.

"I had become a smarter player and also felt a greater sense of responsibility, having married Jill and started a family," he said.

On August 7, 2018, Mikita passed away at the age of 78, surrounded by his family. In a statement, Blackhawks chairman Rocky Wirtz said, "There are no words to describe our sadness over Stan's passing. He meant so much to the Chicago Blackhawks, to the game of hockey, and to all of Chicago. He left an imprint that will forever be etched in the hearts of fans—past, present, and future. Stan made everyone he touched a better person. My wife Marilyn and I, joined by the entire Wirtz family, extend our prayers and thoughts to Jill and the Mikita family. 'Stosh' will be deeply missed, but never, ever forgotten."

2

88 ENDS 49

On June 22, 2007, the day of the NHL's annual entry draft, the Blackhawks had missed the playoffs for eight of the nine previous seasons. But that was the day everything changed for the Blackhawks. With the number one overall pick, the Hawks selected London Knights star Patrick Kane.

The Blackhawks knew they were getting a scorer when they selected Kane. He was coming off a season in which he scored 145 points in 58 games with London. There was no doubt he had the ability to put pucks in nets, but even the Hawks could not have been certain they'd drafted one of the best players in the history of the Original Six franchise.

As of Kane's 31st birthday, he's ranked fourth on the Blackhawks' all-time scoring list, behind only Bobby Hull, Stan Mikita, and Denis Savard. He has won three Stanley Cups and one Conn Smythe Trophy as playoff MVP. He was the first American-born player to win the Art Ross Trophy as the league's leading scorer and has also won a Hart Memorial Trophy as league MVP.

But in a career full of dazzling moments, series-ending hat tricks, and highlight-reel goals, Kane's most memorable goal may have been his most bizarre.

During the 2010 Stanley Cup Final, the Blackhawks held a 3–2 series lead over the Eastern Conference champion Philadelphia Flyers. The teams were locked in a 3–3 tie just over five minutes into overtime of Game 6. Defenseman Brian Campbell had the puck at the left point, then dished the puck to Kane along the left-wing boards. There, he was met by Flyers defenseman (and future Blackhawk) Kimmo Timonen.

Kane head-faked his way past Timonen and headed toward the net. "He had the puck at the hashmarks," Timonen recalls. Kane shot from a deep angle and then began celebrating. The goal light never went on. The referee never signaled goal. Confusion reigned. There

BABY STANLEY

The story of the Zawaski family begins in 2001.

I met my future wife, Hope, at my best friend Jill's college graduation party. Jill and I graduated from Lewis University in Romeoville earlier that day, and we were sitting in her basement with our assembled friends. Lewis is a small school, so even if you don't know someone, you know *of* them. That was the situation with Hope; we had never formally met despite sharing dozens of common friends.

At the party, our first conversation somehow shifted to the Blackhawks. Mind you, in 2001, very few conversations shifted to the Blackhawks in general. Legends like Josef Marha, Jean-Yves Leroux, and Steve Poapst patrolled the United Center ice back in those days. As seemingly the only two Blackhawks fans on earth at that time, our meeting felt like fate.

We started going to a few games together. Then we started going to every game together. Eventually, we became official. After seven years of dating, we were married on May 24, 2008, at Lewis University. Blackhawks radio announcer John Wiedeman emceed our wedding. The groomsmen entered the reception in Blackhawks jerseys and our table cards were the numbers of Blackhawks and Cubs. Needless to say, the Blackhawks were the foundation of our relationship.

Fast-forward to opening night of the 2009–10 NHL season. I was sitting on my couch in Lemont watching Alex Ovechkin and the Capitals paste the Boston Bruins. Hope walked up to me and said, "Hey."

Half paying attention, I grunted a response.

"I'm pregnant," she said.

Now, I'd like to pretend that my response was something romantic or poetic, but I'm not going to lie to you. My response was, and I quote, "Shut the fuck up."

Yep. Quite the Casanova, I am.

Once the shock of the moment wore off, tears of joy were shed, laughter was shared, and a celebratory trip to Buffalo Wild Wings was made. That is the place, after all, where Hope and I celebrate all of life's milestones.

Our baby was due to be born on June 8, 2010, right in the middle of what would be the Stanley Cup Final. Poor planning on my part? Maybe, but who really thinks about those things in the moment, right?

As the months went by, the Blackhawks were proving to be one of the better teams in hockey. They entered that season with high expectations after falling to the Red Wings in the conference final the season prior. Visits to the doctor always ended up in conversations about the Blackhawks.

We chose not to find out if we were having a boy or a girl. We wanted to be surprised. When it was time for the ultrasound, one of the techs started calling our unborn child "Baby Stanley" in reference to the Hawks' hopeful run to the Cup. We'd share a laugh, saying, "Little Marian Hossa Zawaski sounds good, doesn't it?"

In a later ultrasound, it was revealed that our baby would be born with bilateral club foot. When we got the diagnosis, we were devastated, but quickly learned that it was easily treatable. Statistically, it is twice as likely that males are born with clubfoot, so we fully expected that the baby would be a boy.

On the morning of May 21, I was about to walk out the door when Hope's water broke. It was time. I called in to work, got our things ready, and headed out to the hospital. Baby Stanley was coming three weeks early.

When we got to the hospital, things were very slow going. Hope was in labor, but the process had stalled out a bit. Lucky for us, the Blackhawks were facing the Sharks in the Western Conference Final that evening. On the back of Dustin Byfuglien, they won the game 3–2 in overtime, taking a commanding 3–0 series lead. The Stanley Cup Final seemed a certainty, and Baby Stanley would be ready.

At 3:48 AM on May 22, 2010, Adelyn Grace Zawaski came into the world. Yep, Baby Stanley was a girl. A new Blackhawks fan was born, and despite the fact that even at 10 years old she's terrified of Tommy Hawk, she always pays special attention when the Hawks are on the screen.

were two players who saw the puck go behind Flyers goalie Michael Leighton: Patrick Kane and defenseman Nick Boynton.

Kane recalls the moment vividly. "I saw it go in. It was stuck underneath and there was no reaction," he remembers. "Even Timonen was still skating with me after the puck was in the net, and I was, like, trying to skate to get away from him so I could celebrate."

Blackhawks GM Stan Bowman felt confident the puck was in the net when he saw Kane celebrating. "There was confusion, I guess is the best way to put it, because I wasn't positive it went in," Bowman said. "But goal-scorers, they don't react like that. They're never wrong. I was thinking it was a goal, but I didn't want to be the fool to run to the elevator and get downstairs to find out the game was still going on."

The iconic moment for me as a fan was watching the always serious Jonathan Toews sort of celebrating with his teammates, but still looking over his shoulder to make sure it was all real. "Guys were just kind of on the fence, too, not sure if they should yell or throw their stuff off," Toews says. "We just kind of all had to believe Kaner that he knew what was going on. No one saw it. I was one of the last ones down the pile, kind of looking back."

The referees confirmed the call and the celebration was on. Patrick Kane had just ended the Blackhawks' 49-year Stanley Cup drought by scoring a game-winning goal (his eighth point of the series) against Michael Leighton, who wore No. 49.

Typically in sports, the puck or ball is retrieved after a big moment. Be it a first major league home run, first NFL touchdown, or first NHL goal, players are very aware of the importance of their souvenirs and how special they are to those who achieved the feat. But in the confusion of the 2010 celebration, it seems no one remembered to retrieve Kane's game-winning puck.

To this day, the puck hasn't been found. ESPN's Wayne Drehs did a great investigational piece on the missing puck for *Outside the Lines* in 2011.

Several suspects surfaced, and most of Chicago thought the culprit was Flyers defenseman Chris Pronger. But there was video evidence of linesman Steve Miller that said otherwise. Kyle Scott, founder of Philadelphia sports blog CrossingBroad.com, assembled a collection of video clips. Upon completion of his "investigation," Scott said, "I'm very confident Steve picked it up. To me, it's highly unlikely that it was anyone else."

Drehs confronted Miller at a game in Chicago, presenting the linesman with photographic evidence of him looking at the puck, hand open, ready to pick up the object in question. Despite the picture, Miller continued to deny any knowledge of the puck's whereabouts.

"Sure, from that picture there," Miller tells Drehs. "I mean...who knows what kind of angle? Who knows? I never did touch the puck though. So...I never touched it."

"But Steve," Drehs prods, "it's pretty clearly right there."

"It's pretty clear there, yeah, but where's his pad?" Miller asks. "I never touched the puck."

"Every time I see a puck with that NHL logo and 'Game Six' on it, I wonder, 'Could that be it?'" Kane says.

The current location of the puck isn't nearly as important as the outcome of the game. The Blackhawks were Stanley Cup champions. And while Kane would surely like to have the puck in his possession, his trophy case is already a little overstuffed. There's more hardware likely on the way for the player that will be, when it's all said and done, the greatest American-born player of all time. He'll need mantle space for his Hall of Fame plaque, anyway.

3

THE GOLDEN JET

When sports fans compare their lists of the all-time best players, it's almost impossible to reach a solid conclusion. Mainly, that's because it's impossible to compare athletes from before the late 1980s and early 1990s, when training technology, salaries, and expectations changed. Even the best of the best players from eras past would have trouble holding a candle to the finely tuned machines current players have become.

In hockey history, there are a handful of players you could argue could play in any generation, but to me, there's no clearer example than Bobby Hull.

Robert Marvin Hull grew up in a family of 11 children in Pointe Anne, Ontario. He developed his physique chopping wood, shoveling snow, and bailing hay on the farm. "I never lifted weights. I didn't have to. The hay was heavy," Hull recalls.

Hull made his NHL debut at the age of 18, and immediately turned heads. His notable physique (he had 16-inch biceps), combined with his speed, puck-handling, and shooting was deadly. "He was a tremendous, tremendous athlete," says Tony Esposito.

Hull played 15 seasons and 1,036 regular season games for the Blackhawks. He ranks first in Blackhawks history in goals (604), game-winning goals (98), hat tricks (28), shots (4,539), and goals per game (0.58). He ranks second in several categories as well, including points (1,153), plus/minus (259), and power-play goals (152). He's also the team's all-time leader in playoff goals, with 62.

When the conversations about the best Blackhawk of all time begin, you can flip a coin between Bobby Hull and Stan Mikita.

Much like Jonathan Toews and Patrick Kane in the 2010s, Mikita and Hull had their own styles. Like Toews, Mikita was an excellent two-way player. Hull was more like Patrick Kane. He was an electrifying player with a penchant for jaw-dropping goals. He had the ability to bring the fans out of their seats as soon as he touched the puck. "When I came around that net with the puck, I could feel [the fans] getting out of their seats," Hull said. "By the time I got to center ice, they were all out of their seats. By the time the puck was either at the net or in the net, they were all standing and howling. That's what I'm supposed to do. I'm supposed to entertain people."

Admittedly, technology in Hull's era wasn't quite what it is today, but it's said that Hull could skate up to 30 mph and shoot the puck 119 mph. "My brother, Dennis, said I could shoot the puck so hard, it could go through a car wash without getting wet," Hull quips.

"The best part about coming to Chicago was that Bobby Hull was on my side," said Hull's teammate, Hall of Fame goalie Glenn Hall. Hall was traded to the Hawks from Detroit in 1957. "But I still had to face him and his shot in practice. The idea was not to stop that thing, but to avoid getting killed."

One of the scariest reminders of the weapon Hull possessed came in 1961. The Blackhawks were battling Gump Worsley and the Montreal Canadiens when Hull reared back for one of his patented slap shots. "There's 30 seconds to go as he's coming down and I looked in front of the net to see if there was someone he could pass it to. Just as I turned around, the puck was right there. It hit me right in the ear. I went down to a count of about 110," Worsley remembers. Players from both teams, including Hull, gathered around Worsley. The Chicago crowd was silent, fearing the worst. Blackhawks team doctor Myron Tremaine tended to the downed goalie. After about five minutes and plenty of smelling salts, Worsley came to. The Chicago fans applauded Worsley, who amazingly finished the game. "I went down the dressing room, had a shower, and then I was on my way to the hospital," Worsley recalls. "I went out the dressing room door and Bobby Hull was standing there with his shirt, his tie, and his suit and coat, wondering if I was all right or not. He thought he killed me, I guess."

Hull was shaken by the ordeal. "It really scares you. I never want to see it happen again," he said.

Decades later, Tony Esposito declared of Hull, "I still feel he has the best shot ever in hockey."

On March 12, 1966, Hull became the first player to score more than 50 goals in a single season. Two players, Bernie Geoffrion and Maurice Richard, hit exactly 50 goals before Hull, but Hull's 51st made NHL history. "It wasn't so much that I was the first to score more than 50. It was that tremendous ovation from Chicago fans. I came over the bench and Phil Esposito said, 'Bobby, do you have goosebumps like I do?' I said, 'They're the size of robin eggs.'"

Hull finished the season with 54 goals. In the 1968–69 season, he scored a career-high 58.

Hull left the Blackhawks after the 1971–72 season, joining the Winnipeg Jets of the upstart World Hockey Association. Jets owner Ben Hatskin was looking to make a splash by bringing in a big-name player, and he got his man in Hull after offering a $1 million signing bonus.

"Bill Wirtz tried to tell everyone that I was holding the Blackhawks hostage for a million dollars, which was erroneous as could be," Hull said in an interview with HollywoodChicago.com. "I told the WHA from the beginning that I thought I could get a five-year contract from the Blackhawks—I was 32 years old at the time—at $250,000 a year. Never at any time did I 'hold them up' for a million-dollar bonus. I told the WHA I would leave the Hawks for a million-dollar bonus, thinking that if the league folded, I would at least take home what the Winnipeg Jets were offering me, which was the $250,000 I was asking for from the Blackhawks. The nine franchises in the WHA at the time came up with $110,000 apiece, I had my million-dollar bonus, and that was that."

Hull's relationship with the Blackhawks organization remained tense until John McDonough and Rocky Wirtz offered him an ambassador's role as part of the franchise's rebirth. "Our first conversation was pretty profane and rather toxic," McDonough told *The New York Times*. "Bobby felt he'd been wronged, and I had to hear him out." Hull let loose for 45 minutes and left the meeting without reaching an agreement to return to the franchise. Ultimately, Hull decided to rejoin the organization and has been part of the United Center experience ever since.

Looking back on his playing days in Chicago brings a smile to Hull's face. "It was a time in my life that I knew would never come again," he said. "I was playing the game that I loved, in the city that I loved, in front of the greatest fans that ever watched hockey, with some of the greatest players that ever played the game...and we did have fun. We might have been out the night before, but I wanted those guys that I was with to be with me when they dropped the puck at 7:30 at night, because we played guilty, and we played very well guilty. But we had fun."

4

THE CAPTAIN ANNOUNCES HIS ARRIVAL

Before the Stanley Cups, before the Olympic gold medal, the Conn Smythe Trophy, the Messier Leadership Award, and the Selke Trophy, Jonathan Toews was a massive prospect. Before he even made his NHL debut, he was seen as a future captain. Comparisons were being made to legends like Steve Yzerman, Joe Sakic, Rod Brind'Amour, and Mark Messier, and Toews hadn't even pulled the Blackhawks sweater over his head.

No pressure, kid.

Hawks fans would have to wait a year for Toews' debut, however. After being drafted third overall in 2006, Toews decided to play one final season at North Dakota, where he led the Fighting Sioux to the Frozen Four. He also scored the game-winning goal in Team Canada's World Junior Championship gold medal game.

These accomplishments, accompanied by the drafting of Patrick Kane in June of 2007, only made the expectations grow higher.

"He's 19 years old," Hawks head coach Denis Savard said. "But don't let that fool you. There's no big step from the University of North Dakota to the NHL for this kid. He's 19, but he already displays all of the cool and experience of a 30-year-old veteran. He's definitely captain material."

When it finally came time to drop the puck on the 2007–08 season, Toews, and Blackhawks fans, would still have to wait a few more games. He missed the first two contests with an injury. As a Hawks fan, hearing Toews would miss the first two games was crushing. It was torture. I've compared it to waking up Christmas morning with one present on your mind. You open the box, and it's a printout saying, "Your order will be delivered on December 27." Yeah...it was that kind of torture.

On October 10, 2007, the Blackhawks faced the Sharks at the United Center and Toews' debut finally arrived. At the 13:43 mark of the first period, Toews took a pass near center ice from defenseman

Brent Seabrook. Toews chipped the puck past San Jose defenseman Matt Carle and streaked toward the Sharks goal. He put a wrist shot top corner over the shoulder of goalie Evgeni Nabokov.

Toews had scored his first goal on his first shot in his first game in the NHL.

"I was lucky enough to break in and score in my first game. That doesn't happen to a lot of people," he said. "To score early on like that...it definitely gives you confidence. You don't want to be five or 10 games in without a goal or any points. It helped me get on the board."

The debut somehow met the hype that had been building for Toews, but this was nothing compared to the viral moment he'd create just four games later.

The Hawks were off to a 3–3 start on the young season entering a home game against the Avalanche. Toews had points in all four games he had played in up to that point. What occurred at the 6:59 mark of the first period is something I've watched hundreds of times, and I still haven't gotten used to it. It may be, to this day, the most electrifying goal Toews has scored in his incredible NHL career.

Patrick Kane, as he would do hundreds of times as his career went on, fed a perfect pass to Toews, who was streaking down the right-wing boards. As Toews crossed into the Avalanche zone, he shifted backhand to forehand in full speed, splitting the combination of forward Milan Hejduk and defenseman Scott Hannan. From there, he quickly faked to his left, freezing defensemen Brett Clark. When Clark bit, Toews dragged the puck behind himself to create more space. He pulled the puck from his backhand to his forehand, then tucked the puck behind goalie Jose Theodore.

This entire sequence took five seconds to complete. "It happened so fast," Toews said. "I was lucky their D-men were a little flatfooted. I don't think they expected me to come in with that much speed. I was pretty pumped."

"We haven't seen a goal like this in a long time," Savard said after the win. "It was the highlight-tape goal of the week, highlight-goal of the year."

Savvy, it was the highlight goal of a career full of highlight-reel goals, and it happened just five games into Toews' rookie season.

"Unfortunately for me it probably was a once-in-a-lifetime goal," Toews humbly quipped a month later.

This goal was the moment the NHL and fans around the league took notice of what was happening in Chicago. The Avalanche broadcast team of Mike Haynes and Peter McNab were blown away, and their reaction to the moment made the goal that much more memorable and meaningful:

> Haynes: Here comes Toews. Jonathan Toews moving in...what a move! Oh my goodness! Oh man! Wow! I don't care if you're an Avalanche fan...that was one of those great scores that you'll see all season long. Was that wonderful, Peter?
>
> McNab: This is the kind of talent, Mike, that can bring a franchise back from the dead.

That line from McNab was all Blackhawks fans needed to hear. There's something about hearing the visiting team's announcers wax poetic about your team. It's one thing for your team's announcers to sell the product. It's another for the opponents to say, "Screw it...that was awesome."

Kane scored later in the game to make it the first contest in which both he and Toews scored goals. All the fans' hopes and dreams for the new era of Blackhawks hockey were being realized. The Chicago Blackhawks were on their way to something special, and the city—nay, the world—was taking notice.

5

COACH Q

Along the way to their three most recent Stanley Cup championships, there were several important road markers for the Chicago Blackhawks. First came the drafting of Duncan Keith in 2002. Then it was Brent Seabrook and Corey Crawford being part of the 2003 class. In 2006, the Hawks drafted Jonathan Toews. The next season they selected Patrick Kane. Then there was the turnaround of franchise philosophies when Rocky Wirtz and John McDonough took over the front office in 2007. The free-agent signings of Brian Campbell and a year later Marian Hossa warrant mentioning as well.

All these markers, however, may have just been blips on the radar without the hiring of Joel Quenneville.

Quenneville joined the Blackhawks as a scout in September of 2008. He had been fired as head coach of the Colorado Avalanche that summer after amassing a 131–92–23 record over three seasons and earning a reputation as one of the finest bench bosses in the National Hockey League.

When the hire was made, the young Blackhawks, led by their head coach, franchise legend Denis Savard, were preparing for the 2008–09 season. The team entered the year with high expectations, and it was clear to most everyone that Quenneville's presence was a solid insurance policy should things start poorly with Savard. "I knew I had to do well [that] year," Savard said.

The Hawks started the season 1–2–1. Ironically, the firing happened hours after the team won its first game of the season, a 4–1 victory over Phoenix.

"It was a flat camp and we got out of the gate flat," GM Dale Tallon said. "It's about moving forward, about achieving and winning and developing a consistent approach. And we felt we needed a more experienced person in that position, and that's why we made the decision."

When Savard was replaced, Patrick Kane, who considered Savard not just a coach but a mentor and friend, took it hard. "It was definitely a love relationship, where he just wanted to get the best out of me," he said. "It was a tough day. He was a great friend to me."

The Blackhawks went on to win or take at least a point in 14 of Quenneville's first 16 games behind the bench.

"We had such a young team. When he came in, all of a sudden, he had that huge presence in the locker room, and everybody respected him, so we did everything that he wanted and asked for," Duncan Keith recalls. "Our practices just changed overnight. It was quick, hard passes on the tape. Joel just has a real strong presence about him, and for the group of young guys that we were at the time, we really fed into everything he was saying."

Quenneville's presence is a common theme.

He looms larger than he is, at "only" 6-foot-1, and seems larger than life. His eyes are piercing; some say he resembles a wolf. Of course, no Chicago championship coach would be complete without a trademark moustache, and Quenneville's might be the finest of all.

Quenneville, at least behind the bench, does not offer a friendly face.

Some of Q's greatest and most memorable moments have come when losing it on an official. Despite his intense look, Q was typically stoic behind the bench, but when those eruptions occurred, his face would turn red, his arms would flail, and now and again, an inappropriate gesture might be made.

After a 2014 playoff game against the St. Louis Blues, Quenneville was fined $25,000 for grabbing his crotch on the bench (and on national television). I'm not a professional lip reader, but I've always been of the belief that Quenneville shouted, "Grow some balls!" That comment would fit based on the situation. The Hawks and Blues were tied 3–3 in double overtime, and a puck had been knocked out of play by a Blues player, at least in Quenneville's mind. Calling a delay of game penalty for such a violation in such a crucial situation is tough for an official—especially if it wasn't completely clear that it had happened to begin with—but try explaining that to Quenneville. The Blackhawks went on to lose the game 4–3 in triple overtime and the fine was levied. "I was definitely excited, disappointed [in] the call, but I'll apologize for my behavior," Quenneville said. "It wasn't appropriate at all. It was a bush-league move on my part."

The players loved Quenneville, despite his gruff exterior. Every player I've spoken to about him over the years has called him a true players' coach.

"We learned a lot from him. One of the best things about Joel...he allowed us to play the game and not overthink it," Keith remembers. "To me, you have to be able to read and react and think quickly and be natural out there, and that's kind of what I appreciated about Joel the most."

"When we were on the ice, he was all business," former winger Ben Eager says. "But he let the guys control the dressing room."

Quenneville, who played 13 seasons as a defenseman in the league, understood the players' perspective. He knew when he needed to press and when to back off.

"It made us closer as a team," recalls Adam Burish. "Guys would just hang out longer. Quenneville let us run wild."

Former Blackhawk Daniel Carcillo shared a memory about the softer side of Quenneville. Carcillo was very close with the late Steve Montador, who had played 52 games with the 2011–12 Blackhawks. On February 15, 2015, Montador was found dead in his Ontario home. He was 35 years old.

"I'm about to walk into the room to get dressed. My phone is ringing off the hook. I answer. It's a friend crying on the other line saying, 'Steve's gone,'" Carcillo said. "I was in shock. I tried to hide it and get dressed. I broke down once I got to my skates and looked over at his old stall next to [Brent] Seabrook. I hid it well though. Making it on the ice to warm up. I did a few laps and broke down crying again. I couldn't do it. I was spiritually done."

Carcillo, wounded by the loss of his friend, left the ice and headed to Quenneville's office.

"He had just heard," Carcillo said. "I was crying. He was crying. He hugged me in my equipment. I was a mess. I couldn't play. He said he understood. He comforted me. He listened. He didn't force me to play. I'm forever grateful."

On November 6, 2018, the Blackhawks fired Quenneville after 452 regular season wins (second-most in franchise history), 128 playoff games and 76 playoff victories (first in franchise history), and three Stanley Cups (most in franchise history).

"Joel was our leader. It's a tough day to realize...coming to the rink and he's not here today," said Jonathan Toews on the day of Quenneville's firing.

Quenneville's ability to walk the thin line of demanding a high level of performance while remaining a players' coach has helped him to 925 wins (second in NHL history), three Stanley Cups, a Jack Adams Award, and a place in the hearts of Blackhawks fans forever.

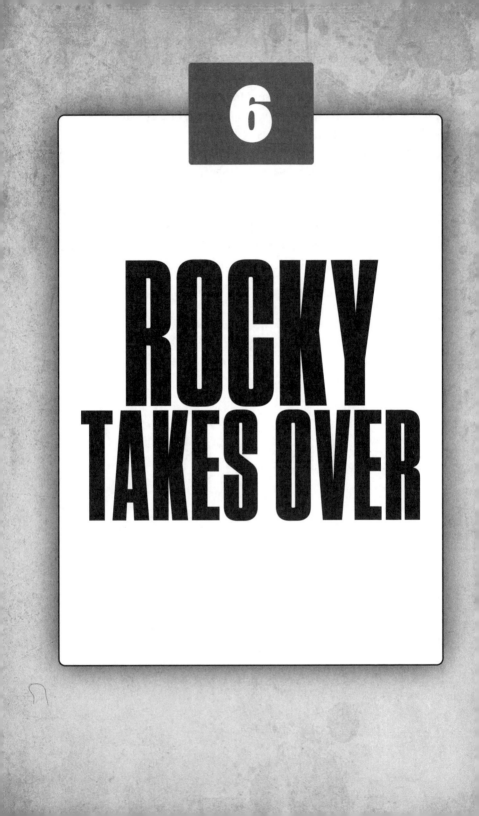

6

ROCKY TAKES OVER

There's no delicate way to write this, but it's reality: the Blackhawks organization changed the day Bill Wirtz died.

When the patriarch of the Blackhawks family passed in September of 2007, so did the ancient policies that had defined the Blackhawks for decades. For years, Wirtz refused to put home games on television, thinking it would hurt attendance. Star player after star player was mistreated and lowballed when it came time to pay for the performances they'd given the organization. Bobby Hull, Jeremy Roenick, Ed Belfour, Chris Chelios, Tony Amonte...these are just a handful of the franchise greats Wirtz insulted and ultimately watched leave town. When top free agents became available to replace these departed stars, Blackhawks fans knew there was no chance they'd be signing in Chicago. There was a reason they called Wirtz "Dollar Bill," after all.

Wirtz's management style led to an ESPN feature in February of 2004 naming the Blackhawks as the worst franchise in North American sports. Here's a nice summary on the state of the Blackhawks in that era from the piece:

> "Sad?" says one who has watched this once-proud franchise fall into disrepair, the tragic victim of neglect and poor planning. "It's not sad. It *used* to be sad. Nobody cares enough to be sad anymore."

Bad drafting. Bad hires. Bad trades. Archaic thinking. Stagnation.

When the Blackhawks held a moment of silence for Wirtz during a pregame ceremony, several fans booed. However you feel about whether that sort of expression is acceptable, it illustrates just how despised Bill Wirtz was amongst many Hawks fans.

"The people who knew him personally knew what a decent man he was," his son Rocky Wirtz remembers. "He would talk to the person cleaning up the street the same way he would talk to the president of a company. He just had that depth. But his public image was not a good one. And he really didn't care. Though he did talk about how it hurt him when his grandchildren would come back and say something they had heard."

When Bill Wirtz's successor was to be named, many expected it would be his son Peter. Peter had served as the team's senior vice president, working at his father's side, but instead it was Rocky who took over. Back in 1962, Bill's father, Arthur, drew up a succession plan that placed Rocky in charge. "We always knew [the plan] but no one ever talked about it for whatever reason," Rocky said.

Before his father's passing, Rocky had been in charge of the Judge & Dolph liquor distribution company, which was owned by the Wirtz family. Suddenly he was the man in charge of an Original Six NHL franchise. "Except for coming for a team picture and then attending a game, that would be the only way you ever would know I was even around on the hockey side," Rocky said.

Before his passing, Rocky would often try to talk his father out of his archaic philosophies. "I'd say, 'Dad, we're losing generations of fans by not televising home games,'" Rocky said. "He said it wouldn't be fair to our fans with season tickets. But we'd gotten down to 3,400 season tickets, which meant maybe 1,500 to 1,700 fans. So we weren't televising home games for 1,700 people? Why bang your head against the wall?"

When Rocky took over, he knew he had to get to work, and fast. "We had to be decisive," Rocky Wirtz told *Chicago* magazine. "We had to be quick. And we had to do things that were dramatic."

Rocky immediately reversed the team's television policy. From there, he shifted his focus to the organization's leadership, reaching out to John McDonough, who had been president of the Chicago Cubs for 24 years, as well as McDonough's right-hand man, Jay Blunk. The Cubs had been "lovable losers" for decades, but no amount of losing could sour their relationship with the fans. If any organization in sports were the opposite of the Blackhawks in terms of fan engagement, it was the Cubs. Lucky for Rocky, McDonough was just a phone call and a limo ride away.

On November 20, 2007, the Blackhawks named McDonough the team's president. "By hiring John McDonough, we are adding one of the top talents in sports management and marketing," Rocky said. "I am thrilled we found a guy who grew up in Chicago, stayed here, and achieved outstanding success here. There are 81 years of history with the Blackhawk franchise and John understands that."

McDonough realized there was tough work ahead if the Blackhawks were going to pull themselves out from the hole that had been dug. "From a professional standpoint, I can't think of a more exciting challenge than the one that lies ahead," McDonough said.

The obvious work—putting games on television, marketing the team correctly—were done, but those things do not create winning hockey. Luckily for Wirtz and company, the Blackhawks had just drafted a duo of franchise stars. Jonathan Toews and Patrick Kane made their NHL debuts in the 2007–08 season, joining a solid core of defensemen Brent Seabrook and Duncan Keith, but would they be willing to totally skirt the "Dollar Bill" philosophy and spend top dollar for a free agent?

The next summer, the team signed the top defenseman on the market, Brian Campbell, to an astronomical eight-year, $56.8 million deal. With Campbell and the young core of stars, the Blackhawks reached the Western Conference Final, falling to rival Detroit in six games. They were close, but they were not Stanley Cup contenders just yet.

Exactly one year after signing Campbell, the Blackhawks shocked the world, signing superstar winger Marian Hossa to a 12-year, $62.8 million contract. The next season, the Blackhawks would capture their first Stanley Cup since 1961, and Hawksmania was born.

In just three short years, Wirtz had converted the Blackhawks from a laughingstock to a dynasty in the making.

Chicago, with the core of Toews, Kane, Keith, Seabrook, and Hossa, would go one to win two more Stanley Cups, one in 2013 and another in 2015. On October 14, 2019, the Blackhawks celebrated their 500th consecutive sellout, and have led the NHL in attendance since the 2008–09 season.

Unlike the boos his father received during his rare public appearances, Rocky is showered with chants of, "Rocky, Rocky, Rocky," at games. He sits among the fans in the 100 level and is happy to chat with them during the game. Any why wouldn't he be? I never thought in my lifetime there would be a beloved Wirtz in Chicago. Today, I'm confident saying Rocky would easily be elected mayor of Chicago if he were to run.

"He's a rock star," Bulls and White Sox owner Jerry Reinsdorf said. "When they put his kisser on the replay board, they cheer and say, 'Hey, Rocky!'"

7

17 SECONDS

Seventeen seconds.

On their own, those two words don't mean too much. It could be how long it takes you to get up from the couch to grab a beer and get back to your seat. It could be the length of one of your all-time favorite guitar solos. But to Chicago Blackhawks fans, it means one thing:

Elation.

On June 24, 2013, the Blackhawks were engaged in an evenly matched and stressful Stanley Cup Final with the Boston Bruins. The Blackhawks won the first game in triple overtime on Andrew Shaw's infamous "I love shin pads!" goal. The Bruins claimed the next two, winning 2–1 in OT and 2–0, respectively. Chicago took Game 4 on Brent Seabrook's overtime goal and Game 5 after Dave Bolland's late empty-netter.

With a 3–2 series lead, the Blackhawks wanted no part of a Game 7, despite having home-ice advantage. The series was too close and too many crazy things had happened up to that point.

"You've got to be careful," Blackhawks winger Patrick Sharp said. "You've seen a couple years ago [in 2011], Boston was down 3–2, they won at home, and then won Game 7 in Vancouver. We know this [Bruins] team is capable of coming back."

Boston began Game 6 with a huge focus on physicality and dominated the first period. "They threw everything at us to start the game," head coach Joel Quenneville said. "We were surprised and caught off guard." The Bruins outshot the Hawks 12–6 in the first period and were rewarded for those efforts when Chris Kelly gave Boston a 1–0 lead. "For a second there it was kind of scary. They were almost invincible, the way they were playing," Jonathan Toews said.

"After that period, we had to be harder to play against," Quenneville remembers.

Chicago bounced back with a strong second-period effort. On a two-on-one, Toews wristed a fluttering puck between the legs of Bruins goalie Tuukka Rask and the game was tied with only 4:26 gone in the period. The teams remained tied 1–1 through 40 minutes.

GM Stan Bowman recalls a conversation he had with his father, Scotty Bowman, between the second and third periods. "I just said, 'All we need to do is win one period to win the Cup.'" But it wouldn't be that simple.

With 7:49 left in the third period, the Bruins struck. Hawks goalie Corey Crawford was behind his net, trying to play a puck. Bruins forward Milan Lucic disrupted Crawford just enough to squirt the puck loose to Duncan Keith, who attempted to clear the puck out back behind the net when Boston forward David Krejci intercepted the pass. Krejci flipped the puck in front of the net and Lucic was there to put the puck past Crawford.

"You kind of get that sinking feeling in your stomach," Toews recalled of Lucic's goal. "You just gotta let it go and move on to the next shift and the next play."

The Hawks did just that.

Down 2–1 with just over 90 seconds left in the game, the Blackhawks called Crawford off for the extra attacker. As their netminder raced toward the Chicago bench, winger Patrick Kane weaved his way through center ice and into the Boston zone. After putting a weak and contested shot into the pads of Rask, the puck bounced into the left-wing corner. Boston defenseman Dennis Seidenberg and Krejci both had chances to control the puck and clear, but Jonathan Toews was too determined. The captain lifted Krejci's stick and knocked the puck free to Kane, who then sent the puck to a waiting Duncan Keith. Keith calmly sent the puck back to Toews, who was standing on the Bruins' goal line to the right of Rask. Toews centered the pass to a streaking Bryan Bickell, who had made his way to the front of the net. Bickell didn't miss his opportunity, burying the puck behind Rask. The game was now tied 2–2 with 1:16 left.

"I don't think I've ever jumped that high," Brandon Saad remembered.

BEHIND ENEMY LINES

My job at 670 The Score has given me many priceless and incredible sports opportunities. I've attended World Series games, Super Bowl weeks, Final Four tournaments, and have met more sports legends than I can possibly recall.

None of them, however, were as memorable as my experience for Game 6 of the 2013 Stanley Cup Final in Boston.

The show I was producing at the time, hosted by Dan McNeil and Matt Spiegel, was stationed at a bar near the TD Bank Garden. I was also on postgame hosting duties, so instead of heading to the game with McNeil and Spiegel, I hunkered down in a studio at our sister station, WEEI. Like The Score, WEEI shares its studios with several other CBS Radio stations, including FM rock station WAAF.

As I settled down for my show, I could see directly into the FM studio. There was a DJ in the room decked out in a Bruins jersey and hat, ready to do his show. We exchanged pleasantries through the glass, and I started watching the game.

As the game ebbed and flowed, we could see each other react in real time.

Chris Kelly scores, and the Boston DJ pumps his fist. Jonathan Toews ties it, and I react in a similar fashion. All the while, we were looking at each other while not *really* looking at each other.

With just under eight minutes left in the third period, Milan Lucic scores and the Boston DJ jumps up and down. For the remainder of the game, he's standing. I'm sitting, looking calm and professional, but well into "barf, cry, die" mode, as the Blackhawks' social media community called the feeling during the Cup runs.

Then, Bryan Bickell puts the puck behind Tuukka Rask. The DJ is still standing, but with his hands clenched tightly over his mouth. Seventeen seconds later, Dave Bolland throws off his gloves in celebration. The DJ is no longer standing. He's now in a squatting cocoon of pain, head firmly in hands, pulling at his long blond hair.

I sit back with a wry smile. He didn't see that.

Moments later, I'd be on the air in Chicago talking to Bolland, Bickell, Michael Frolik, John McDonough, Stan Bowman, and others as they celebrated on the ice just miles away. By the time I could catch my breath and look around, I noticed the DJ had turned the lights off in his studio and was working by the light of his computer alone.

Good times, good times.

Watching the tying goal on replay reveals a lot about this moment. While Bickell's maniacal, toothless shout is iconic, I find myself drawn to Brent Seabrook's casual fist pump. For such a huge and emotional moment, Seabrook knew the Hawks' work wasn't done.

The focus for Chicago, at that point, was to get the game to overtime.

"When you score a goal that late to tie the game, you're always pretty confident you're going to win in overtime," Toews said.

The next shift, Joel Quenneville's defensive stalwarts took the ice. Dave Bolland centered Marcus Kruger and Michael Frolik. Niklas Hjalmarsson and Johnny Oduya, both shot-blocking machines and stay-at-home defensemen, took their spots on the blue line. Boston answered with Krejci, Lucic, and Nathan Horton up front.

The Bruins won the faceoff, but Hjalmarsson quickly took control of the puck at the Hawks blue line, sending it to Bolland near center ice. Bolland rushed into the Bruins zone, sending a drop pass to Frolik, who sent a weak shot on goal to Rask, who steered the puck to the left-wing board to a waiting Kruger. Kruger then sent the puck to Oduya at the left point. His shot deflected off Frolik's stick and the post, and out in front to a waiting Bolland.

"All I knew was [the puck] was sitting there in front of me, so I had to tap it in," Bolland said.

The Hawks center buried the puck behind Rask. In the commotion, Bolland's glove and stick came off. Along with Bickell's iconic toothless grin, Bolland flipping the gloves off in slow motion will be etched in the memory of Blackhawks fans for decades.

"My gloves got caught, actually. Once I slipped my hands back, my gloves just came off and...there we go," Bolland said.

Seventeen seconds after Bickell had tied the game, the Blackhawks had a 3–2 lead in the game and the series. The Bruins pulled Rask and tried to get back in the game but save for a weak flip shot Crawford had to push away, the Bruins never threatened.

"All the guys on the bench are holding their breath the whole time. I looked up and saw there were three seconds left," Toews remembered. "The next thing you know, we're walking away with the Stanley Cup. It almost felt like we stole it."

The celebration was on. The Blackhawks were Stanley Cup champions for the second time in four seasons.

"We never give up as a team," Bolland told CBC during the Cup celebration. "We die hard. We do the right things. We always battle to the end."

That mentality was a defining trait of the Blackhawks in that decade. No deficit seemed too large. No odds seemed too great. During a 2014 playoff series with the Blackhawks, then Blues head coach Ken Hitchcock remarked, "It's their resolve. That's what makes them special players. It's not their skill. There are lots of people with just as much skill. It's their ability to stay with it."

The 2013 Blackhawks, and their remarkable 17 seconds in Boston, solidified their reputation as one of the hardest-working and resolute teams in recent memory.

8

CHRIS CHELIOS

On June 29, 1990, the Chicago Blackhawks made one of the biggest blockbuster trades in the history of hockey, shipping superstar Denis Savard to the Montreal Canadiens for defenseman and Illinois native Chris Chelios and a second-round pick.

Savard and new Hawks GM and coach Mike Keenan had famously clashed during their time together, and some felt those issues led to the trade. "Keenan would tell me something one day...that he loved me and wouldn't trade me," Savard told the Montreal press after the trade. "Then he'd tell me something that's completely different the next day. Keenan told me a lot of things. This is a business move that will benefit both clubs."

"I didn't have any personal vendetta or dislike for Savard. He wanted to win as badly as I did," Keenan said.

Before the trade, Chelios, who won his first Norris Trophy in 1988–89, served as co-captain of the Canadiens (alongside Guy Carbonneau), who had just suffered a disappointing second-round playoff loss to the Bruins, one year removed from winning the Wales Conference championship. "Someone's going to go when you lose out early in the playoffs," Chelios said.

The defenseman was also coming off a left-knee injury. "I blew my knee out early...I think I missed nearly 40 games. The rumor was they better get rid of me because my knee will never last."

He was 28 years old that season. He played until he was 48.

"I really loved playing in Montreal," he said. "I was just starting to settle down. I got married, I had my first kid. I said, 'I'm ready to accept this responsibility as a captain and mature a little bit,' and be what they wanted me to be, but to go home? I got over it really quick. It was great to come home. It worked out perfect for me."

Chelios moved his parents back to the Chicago area so they could watch him play. "It was kind of cool to be able to play in front of my friends and family," he said.

The Blackhawks couldn't have been happier with the deal, either. They knew they were trading for a great defenseman. Keenan called him one of the top defensemen in the game when the trade was made, but I'm not sure they knew they were trading for arguably the greatest American-born player ever.

Chelios, who stood 6-foot-0 and weighed 190 pounds (smaller than Duncan Keith, for the record), played like a giant. There was no safe corner or board for a puck-carrier entering the Blackhawks end. The front of the Hawks net became a danger zone as well. Chelios would abuse any player who dared attempt to screen his goaltender. Opponents learned to fear and respect his game.

"He was tough as nails," remembers Carbonneau.

But Chelios' game wasn't just about toughness and intimidation. He was one of the best two-way defenders in the NHL. He logged huge minutes, playing more than 27 minutes some nights. In 664 games with the Blackhawks, he scored 92 goals and tallied 395 assists. He also won two more Norris Trophies and led the Blackhawks to the Stanley Cup Final in 1991–92. The team would ultimately get swept by a star-studded Penguins team, headlined by Mario Lemieux.

"It would have been the best thing to win a Cup in your hometown and be in that situation, but they were a great team," Chelios said. "[Rick] Tocchet, [Joe] Mullen, [Jaromir] Jagr, [Ron] Francis...[Larry] Murphy on D. It's just unfortunate we didn't put up a better fight."

Despite all he had done for the franchise over his nine seasons with the Blackhawks, the team decided to trade him to the hated rival Detroit Red Wings in March of 1999. He joined Ed Belfour and Jeremy Roenick as members of the team core to be traded, and it was another example of Bill Wirtz and the Blackhawks cheaping out on one of the best players in franchise history.

"That was horrible," Chelios remembers. "It was just a matter for me of wanting to get out of Chicago, the way I was getting treated at the end. It was the right time for me to leave...I [just] didn't like the way certain people handled it. They were telling me I should retire that year and they'd put me up in the front office. I said, 'I feel I can still play.' I lasted another 10 years and had some great years in between."

I'll never forget the day Chelios was traded. I was numb. So many of my favorite players had been traded before that it had become the norm, but not Chelios. He was from Chicago. He was one of us. At the time, I was a student at Lewis University in Romeoville. A friend of mine, Dee, brought me a newspaper. The cover was Chelios' face with the Red Wings logo superimposed over it. She may as well have shown me a picture of a dead relative. Thanks a ton, Dee.

He went on to play 578 games with the Red Wings and win two more Stanley Cups.

Chelios, who famously told The Score's Mike North that he'd never play for the Red Wings, seemed to take some joy in rubbing the Blackhawks' face in his Detroit success. He'd bring the Stanley Cup to Wrigley Field for Cubs games in the summer. He'd bring the Cup to Chicago bars and restaurants. It felt like a personal slap in the face to me and Hawks fans like me.

The biggest insult came when the Blackhawks named their 75th anniversary team in 2001. The organization got a collection of great players for an on-ice ceremony before a game with the Red Wings, of which Chelios was still a member. Hawks legends of every era posed in their Hawks jerseys at center ice. The Blackhawks presented Chelios with a Hawks jersey of his own, but he didn't put it on, forever sullying the photo with a damn Red Wings jersey.

To be honest, it pissed me off. It felt like he was intentionally hurting Blackhawks fans. I held a grudge for a long time. Like, a really, really long time. In fact, I think I finally got over it while writing this book. In reminding myself about the team's history, I've realized that Chelios wasn't sticking it to the fans, but to the organization that had treated him so poorly. So as much as I'd like to delete my September of 2010 Chicago Now piece titled, "Traitor Chelios Undeserving of Heritage Night," or my December of 2010 670 The Score column titled, "Chelios Should Stay in Detroit," or better yet my July of 2018 The Score op-ed titled, "The Red Wings Can Keep Chelios," after

Chelios rejoined the organization as an ambassador, those pieces need to live online as a reminder of my angrier days.

To me, he is the greatest American-born player to ever play the game—"So far," I say, looking in Patrick Kane's direction—and he had the best seasons of his incredible career in his hometown of Chicago.

This is the first time I'm admitting it, but I forgive Chris Chelios.

9

THE OLD BARN

The newest generation of Blackhawks fans didn't miss much before the Stanley Cup–winning teams of the 2010s. In their lifetimes, the teams that came before Jonathan Toews, Patrick Kane, and company didn't leave memories so much as they did years of disappointment.

But there is one part of Blackhawks history this generation will sadly never fully understand: attending a game at the Chicago Stadium.

While the Blackhawks' current home arena, the United Center, refers to itself as "The Madhouse on Madison," it more often resembles a morgue when compared to the lunacy of the Chicago Stadium. That building, which opened in 1929, is often referred to as "The Old Barn." The building's shape and design lent itself to that description. Steel trusses that spanned 266 feet without supports gave Chicago Stadium attendees a wide-open space with very few obstructed views, if any. That open space also helped the sound of the rabid, screaming fans to travel. Add in a 3,663-pipe Barton Organ and you have the makings of a true sports "madhouse."

The atmosphere in the building had a multiplying effect. As the building got louder and louder, the fans got more and more riled up. Of course, beer sales helped as well, but there was a pride in attending a Blackhawks game at the Stadium. You didn't want to be the one fan not participating in the chaos.

In a 1985 *Hockey Night in Canada* feature, broadcaster and former Bruins and Flyers player Gary Dornhoefer recalled what it was like to be an opposing player at the Stadium:

> The dressing room was below the ice surface. You were in the basement. And 15 to 20 minutes prior to the start of the game you can hear the fans starting to make noise. They're pounding on the floor and you feel like you're in an earthquake. All of a

> sudden, you're preparing yourself mentally for the game, then it's a long walk up the steps, it's about 25 steps, and once you hit the ice, the excitement is there, you can feel it, and you're ready to play.

Dornhoefer's broadcast partner and former Blues and Rangers player John Davidson recalled the steps as well: "I hated the steps. Being a goaltender wearing that equipment, to get up them was tough enough. But when the game was over, if you happened to have lost it, to get back down those steps was no fun at all. There's no building like the Chicago Stadium."

You don't have to look far to find athletes, commentators, and hockey people sharing memories of the Chicago Stadium, but to truly understand, you must get the perspective of the fans.

I asked lifelong season ticket holder and schoolteacher Dan Hunt about his memories of the Stadium:

> Growing up in the late '80s and early '90s, going to Blackhawks games at the Stadium is what caused me to fall in love with hockey. All the things you hear are true...the noise, the organ, the physical brand of hockey on the small rink, the connection between the team and fans, and so on. But to me, the memory that I keep of the Stadium the most is how the Hawks almost always seemed to come out in the first 10 minutes of the games. In many ways, it was how all those things came together. The anthem, followed by those first few minutes of the game, was pure entertainment, especially if you enjoyed the intimidating, physical style the Hawks played at the time. It felt like they were winning 2–0 every night.
>
> Winter Sundays seemed to take forever, excited and nervous all day, waiting for 6:00 PM to come around when my dad and I would leave our Portage Park home, grab a beef sandwich at Bob-O-Rino's, and head down for the 7:35 start. Those are nights I'll never forget and some of my most cherished memories.

Another lifelong Blackhawks fan and Chicago sports radio icon, Dan McNeil, shares his memories of the Old Barn as only he can:

> A dozen or so years ago, my showmates and I were giggling at the expense of Blackhawks Hall of Famer Denis Savard. Singing the praises of Chicago Stadium, Savy proclaimed, "It was the greatest building that ever lived."
>
> After further review, I think Savard chose the perfect words to describe the house at 1800 W. Madison St., which sat hard on the once decayed and depressed West Side. I often referred to the Stadium as "she," as in "she's a grand old barn."
>
> She belched cigarette smoke and the malodorous waft of stale beer. But she was to hockey fans what Grandma's house was to Thanksgiving dinner, providing a warm nest when the weather was turning to shit. In her bosom, she comforted 18,472 family members, convened in a cozy, intimate setting on Wednesday and Sunday nights for six straight months. If I close my eyes and flash to memories of the big barn, there are two feet of snow on the ground that envelops her.
>
> Making her unique, the classic organ loft nestled above the mezzanine behind the goal the Hawks defended twice. At the other end, a cramped press box so tiny it couldn't house a cooler of beverages. Working media, team personnel, and league types dined pregame in the bowels of the Stadium where the always-affable Chef Hans would be sweating over the carving station, replete with steaming hunks of roast pork or prime rib.
>
> I loved her, and while the United Center checks far more boxes for enhancing the fan experience, it lacks the charm of the Stadium. I've seen three Stanley Cup teams grace the UC. Been to several terrific Rolling Stones shows there. Disney on Ice. The Who. AC/DC. I've had more expendable cash since the United Center opened its doors in '94, so it's afforded me more experiences. But I always will remain attached to the less cavernous, zero–country club atmosphere of the Stadium.

> Like going to the drive-in theater with your high school sweetheart, back when you had only the scratch for a case of Little Kings and some White Castles, it was more than capable of torturing you with pleasure. You never forget your first girl.

I myself had the privilege of attending several games at the Stadium, but two specific games stand out the most.

I couldn't have been more than eight or nine years old when my uncle took me to my first game at the Stadium. As a typical eight-year-old, I didn't grasp the importance of the experience until much later. I don't recall the opponent. I don't recall the outcome of the game, but I do recall one specific goal for a very painful reason.

The Blackhawks scored, the horn blew, and the crowd erupted. I was witnessing my first NHL goal in person. The Stadium seats, like most arena seats, would fold up when you stood up. When the celebration ended, I went to sit back down but foolishly put my right hand under the seat. As the seat went down under my weight, my fingertip got trapped. When I realized what had happened, I looked at my hand. It was gushing blood and half of my fingernail was gone.

My uncle, a fireman, looked at me, somewhat panicked. He looked at my finger, looked at the scoreboard, then back at me.

"Are you OK? Do we need to go?" he asked, praying I wouldn't say I did.

Of course, we didn't leave. We pulled some napkins from our pregame meal off the floor and the game rolled on. That was the end for me. It was Blackhawks for life.

The second game took place on January 19, 1991. The Gulf War was ending and the NHL's best players had gathered at the Chicago Stadium for the annual All-Star Game. There was, to quote Jim Carr in *Slap Shot*, an "air of expectancy" in the building.

One group of fans had a sign that read, "Let's Show the World How We Do It in Chicago." Cheering throughout the entirety of the anthem was becoming a tradition, and combined with the knowledge that a national TV audience was watching, it resulted in the loudest and most popular anthem performance in recent memory, aside perhaps from Whitney Houston's Super Bowl XXV performance in Tampa. The crowd was in a frenzy before singer Wayne Messmer or organist Frank Pellico even struck a note.

"The patriotism that all the fans showed...it was the loudest that I've ever heard the national anthem. Still thinking about it chokes me up," recalls former Blackhawk Jeremy Roenick.

Yes, I was in the building for that game, and I can tell you firsthand that anthem was every bit as loud and memorable as the tallest tales describe. Every hair on my body was standing up, my eyes welled with tears, and my ears rang. It's a memory I will never forget and a memory that will likely never be duplicated in my lifetime.

10

TONY O

Anthony James Esposito, or "Tony O" as he's known to Blackhawks fans, was one of the greatest goaltenders in the history of the National Hockey League.

He won the Calder Trophy, awarded to the league's best rookie, in 1970, after posting a league-leading 15 shutouts (still an NHL record), a 2.17 goals-against average, and an NHL-best .932 save percentage. He is a three-time winner of the Vezina Trophy, given to the NHL goaltender "adjudged to be the best at this position." He was a six-time All-Star, saw his No. 35 retired by the Chicago Blackhawks in 1988, and in 1997 was named to the NHL's Top 100 players of all time list. He is the Blackhawks' all-time leader in wins (418), shutouts (74), and games played for a goalie (873). For these accomplishments, Esposito was inducted into the Hockey Hall of Fame in 1988.

"Tony was the backbone of our team," Bobby Hull recalls. "He won many games for us."

However, Esposito wasn't just a great goalie. He was also a great innovator. He was one of the early adopters, along with Vladislav Tretiak and Jacques Plante, of the butterfly style of goaltending, which remains the dominant style even in today's NHL. The butterfly style is distinguished by a goaltender dropping to his or her knees and spreading the leg pads wide in each direction to take away the lower portion of the net. Esposito's adoption of the style, along with his lethal glove hand, made him one of the most difficult goaltenders to beat.

Esposito also revolutionized the goalie mask and pads. His plain white mask, which resembles the one worn by horror movie icon Jason Voorhees, was designed to fit Esposito's face exactly. It was made of aircraft fiberglass, among the strongest materials available at the time. Despite the mask's durability, it did not protect Tony O from lacerations. Often when Esposito would take a puck in the face, his bones would cut his skin from the inside out. Those cuts were easy to heal, though.

"They were straight cuts, not jagged," Esposito said. "When you got cut without a mask, it tore you badly, so you had terrible scars. Mine were fine and stitches healed up. Plus, I've got that Italian skin. You don't get as many wrinkles as you age."

The mask served him well until the 1974–75 season, when Tony O took three separate shots off the eye. The third shot did some damage, affecting his sight. Esposito took it upon himself to add a protective cage around the eye area.

"I put these bars on the cage because I got hit in the eye a couple of times," Esposito remembers. "The last time was severe, and I had vision problems for a little while. I decided to do something if I wanted to continue to play. I came up with my hacksaw and cut off the bars and made it fit and taped it on." The bars became something of a prototype for the modern goalie mask.

Later that season, Esposito added another element to his mask by extending the protection higher on his head. What once covered only his face now extended to cover the upper part of his skull. "I got zinged in the forehead a few times, so that would deflect the puck," Esposito recalled.

This wasn't the only time Esposito updated his equipment because of injury. During a practice in 1971, teammate Lou Angotti fired a slap shot at Esposito. The puck struck the goalie in the throat.

"I thought I was dead," recalled Esposito.

Consequently, the goaltender added a neck piece to his mask. To this day, Esposito speaks with a rasp in his voice as a result of the shot. Angotti, who is a close friend of Esposito's, still hears about the incident to this day.

Esposito also adapted some of the equipment designed to protect his lower body. Early in his career, he sewed a 12x6 piece of thin elastic mesh between the legs of his goalie pants. The mesh functioned as a net preventing pucks from slipping through his five-hole. During one particular game, the mesh worked so well the puck rebounded to one of Esposito's opponents as if thrown off a trampoline.

He used the mesh until the NHL was forced to adopt a rule outlawing its use. Once the webbing was no longer an option, Esposito resorted to sponges to minimize his five-hole. He cut the material inside his pants and sewed in the rolls. If you look at modern goaltending pants, you'll see a similar design.

STAN'S STICK

Tony Esposito wasn't the only Blackhawks innovator of that era.

Stan Mikita is to this day considered the inventor of the curved stick blade. During a practice in the mid-1960s, Mikita accidentally bent his stick blade.

"My invention started like all great inventions do—by accident. It happened that my stick got caught in the doorway of where the players come in and out of the bench, and somebody pushed me forward even more and the stick cracked. It didn't break, but it cracked," Mikita recalled. "As I pulled it out and I saw the 'L' shape in the stick, I got a little upset because now I had to go all the way downstairs to get another stick, and I didn't really want to do that. I saw a puck laying there and I slammed it against the boards in anger, and there was a different sound that I heard. I shot a couple more, and it turned out to be the same."

Mikita quickly learned he could bend stick blades by heating them up, which he did with a propane torch, a technique still used today.

Mikita's discovery quickly caught on around the league, and the curved blade is essential to all hockey players, from NHLers to kids trying to curve the plastic blades of their sticks in gym class.

Mikita was also one of the first players to adopt wearing a helmet after losing part of his ear.

"I guess I was too stupid to put on the helmet until I got hit in the head and it woke me up a little bit," Mikita joked. "The most important part of our body, the head, we didn't have much protection."

Mikita then realized that the NHL helmet could be improved and provide more protection than they were at the time.

"I got together with an engineer from Riddell Company, and we came up with one with a suspension in it that the football players used to use. Then we got into the rubber foam afterwards. It saved me an awful lot of headaches," Mikita said.

When Esposito played, every goaltender used the same glove or something very similar. Tony O noticed that sometimes pucks would deflect off the sleeve of his glove and into the net, so he decided to do some research. The official rulebook stated that the glove could not be more than eight inches wide, but it didn't specify *which* part of the glove. Esposito molded a piece of hard plastic and attached it to the sleeve of his glove. Now the entire piece was eight inches wide. The plastic was also curved upward to deflect pucks away from the goal.

There was one final piece to Tony Esposito's James Bond-esque equipment innovations (that we know of). Esposito added furniture stuffing to his leg pads, adding about three inches of coverage to each leg. When equipment inspections came during the playoffs, Esposito and the Blackhawks staff would put heavy weights on the pads to temporarily compress them so they could pass league inspection.

Throughout his career, Esposito looked for every advantage he could find, usually within the rules, sometimes not. NASCAR driver Richard Petty once said, "If you ain't trying to cheat a little, you ain't likely to win much." Tony O was trying to win. So were his opponents. It's a shame Esposito didn't patent any of these ideas, as many have been adapted and are used in the game today.

11

SAVOIR FAIRE

Denis Savard.

Saying that name to any Blackhawks fan evokes a big, fat grin, and with good reason. The memories he created with his swift skating, dazzling stick-handling, and scoring ability made him one of the most electrifying players of his era and in Blackhawks history, and he may be an even finer human being.

Nicknamed "Savoir Faire" after the mouse that feuded with Klondike Kat in the 1960s cartoon series, Savard was chosen third overall by the Blackhawks in the 1980 NHL amateur draft. He was passed over by his hometown Montreal Canadiens, who chose center Doug Wickenheiser, and the Winnipeg Jets, who chose defenseman Dave Babych.

The selection certainly raised some eyebrows around the league. Savard, who stood just 5-foot-10 and weighed in at 170 pounds, was small by NHL standards. "You always have that insecurity when you get to the NHL. From the get-go, I knew I was going to be OK," he said. "I was going to be able to play with these guys."

It didn't take Savard long to prove his doubters wrong. Before he played a single NHL game, Savard shared a tearful moment with his parents, brothers, and friends in the Montreal airport. With tears in his eyes, he said to the group, "I'm not coming back until summer. I'll make the team in Chicago." Savard boarded the plane and never looked back.

In his rookie season, Savard scored 28 goals and tallied 47 assists for a total of 75 points. Only two rookies in team history would have better freshman campaigns: Steve Larmer scored 90 points (43 goals) in 1982–83 and Artemi Panarin registered 77 points (30 goals) in 2015–16.

As impressive as his debut season was, Savard's sophomore year put him in another stratosphere. His 119 points (32 goals) set a club record until it was broken the next season...by Denis Savard. In 1987–88 he set the club record for points (131), a record that still stands to this day. The only player who has come close is Patrick Kane, who scored 110 points in 2018–19.

"I was a good skater. I was able to generate a lot of stuff offensively because of my skating ability and my puck-handling," Savard demurred.

That's an incredible understatement. Savard was a human highlight reel.

"He could spin and turn and absolutely razzle-dazzle you," former goalie and current broadcaster Darren Pang said.

"Even playing with him...I found myself standing around watching him," laughed Steve Larmer.

"Denis Savard could stop on a dime and give you nine cents change," said broadcaster Jim Hughson.

Savard's trademark maneuver was the Spin-O-Rama. Savard would close in on a hapless and typically panicked defenseman, dip his shoulder, and spin 360 degrees to his backhand, never losing control of the puck.

"That particular move gave me the space that I needed, as an offensive player, to be able to gain the blue line to back the defenseman off. Once you get two or three feet inside the blue line, you're able to make plays," he said.

As always, Savard is underselling his abilities. Yes, he used the Spin-O-Rama as an evasive maneuver and to create space, but he also used the move, many times, to put the puck behind the stunned and defenseless goalie. "It was fun to watch," Steve Larmer recalls with his typical dry wit.

After 10 seasons and 1,013 points, the Blackhawks traded Savard to his hometown Montreal Canadiens ahead of the 1990–91 season. In exchange for Savard, the Blackhawks acquired defenseman and eventual franchise legend Chris Chelios, and a second-round pick in the 1991 entry draft (Michael Pomichter).

In 1993, Savard played an integral role with the Montreal Canadiens en route to their 24th Stanley Cup in franchise history. That season, the 31-year-old Savard tallied 50 points in 63 regular season games. He appeared in 14 playoff games but injured his knee in Game 1 of the

Stanley Cup Final. Hockey historian Dave Stubbs recalls the moment the Canadiens captured the Cup: "One of the most famous pictures is of Denis Savard coming out with a suit in 1993. You could have turned off all the lights in the Montreal Forum and his smile would have lit up the entire building."

That summer, Savard signed a free-agent deal with the Tampa Bay Lightning but was traded back to Chicago halfway through the 1994–95 season. Savard finished his career where it began, in Chicago, this time at the United Center.

After 13 seasons and 881 games with the Blackhawks, Savard is third in team history in points (1,096), behind only Stan Mikita (1,467) and Bobby Hull (1,153). On March 19, 1998, the Blackhawks retired Savard's No. 18. He was inducted into the Hockey Hall of Fame the following year, but his time with the Blackhawks wasn't over yet.

On November 27, 2006, Savard was named interim head coach of the team, replacing the fired Trent Yawney. He coached one more full season and four games of the next before being replaced by Joel Quenneville, who then led the Blackhawks to three Stanley Cups (2010, 2013, 2015).

"It's a tough day, no question. I'm hurt," Savard said in the wake of the firing. "I worked hard to do the best I could to get the team on its way to the Stanley Cup."

Even in the painful days and weeks after his firing, Savard's class remained. "This is a business, and in business, there is always change," he said. "This team is not about Denis Savard. Joel Quenneville is doing a great job and he's a great guy. I love what he's doing."

Many of Savard's players, including Patrick Kane, were saddened by the move. "He was my first coach in the league," Kane said with tears in his eyes. "I think more than anything, a great friend."

"Denis is a true, genuine, great person," says former teammate Murray Bannerman. "Saying that about him, to me, is more important than any points records or anything he might have done."

"There's only one Denis Savard," says Darren Pang. "He was worth the price of admission."

12

LIKE FATHER, LIKE SON

The story of the Wirtz family's rise to power in Chicago could've been written in Hollywood. The Wirtz family is hockey and American royalty, and it all started with Arthur Wirtz.

Arthur Michael Wirtz was born on January 23, 1901. His father, Frederick, was a Rogers Park police officer; his mother, Leona, was a homemaker. They were as typical an American family as there was in those days, often finding it difficult to make ends meet. It's hard to imagine a couple like this raising one of Chicago's most successful and driven businessmen. Some attribute Arthur's drive to the abusive nature of his stepmother, whom Frederick married after Leona passed away.

Arthur attended the University of Michigan while courting Virginia Louise Wadsworth, the daughter of a wealthy family from Chicago's Edgewater neighborhood. He graduated in 1922. Upon his return home, he married Virginia, despite the grumbling of her parents, and found gainful employment as an assistant surveyor at a railyard. He enjoyed the job but had bigger ambitions.

In 1927, with $10,000 in capital, Arthur partnered with W. Francis Little and Rolland E. Huburt, two New York realtors, and their company quickly grew from a single 16-story apartment building to an empire of close to 80 buildings and 3,000 rental units. Shortly thereafter, the Great Depression struck, crushing the nation's economy and causing fortunes to vanish overnight.

Fortunately for Arthur, he was able to survive. When he purchased a property, he did so with as little debt attached as possible. He had also invested his proceeds in gold, giving him loads of cash when most Americans had little to none. Among those affected by the Depression were Virginia's parents, the Wadsworths, whom Arthur was able to rescue from financial ruin. Although they looked down their noses at young Arthur, he never hesitated to help and never held it over their heads.

James E. "Pop" Norris, a Canadian businessman who had made his fortune as a grain speculator at Chicago's Board of Trade, took notice of Wirtz's early real estate success. The heir to a family fortune, money was never an issue for Norris. When the Great Depression hit, Norris was ready to pounce, just as Wirtz had. Norris eyed several prime locations in downtown Chicago, including a spot on Randolph St. and Michigan Ave. Norris brokered Wirtz to close the deal and a new partnership was born. Within 10 years, the pair would become two of the wealthiest men in the country.

Norris and Wirtz would soon turn their real estate attention to sports arenas. Though Arthur was a great athlete, he wasn't a sports fan. He saw sports fans as customers and means to an end; if you're a longtime Blackhawks fan, that sentence made you roll your eyes or laugh, because that belief might as well have been emblazoned on Arthur and Bill Wirtz's foreheads.

Pop Norris was the opposite. He followed the teams he owned as if he was a season ticket holder. He loved the games and prioritized winning. Somehow, the combination of personalities made Norris and Wirtz's partnership work.

One of their first arena acquisitions came in 1933, when they purchased Detroit's Olympia Stadium. Detroit, still reeling from the Depression, had 200,000 unemployed at the time. The arena's owners, desperate to unload the $2.5 million property, sold it to Wirtz and Norris for 10 cents on the dollar. To seal the deal, they threw in the floundering Detroit Falcons franchise for another $100,000.

Wirtz and Norris were now the new owners of a stadium and an NHL franchise. They quickly renamed the team the Red Wings. Arthur was placed in charge of the business end of the team, while Pop Norris and his son, Jimmy, handled the hockey side, quickly turning the Wings into one of the league's top teams.

Two years later, Wirtz and Pop Norris, along with the emerging business acumen of Jimmy Norris, took control of the biggest indoor stadium in the world, the Chicago Stadium. The Stadium opened in March of 1929. Nine months later, the NHL's Chicago Blackhawks, owned by coffee magnate and WWI Major Frederic McLaughlin, made the Stadium their home. Despite winning two Stanley Cups under

McLaughlin's 18-year ownership, the team and the franchise struggled with losing, coaching changes, and disagreements with figures around the league.

Norris had long waited to buy the Blackhawks from McLaughlin. When the Major passed in 1944, Norris had his chance. But there was a catch—because Norris owned a stake in other NHL teams, he wasn't allowed to buy the team outright. He convinced longtime Hawks president Bill Tobin to front a group that took over as de facto owners. Jimmy Norris and Arthur Wirtz were part of that group. Despite his long pursuit of the Blackhawks, Pop Norris neglected the team, as he was more focused on his beloved Red Wings. The Blackhawks stayed at or near the bottom of the league.

In 1945, another Chicago business, the Walgreen Drug Co., announced it would be selling liquor wholesaler Judge & Dolph. Arthur jumped at the opportunity to extend his Chicago empire. Judge & Dolph became a cornerstone of the Wirtz family fortune and it continues to this day.

Jimmy and Arthur became close friends and partners on their own, founding the International Boxing Club in 1949. This was the golden age of boxing, and Jimmy and Arthur knew it. The company produced several prepackaged boxing shows for television. Because of their control of the nation's best sports arenas, including New York's Madison Square Garden, they controlled who would fight who, who was the number one contender, and so on. From 1949 to 1955, IBC promoted 92 percent of the championship fights held in the United States. With their success, whispers of a monopoly began to surface.

In 1954, Arthur's oldest son, William Wadsworth "Bill" Wirtz, began working for his old man in the real estate and liquor segments of the family empire. Just as his father had, Bill became fast friends with Jimmy Norris. "We called him Uncle Jimmy," says Bill's son Rocky.

It was around this time, however, that the feds and the New York Athletic Commission began looking into the IBC. Norris, as the face of the organization, was the main target. New York Athletic commissioner Robert K. Christenberry called the IBC's stronghold on boxing "the gravest crisis in [boxing] history."

"It is already a matter of record that crooks have fixed fights in the course of pulling off betting coups," Christenberry said. "More importantly, they have muscled in on fighters, managers, and promoters to fleece them of their earnings."

At the same time, the federal government sued the IBC under the Sherman Antitrust Act. The charges accused Arthur and Jimmy Norris, who were defendants in the suit, of fixing bouts, doctoring their financials, consorting with mob figures, and use of intimidation. The government won the case. In 1959, Arthur and Jimmy dissolved their interest in the IBC. A year later, Norris testified that he had been involved with mobster Frankie Carbo, who was sentenced to 25 years for extortion and conspiracy.

Despite the outcome of the lawsuit, Arthur and Jimmy avoided jail time. In fact, their wealth only grew. They sold their stock in Madison Square Garden for $4 million and later sold the St. Louis Arena.

During all of this, the Blackhawks had begun to make some noise. After Pop's passing in 1952, Jimmy took a stronger interest in the Blackhawks. In July of 1954, Jimmy made his best hockey move, prying coach Tommy Ivan, who had won Cups in 1950, 1952, and 1954, away from the Red Wings. Ivan was named coach and GM.

"I wanted a new challenge other than coaching, and I got one in Chicago," Ivan said.

Upon his arrival in Chicago, Ivan convinced Arthur, who was entrenched in his role as Blackhawks president, to buy two minor league clubs, the St. Catharines Teepees and the Buffalo Bisons. Those clubs produced Bobby Hull and Pierre Pilote, two of the franchise's greatest players. In 1961, Hull, Pilote, and Stan Mikita led the Blackhawks to their first title since 1938.

Jimmy Norris passed away in 1966, leaving Arthur in charge of the organization. Arthur gave immediate control of the hockey team to his sons; Bill would serve as team president and Michael would be the organization's senior vice president. Arthur also ordered that Bill join the NHL Board of Governors. At the time, the move felt like a formality, but it would shake the foundations of the entire league years later.

The Blackhawks enjoyed success the first couple of years under Bill's reign as president. In 1966, Hull broke the NHL goal record, scoring 54. No player before had ever surpassed 50. But in 1969, the Blackhawks found themselves at the bottom of the league.

Wirtz didn't take well to losing. He unleashed a tirade to a *Chicago Tribune* reporter. The next day, the headline read "Bill Wirtz Vows 'Sweeping Changes' to the Hawks." In the piece, Wirtz questioned the players' commitment and heart. He called them soft; only Hull avoided Wirtz's wrath.

"My father put me in charge of this club," Wirtz said, "and I may be fired. But I wouldn't be the only one to change uniforms. It isn't the losing that irritates me, it's the way they lose; the lack of desire. I don't go for the injuries excuse."

Over time, Bill Wirtz became a villain to Chicago sports fans. He earned the nickname "Dollar Bill" for his penny-pinching management style. During his tenure, the Blackhawks shipped off so many stars over contract disputes, names synonymous with Blackhawks hockey including Hull, Jeremy Roenick, Chris Chelios, Ed Belfour, and Tony Amonte. Gil Stein, a longtime hockey executive, claims to have heard Wirtz say, "Every time Chicago fans boo me, I raise their ticket prices."

Aside from cheaping out on stars and ripping the fans, Wirtz refused to televise Blackhawks home games, a policy held by Arthur in his time as president. Wirtz claimed that "giving away the product for free" would be a slap in the face to season ticket holders and would lower attendance. Wirtz's inability to evolve with the times, on the ice and off, led to his becoming one of the most despised figures in Chicago sports history.

"Club presidents aren't in the business of being loved by fans," Bill would say. "I learned that from my father."

Bill Wirtz passed away on September 26, 2007. I remember getting the email from Blackhawks media relations and reading it with mixed emotions. The human being in me knew a lot of people who loved Bill Wirtz, and I felt for them and their loss. The Hawks fan in me had a sudden surge of hope. Maybe, just maybe, Bill's successor would change things.

All I wanted was home games on TV.

We got so much more.

13

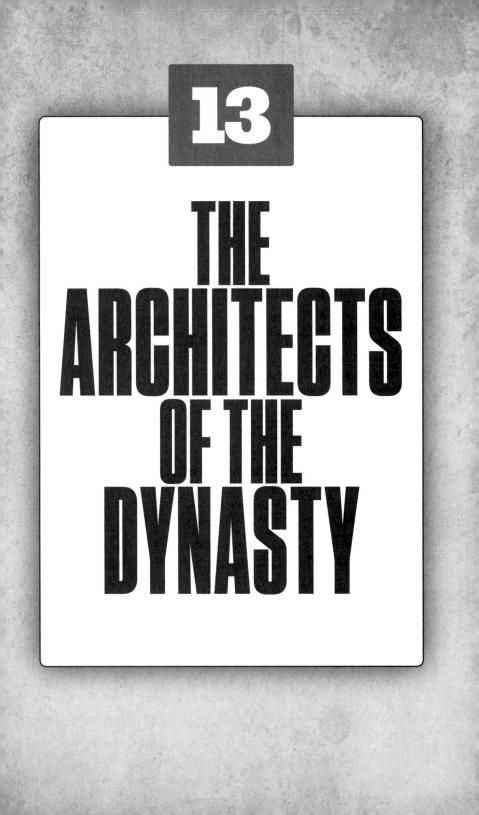

THE ARCHITECTS OF THE DYNASTY

If more than 20 years in sports radio has taught me anything, it's that when a sports franchise is in the midst of a really strong run, or more rarely a dynasty, fans still need something to argue about. Total happiness is not an option.

When it came to the Blackhawks of the 2010s, the arguments focused on general managers Dale Tallon and Stan Bowman. Who should get the most credit for the Cups? Who should get blame for the things that didn't work out? Dale Tallon was mistreated! Dale Tallon screwed up! Stan Bowman only got the job because of his father! Stan Bowman was incredibly qualified for the job!

The bulk of these arguments are simultaneously true.

Before we get into all of that, though, there is a name that hasn't received much credit at all: Mike Smith.

Smith was the team's GM from September of 2000 to October of 2003, and while many of his moves were disastrous (trading Bryan McCabe for Alexander Karpovtsev, naming Alpo Suhonen head coach), there may not be a Blackhawks dynasty without him.

In 2002, Smith used a second-round pick to select Michigan State defenseman Duncan Keith 54th overall. Keith went on to win three Stanley Cups, two Norris Trophies, a Conn Smythe Trophy, and will be enshrined in the Hockey Hall of Fame as soon as he becomes eligible.

The next season, Smith drafted Keith's longtime defensive partner, Brent Seabrook, with the 14th overall pick. Seabrook provided the Blackhawks with solid defense and the ability to play on the power play and penalty kill. Seabrook also scored one of the biggest goals of the dynasty era, beating the Detroit Red Wings in overtime of Game 7 during the second round of the 2013 Stanley Cup playoffs.

Thirty-eight picks later, Smith chose Moncton Wildcats goalie Corey Crawford. Crawford would lead the Blackhawks to their 2013 and 2015 Cup championships, and is the franchise's third-winningest goalie, behind only Tony Esposito and Glenn Hall.

Without Keith, Seabrook, and Crawford, chances are those Blackhawks teams don't win any of their three Stanley Cups.

There. Credit given to Mike Smith.

Now, on to the argument at hand...Tallon or Bowman?

Tallon has a leg up on Bowman with most Hawks fans for several reasons:

He played for the team.
He was a beloved broadcaster.
He's a no-nonsense, "Chicago-type" guy.

Bowman, on the other hand, isn't quite what fans think of when they think of hockey:

He's an intellectual, with a degree in finance and computer applications from Notre Dame.
He was born with a silver spoon, or hockey stick, in his mouth; his father, Scotty, is hockey royalty and certainly played a role in him getting a job in hockey.
He's soft-spoken, calculated, and unemotional.

Anyone who lives or has lived in or around Chicago can see why fans prefer Tallon's personality to Bowman's. Tallon was a larger than life figure. Bowman, despite being part of the organization since 2001, where he started his career as special assistant to Smith, is not.

The argument for Tallon, who was GM of the Blackhawks from June of 2005 until July of 2009:

Drafted Jonathan Toews and Patrick Kane.
Traded for Patrick Sharp in one of the most one-sided trades in sports history.
Traded for Martin Havlat.
Traded Tuomo Ruutu for 2010 Cup winner Andrew Ladd.
Signed Brian Campbell.
Signed Marian Hossa.
Signed Tomas Kopecky.

Signed 2010 Cup champion John Madden.
Drafted Niklas Hjalmarsson in the fourth round
Drafted Marcus Kruger in the fifth round.
Signed Antti Niemi, the 2010 Cup-winning goalie.
Traded for Kris Versteeg.

The arguments against Tallon:

Drafted Jack Skille seventh overall in 2005.
Drafted Kyle Beach 11th overall in 2008.
Signed Cristobal Huet, who was replaced by Niemi.
Filed free-agent paperwork late, costing Hawks significant cap space.
Aside from Toews and Kane, acquired no one of note during the 2006 and 2007 drafts.

The arguments for Bowman:

Drafted Brandon Saad in the second round in 2011.
Signed goalie Scott Darling, who got the Hawks out of the first round in 2015 when Crawford struggled.
Drafted Andrew Shaw in the fifth round in 2011.
Traded for Michal Handzus ahead of the 2013 Cup.
Drafted 2015 Cup champion Teuvo Teravainen 18th overall in 2015.
Traded for Antoine Vermette ahead of 2015 playoffs.
Traded for defenseman Johnny Oduya, who won two Cups with the Blackhawks.
Signed Brad Richards, a key contributor to the 2015 Stanley Cup winner.

The arguments against Bowman:

Signed Bryan Bickell to a four-year deal. Bickell struggled and moving his contract necessitated losing Teravainen.

Losing Brandon Saad, another cap casualty, for Artem Anisimov and Marko Dano.
Drafted Mark McNeill 18th overall in 2011.
Traded Nick Leddy for Ville Pokka.

Remember, we're only analyzing their moves as they pertain to the dynasty. Since then, Bowman has made several bad decisions,

ONE SHARP TRADE

While history will look back at the Blackhawks of the 2010s and think of Jonathan Toews, Patrick Kane, Brent Seabrook, and Duncan Keith primarily, what truly separated those teams from their competition was their depth. They had the ability to roll four lines most nights, and all four of those lines were good enough to be second or third lines on most teams. Because of their star-studded lineup, players who would have been stars in other cities were in supporting roles for the Hawks.

Patrick Sharp was probably the best of these players. He was part of all three Stanley Cup champions, was an alternate captain, and put up big numbers even in the shadows of Kane and Toews. Sharp played 11 seasons with the Blackhawks, appearing in 749 games and scoring 249 goals and tallying 283 assists for 532 points. That's 15th all time in team history, ahead of Al Secord, Dirk Graham, and other Blackhawks legends. In 117 playoff games with Chicago, Sharp added 42 goals and 38 assists for 80 points, which is tied for ninth all time in team history.

As these numbers clearly show, Patrick Sharp is a huge part of Blackhawks history. What makes it even more amazing is how little GM Dale Tallon gave up to acquire him.

On December 5, 2005, the Blackhawks received Sharp and winger Eric Meloche from the Philadelphia Flyers for winger Matt Ellison and a third-round pick in the 2006 draft. Ellison went on to appear in all of seven games for the Flyers before walking away from the game. He registered one assist.

Sharp picked up a total of 612 regular season and playoff points for the Blackhawks. Ellison had one career point. I wonder if a +611-point trade would qualify as the most one-sided trade of all time. Maybe the three Stanley Cups put it over the edge.

including moving on from Artemi Panarin and signing Seabrook to an eight-year contract while his decline was already underway.

When we look at the score sheet, the edge must go to Tallon. His moves, especially the signing of Hossa, solidified an already emerging core. Bowman did a good job of keeping the team competitive despite cap issues, but without Tallon's drafts and especially his free agency savvy, the Hawks don't win.

14

THE FREAK OF NATURE

"Too small."

"He can't play in the NHL at his size."

"He'll never make it."

These are some of the things scouts and observers had to say about eventual three-time Stanley Cup champion, two-time Norris Trophy winner, Olympic gold medalist, and future Hall of Famer Duncan Keith ahead of the 2002 NHL draft.

"Everybody wanted big players," Keith says. "It was the old NHL rules, where you were allowed to hook and hold, and there weren't any small guys in the league."

By today's standards, Keith isn't really all that small. He stands 6-foot-1 and weighs in at 192 pounds, but at the time he was selected the NHL was a league built on obstruction, clutching and grabbing, and an overall slower pace to the game. Hulking defensemen like Dallas' Derian Hatcher thrived in that era, but Blackhawks GM Mike Smith wasn't deterred. He selected Keith 54th overall in the second round of the draft and described the Michigan State product as a "Phil Housley–type defenseman," and a "great skater with good skill."

Housley, who played 21 seasons (1982–2003) in the "Old NHL", was one of the exceptions to the rule of the era. Despite his 5-foot-10, 185-pound frame, he was one of the premier offensive defensemen in the league. He played 1,495 NHL games and picked up 1,232 points, good for fourth all time among defensemen behind only Ray Bourque, Paul Coffey, and Al MacInnis.

Smith's comparison was dismissed at the time as a bit of GM hyperbole; every team likes to pretend it has selected the next Wayne Gretzky on draft day. Thing is, Smith was right when he made the pick. Sure, Keith will never come close to Housley in points, but Housley couldn't hold a candle to Keith's defense. Keith was the steal of the 2002 draft.

"When you're talking about the elite of the elite, a lot of times you're talking about offensive production. Points and goals. And Dunc's able to put those up," Brent Seabrook says. "But the best part of his game is his defensive game. His gaps. His ability to read rushes. His ability to play pucks to the corners and get them to our forwards."

The NHL locked its players out ahead of the 2004–05 NHL season. The entire 82-game season and playoffs were canceled. Once the league and the players union finally reached an agreement, sweeping rule changes were announced. Keith made his NHL debut the next season. Two of the changes the league made helped make Keith's transition to the NHL a smooth one:

1. Lifting the prohibition of the two-line pass.
2. The "zero-tolerance" policy as it pertained to hooking, interference, and holding.

The two-line pass allowed puck-moving defensemen to find streaking forwards and send them rushing the other way. In fact, a major part of Joel Quenneville's system during the 2010s dynasty was built on the long stretch pass. Puck-moving defensemen were an absolute necessity to make the system work, and Keith was the prototype. The team's defensive corps were always loaded with puck-movers; Seabrook, Brian Campbell, Johnny Oduya, Niklas Hjalmarsson, Nick Leddy, and others all had the ability to move the puck forward with accuracy and speed.

Speaking of speed, during his prime years, Keith was among the fastest defensemen in hockey. "He's so quick," says Montreal Canadiens defenseman Shea Weber. "You rarely beat him. Forwards can't beat him."

"He's a great skater," agrees Los Angeles Kings forward Anze Kopitar. "It's really tough to create some space for yourself out there."

But a lot of defensemen are fast. A lot of defensemen can move the puck. What makes Duncan Keith so special? His endurance.

Throughout his career, Keith has averaged more than 25 minutes per game. He plays at even strength, and on the power play and penalty kill. He's unstoppable. Even late in his career, at age 36, he's averaging 24 minutes of ice time. People keep expecting him to slow down, and he doesn't.

Mike Vorkapich has been the strength and conditioning coach for Michigan State since 1998. He has a firsthand account of Keith's freakish endurance. The VO2 Max test basically measures a player's fitness and willingness to work through pain and distress. If you've ever seen an NHL prospect throw up at the combine, it's typically after the VO2 test.

The test takes place on a treadmill. Level 1 is a zero incline, six-mph jog. An incline is introduced at Level 2, and with each incremental level, the challenge gets faster and steeper. Vorkapich, who compares Level 4 to a typical NHL shift, says that only three MSU hockey players have gotten through Level 6, and only one was able to run for a minute at Level 7, which is 11 mph uphill. That player was Duncan Keith.

"I don't know how many overtimes that would be equal to," Vorkapich says.

Remember, this was achieved during Keith's collegiate days. Since then, he's played in 15 NHL seasons, using professional strength and conditioning coaches and equipment. He's also played 25 minutes in more than 1,000 NHL games. If anything, he's more fit than ever.

Blackhawks skating coach Dan Jansen ran the team's preseason physicals. In or around 2013, he gave Keith the VO2 Max test again and noted that the only athlete he's seen with a higher test result was Tour de France winner Lance Armstrong.

"He's a freak," Patrick Kane said. "I try not to compare my [VO2 Max] score to his."

"He's superhuman," says Oduya. "He had, obviously, physical ability other guys don't have. His lung capacity and ability to process oxygen is unbelievable."

Maybe Keith has some genetic advantage over other players. Maybe he just outworks everyone. Maybe it's both.

"He hates to lose. When the chips are down, you want him in the corner. His willingness to do what it takes to win is not matched by many people," gushes Seabrook.

"I think there's a part of you that just focuses on the shift in front of you and nothing more," Keith says. "There's also a sense in the back of your head that it's do or die, and this next shift could be your last shift."

There's no telling when Keith will stop, but whenever his career ends, he will go down as the best defenseman in Blackhawks franchise history. Chris Chelios and Pierre Pilote certainly have claims to the throne, but three Stanley Cup championships, two Norris Trophies, and a Conn Smythe Trophy might trump any statistical argument against him.

Keith's No. 2 will hang from the United Center rafters for eternity. His place in the Hockey Hall of Fame is already secure.

15

SEABS

The 2010s Blackhawks never lacked for leadership. Jonathan Toews, aka Captain Serious, was, and is, renowned as one of the best captains in NHL history. Duncan Keith, Patrick Kane, and Marian Hossa led those teams by example on the ice. Throughout the era, depth players like Craig Adams, Adam Burish, Jamal Mayers, and others stepped into leadership roles, but one man held the mantle as the team's vocal leader for the entire dynasty: Brent Seabrook.

The Blackhawks selected Seabrook with the 14th overall pick in the 2003 NHL draft. The defenseman made his NHL debut during the 2005–06 season, during which he appeared in 69 games and recorded 32 points. On top of his three Stanley Cup championships, Seabrook won a gold medal for Team Canada in the 2010 Olympic Games in Vancouver and was named an All-Star in 2015. He ranks third all time in franchise history in games played, behind only Keith and Stan Mikita.

The big defenseman's tenure, accomplishments, and level of play have earned him respect from his teammates and opponents.

"He's such a great leader, such a big part of this locker room," says Patrick Kane. "[He] takes in every guy just like he's known him his whole life. I mean, he's an unbelievable teammate."

"Biscuit," as he's known to his teammates, can be seen and heard ushering the team onto the ice before the opening faceoff: "Let's go boys, eh? Let's go, red!"

The best illustration of Seabrook's leadership and influence came during a 2013 playoff series with the Detroit Red Wings. The Blackhawks finished the lockout-shortened 48-game season with an incredible 36–7–5 record and were the clear favorites to win the Stanley Cup. The Hawks dispatched the eighth-seeded Minnesota Wild in five games, while their old Original Six rivals from Detroit surprised second-seeded Anaheim, winning the series in seven games. The stage was set for one final playoff series before Detroit moved to the Eastern Conference the following season.

Many observers, myself included, felt the Hawks were lucky to not be facing the Ducks, and the Wings would just be a speed bump on the way to the conference final; after a convincing 4–1 win in Game 1, those feelings seemed to be justified. But perhaps the Blackhawks took the Wings a little too lightly, as well.

The Red Wings went on to win the next three games, putting the Blackhawks on the brink of elimination. During Game 4, Jonathan Toews was melting down. "I kinda hit rock bottom. I wasn't scoring. Things weren't going very well," Toews remembers. He was mired in a nine-game goalless streak and had just taken three consecutive penalties on three consecutive shifts.

Moments after Toews' third penalty—a high-sticking call against Jonathan Ericsson—the captain angrily skated toward the penalty box, again. This time, No. 7 was right behind him. Seabrook stepped into the box with Toews and got in his face, patting him on the head and encouraging the captain to wake up.

"I was feeling pressure to finally contribute," Toews says. "[Seabrook] came over, all the way to the box, to try to cheer me up and get me to snap out of it."

"I just tried to calm him down," Seabrook said. "We need him. He's the best player on the team and our leader. If the rest of the group sees him like that it's going to trickle down, so we need him to be focused and be ready. He's a heart-and-soul type of guy, and he was frustrated. Our whole team was frustrated. I just needed to let him know it's OK, we'll get it figured out."

"I don't know if it's something that goes with the relationship and the friendship we've had over the years, rooming with him my rookie year here in Chicago...but he's always kind of looked after me that way," Toews said.

The Blackhawks ultimately lost that game 2–0, but it was a turning point in the series. Toews responded in Game 5. With a 2–1 lead and a power play, Marian Hossa, who was manning the right point, found Toews alone near the Red Wings' goal line. The captain picked his spot and didn't miss. Relief and exhilaration on his face, Toews went to a knee, then leapt into Hossa's arms in celebration.

The monkey was off Toews' back, and the Blackhawks were ready to roll. They won Game 6 in Detroit 4–3 (Toews had two assists), forcing Game 7 at the United Center.

What happened in that game will go down as the defining moment of Brent Seabrook's career.

The Blackhawks ended the second period with a 1–0 lead on Patrick Sharp's goal, but 26 seconds into the third, Henrik Zetterberg knotted things up with a goal of his own. Tension was building, with every shot more meaningful and stressful than the last.

With 1:47 left in the third, Andrew Shaw fed defenseman Niklas Hjalmarsson, who was wide open at the point. Hjalmarsson blasted a slapper past Red Wings goalie Jimmy Howard. The United Center was up for grabs, but something wasn't right. Behind the play, Hawks winger Brandon Saad and Detroit's Kyle Quincey were tied up along the benches. The players were called for offsetting roughing penalties, and the goal was negated. The typically level-headed Hjalmarsson almost threw his stick in frustration.

The third period ended with the game was still tied. Overtime was next.

Just 3:35 into the extra period, Seabrook corralled a loose puck and flipped a fluttering puck toward Howard and past his glove. The Blackhawks had done it. For the first time in franchise history, they had come all the way back from a 3–1 series deficit and were headed to the Western Conference Final.

"I felt like I had a lot of room," Seabrook told NBC Sports Network. "I just tried to shoot it."

Perhaps if Seabrook hadn't followed Toews to the penalty box in Game 4, he never would have had the opportunity.

16

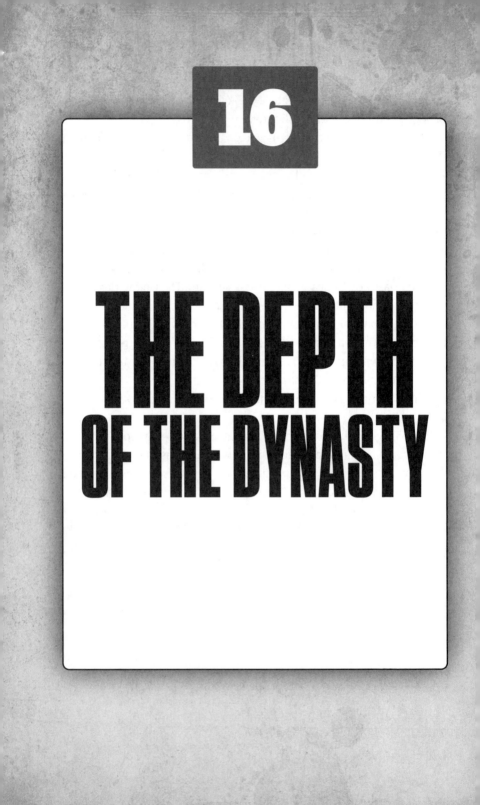

THE DEPTH OF THE DYNASTY

The 2010s Blackhawks will be remembered as a team loaded with superstars, and with good reason. When it's all said and done, those rosters should have four Hall of Famers. Patrick Kane, Jonathan Toews, and Duncan Keith will all join Marian Hossa when their times come, but the Blackhawks won their championships because of their unmatched depth.

In this chapter, we will sing the praises of the Blackhawks without whom the three Stanley Cup championships would not have been possible.

The Other Stars

Patrick Sharp - Winger - 117 playoff games - 42 goals - 38 assists - 80 points - +9

2010, 2013, 2015 Cup winner

On lesser teams, Patrick Sharp could have been a superstar. With his Hollywood good looks, blazing speed, and scoring ability, Sharp was one of the Blackhawks' most dependable and versatile players in an era loaded with them. During the 2010 Stanley Cup run, Sharp recorded 11 goals and 11 assists in 22 games.

After being acquired from Philadelphia in exchange for forward Matt Ellison—one of the most one-sided trades in sports history—Sharp played seven seasons with the Blackhawks. He scored 249 goals and added 283 assists in 749 regular season games.

Brandon Saad - Winger - 67 playoff games - 15 goals - 19 assists - 34 points - +16

2013, 2015 Cup winner

The soft-spoken Saad is one of his generation's better power forwards. While he never has, or will, put up huge numbers, he'll provide a "wow" moment once a game. He uses sneaky speed to gain distance after muscling through defenders. Saad can play in all situations and is the kind of depth scorer every Cup team needs. Like Sharp, Saad would be a star player on a lesser team. He's been called "Baby Hossa" because of the way he plays, though he hasn't been able to take that "next step" offensively in his career.

Niklas Hjalmarsson - Defenseman - 128 playoff games - 2 goals - 26 assists - 28 points - +22
2010, 2013, 2015 Cup winner
One word comes to mind when describing Hjalmarsson: warrior. Hjalmarsson was the Blackhawks' best pure defender of the era, and while he didn't stack up points like some of his defensive teammates, he could move the puck very well. "He's one of those guys that you have an appreciation to watch," says Joel Quenneville. "[Seeing] how he competes and seeing what he fights through to stay on the ice in a lot of games." Hjalmarsson was a willing and skilled shot-blocker. In 751 regular season and playoff games, the Swede blocked 1,484 shots.

When the Blackhawks traded Hjalmarsson to Arizona in the summer of 2017, it's reported that Quenneville stormed out of a meeting upon hearing the news. In exchange for Hjalmarsson, the Blackhawks received defenseman Connor Murphy, who since joining the Blackhawks has played quite well. But Quenneville could never warm up to Murphy. He was too upset to see one of his favorite "warriors" leave.

The Grinders

Dave Bolland - Center - 67 playoff games - 17 goals - 26 assists - 43 points - +9
2010, 2013 Cup winner
Blackhawks fans might love Bolland, nicknamed "The Rat," as much as Canucks fans hate him. Bolland was a thorn in the side of every opponent. He was a pest, often getting under the skin of players who were rarely thrown off, most notably Vancouver's Daniel and Henrik Sedin. "I played so many games against them in the past. If you let them go for a second or two, they'll be putting the puck through your

legs and in the back of your net. So when we do go in there, we've got to be ready for them," Bolland said. "When you get under guys' skins, you get them off their games. It's huge for your team and it's huge for confidence when you get them off their games."

Categorizing Bolland as "just a pest" is terribly underselling his value and skill. He was an excellent two-way centerman and penalty-killer. He also had a penchant for scoring big goals, none bigger than the 2013 Stanley Cup winner, completing the sequence of 17 seconds. The iconic image of Bolland throwing off his gloves in celebration will live in the minds of Blackhawks fans forever.

Bryan Bickell - Winger - 75 playoff games - 20 goals - 19 assists - 39 points - +21
2010 (four games), 2013, 2015 Cup winner
A prototype power forward, Bickell has three Stanley Cup rings with the Chicago Blackhawks. In 2010, he appeared in only four games during the team's Cup run but burst on to the scene during the Blackhawks' quest for the 2013 Stanley Cup. In 23 games, he picked up nine goals and eight assists. He scored the game-tying goal of the Cup-winning game, 17 seconds before Bolland broke the deadlock. Bickell's performance landed him a four-year, $16 million contract. However, his consistency and level of play dipped considerably. In November of 2016, while a member of the Carolina Hurricanes, it was revealed that Bickell was diagnosed with multiple sclerosis. "Since the 2015 playoffs, I've been struggling to understand what was going on with my body," Bickell said. "Again during the past few weeks, it felt like something wasn't right. Obviously, this is a bit of a shock for my family and me, but I am hopeful I will be able to return to the ice and continue playing the game that I love." Bickell did return to the ice. In his final NHL game, Bickell scored during the shootout in a win over the Flyers. "I think I sweated all the tears out, so I don't have much left," Bickell said after the game. "It's been an emotional week leading into this day. Seeing my family here, all the people that supported me through it all, I'm just happy."

Andrew Shaw - Center/Winger - 67 playoff games - 16 goals - 19 assists - 35 points - +2
2013, 2015 Cup winner
"I love shin pads!" screamed Andrew Shaw. He had just redirected a puck into the net off Michal Rozsival's shot, giving the Blackhawks a 4–3 triple-overtime win over the Bruins in Game 1 of the 2013 Cup Final. Ugly goals, grindy goals, greasy goals—whatever you want to call them, Shaw scored them. He's hated by his opponents and walks the line between "beloved" and "tolerated" with his teammates. Quenneville, ahead of Shaw's restricted free agency in the summer of 2016, called the forward "irreplaceable."

Shaw can play center, wing, on the power play, or on the penalty kill. He can score beautiful goals and ugly goals. He can take a hit and make a hit. Shaw is the kind of player who thrives in the NHL playoff atmosphere. Sure, you'll have to tolerate a frustrating penalty here or there, but Shaw's ability to play on the edge is what gives him an advantage over his opponents.

Marcus Kruger - Center - 87 playoff games - 6 goals - 10 assists - 16 points - minus 14
2013, 2015 Cup winner
Listing Kruger's stats does him a disservice. He was not a goal-scorer, but during his prime, Kruger was the best fourth-line center in the NHL. Kruger consistently drew the toughest matchups for the Blackhawks. When the opponent's top lines were on the ice, Kruger was there to shut them down. The fact that he's only a -14 over 87 games is incredible considering the level of competition he faced. Kruger accepted his role, even though most knew he was capable of being more than just a fourth-line center. "I think everybody wants better opportunities. I think even Krugs is a guy who handled it, he accepted it, but I think he would have still liked more," Quenneville remembered. "He would have liked more quantity, more quality. Yeah, I think that's one thing about a player; every guy wants more quantity and more quality. That's the nature of hockey players."

Kruger's ability to shut down the competition freed up Jonathan Toews to focus on the offensive side of his game. Without Kruger, it's hard to envision the Hawks winning the 2013 and 2015 Cups.

The Last Lines of Defense

Johnny Oduya - Defenseman - 75 playoff games - 5 goals - 18 assists - 23 points - +5

2013, 2015 Cup winner

The Blackhawks acquired Oduya from the Winnipeg Jets at the 2013 trade deadline. At the time, it felt like a depth trade, but Oduya provided more than anyone could have expected. His chemistry with Hjalmarsson was immediate. Oduya was built like a Greek god. He was a rock-solid defender and a plus puck-mover, making him a perfect fit for Quenneville's system. The trade was one of the best and most successful Stan Bowman made during his tenure as general manager.

Antti Niemi - Goaltender - 22 playoff games - 2.63 GAA - .910 save percentage

2010 Cup winner

International free agent Antti Niemi signed with the Blackhawks in May of 2008 after years of stellar play in the Finnish league. That season, the tandem of Nikolai Khabibulin and Cristobal Huet got the bulk of starts for the Blackhawks, blocking Niemi's full-time arrival until the next season. Even then, Niemi was expected to merely back up Huet, but things didn't go as planned. Huet struggled, and Niemi took over.

Niemi's play was a huge part of the 2010 Cup win. He recorded a pair of shutouts and made several highlight-reel saves in every game. In the summer of 2010, former Hawks defenseman and current San Jose Sharks GM Doug Wilson signed Niklas Hjalmarsson to an offer sheet, knowing the Hawks would have to choose between Hjalmarsson and Niemi. The Hawks correctly chose Hjalmarsson, and Niemi signed with San Jose.

Without these players, the Blackhawks likely don't win their Stanley Cups. Many of these names have left town, and Bowman hasn't been able to find adequate replacements for their talents. Since the 2015 Cup, the Blackhawks have failed to be serious contenders.

Stars win games. Depth wins championships.

EDDIE THE EAGLE

In a star-studded era of Chicago hockey, Blackhawks goalie Ed Belfour was one of the finest and most memorable. His place in franchise and hockey history is secure.

Belfour joined the Blackhawks in 1990–91 as an undrafted free agent after a phenomenal season at North Dakota, where he led the Fighting Sioux to a 40-win season and a national championship. He promptly won the Calder Trophy as the NHL's top rookie. That season, he set the Blackhawks' single-season record for wins with 43, a record that still stands to this day.

He was elected to the Hockey Hall of Fame in 2011 and is among the franchise leaders in several goaltending categories. He's fourth all time in games played (415), wins (201), and shutouts (30). Belfour was a five-time All-Star, a two-time Vezina Trophy winner, and a four-time Jennings Trophy winner. All that in only eight seasons as a Blackhawk.

Belfour had a penchant for making miraculous saves at the biggest moments. He was one of the first goalies to wear a customized goalie mask, and his iconic eagle artwork remained on his helmet for his entire career. The mask from his rookie season is in the Hockey Hall of Fame.

For Blackhawks fans of a certain age, Pat Foley's enthusiastic "Belllll-foooour!" after a big save, as well as the chants of "Eddie, Eddie, Eddie" echoing through the Chicago Stadium rafters, provided a soundtrack for one of the most memorable eras of Blackhawks hockey.

"I'll never forget the 'Eddie, Eddie' chant. [Hawks fans] are the ones who started it," Belfour said. "I think they're some of the best fans in the world. It always gave me inspiration and made me play better. I'll never forget it."

There's one Blackhawks record Belfour holds that will never be broken: penalty minutes as a goalie. His 242 are most in Blackhawks history. When I think of Eddie Belfour, after all the obvious accolades and incredible performances, I think of his hot temper. He was never shy about whacking an opponent as they crossed his crease, or uppercutting a groin or two with his goalie paddle.

"Eddie had an edge to him," recalls Blackhawks historian Bob Verdi. "He wore that proudly."

"Eddie was the guy who wasn't going to take any guff. If you came into his crease, you were going to feel a little lump," says Foley.

In 1993, the Blackhawks were swept out of the first round by the St. Louis Blues on a Game 4 overtime goal. The Blues finished the regular season 21 points behind the division-winning Blackhawks. No one expected the Blues to win the series, let alone sweep. During the game, the teams exchanged huge hits and scoring chances while Belfour and St. Louis goalie Curtis Joseph made big save after big save. With the game tied 3–3 in overtime, Belfour ventured outside of his crease, which was something the netminder did well and with regularity. As he attempted to get back to the net, he collided with Blues winger Brett Hull. Belfour fell to the ice, and Craig Janney ended the game.

Belfour threw both arms in the air wildly, arguing that he had been interfered with, but referee Rob Shick was having none of it.

"Interference?" Hull asked after the game. "He hit me. It should have been interference on him."

The game and the Blackhawks' season were over. Belfour furiously chopped the crossbar with a two-handed overhead swing of his stick. When it failed to break, he took his temper out on the post. The stick broke and Belfour threw what remained of the handle down the ice in Shick's direction.

The tantrum wasn't over once he left the ice. Belfour reportedly caused thousands of dollars of damage to the locker room, smashing a television, a hot tub, a fan, a coffee maker, and more.

"Referees are nothing but a joke," a raging Belfour said in the postgame dressing room. "I can't talk right now, but that's what I feel. I'm too upset. I'll lose it."

While this meltdown is Belfour's most famous, it was neither his first nor his last. In fact, early the following season, in an October game against the Maple Leafs, even his head coach, Darryl Sutter, grew aggravated with Belfour's temper.

Toronto's Mark Osborne made light contact with Belfour behind the Blackhawks goal. As the players came apart, Belfour slashed and punched Osborne. "I was surprised," Osborne said of Belfour's reaction to the collision. "I think he was frustrated [the Blackhawks were trailing 3–1 at the time]."

During the scrum, Hawks defenseman Bryan Marchment came to Belfour's aid and was thrown out of the game for being the third man to enter a fight. Sutter immediately removed Belfour from the game, replacing him with Jeff Hackett. "I'd seen enough," Sutter said. The coach went on to add that Belfour's antics were "unacceptable and inexcusable."

Belfour's teammates weren't safe from his wrath, either. During an interview with Dan McNeil and Danny Parkins on 670 The Score, Belfour recalled an encounter with Hawks defenseman and tough guy Dave Manson in practice. Manson, who owned a wicked slap shot, sent a few pucks a little too high for Belfour's tastes.

"Everybody shot to score [in practice], and [Manson] had an awesome slap shot, but every once in a while, he'd let one rip right by my ear," Belfour said. "The first one was OK, and he'd do it again... the third time coming down the ice, I'd go, like, 'That's it, I'm not even going to let him get a shot off.' Out came the blocker, and one thing led to another and there was a bit of a melee."

Jeremy Roenick, who had relayed the story to the radio hosts, reported less of a melee and more of a flat-out punch.

To what does Belfour attribute his edge?

"I think I was born with it," he said. "I've always been a real competitive athlete ever since I was a little kid. I hated to lose. It didn't matter what I played. It could have been a game of Monopoly. I hated losing that game. We'd play floor hockey every day, and there'd be fights. I was born with it. It was what drove me to have big dreams and want to play in the NHL."

Despite the occasional meltdown, Belfour's fire and attitude helped him more often than it hurt him.

"'Intense' is a good word. I think 'competitive' is a really good word too," remembered former Hawk defenseman Steve Konroyd. "His team fell in love with him because of what a battler he was."

"He was a special one. He was a battler, he was a winner, and he was a great goalie for a long time," says Denis Savard.

Most of the time, Belfour was able to control his temper and use his emotions as a catalyst for his Hall of Fame career.

"He had a mindset that said, 'I'm going to play in the NHL and I'm going to be great,'" recalls former teammate Troy Murray. "That's the way he came into the NHL and that's the way he left."

18

MR. GOALIE

Glenn Hall is among the top two or three in most important goaltending categories when it comes to Blackhawks records. You'll find him and Tony Esposito at or near the top every time.

"Glenn Hall was one of the greatest, if not the greatest goaltender, that ever played. He was the backbone of our team," says Bobby Hull.

Hall was a 13-time All-Star, a three-time Vezina Trophy winner, a Calder Trophy winner, and, of course, a Stanley Cup champion.

On top of these great accomplishments, Hall holds one record that will never be broken.

While Joe DiMaggio's 56-game hit streak gets more attention as the "unbreakable record," there have been some players, such as Pete Rose and Paul Molitor, who have at least gotten within striking distance.

Glenn Hall's record of 502 consecutive starts in goal will *never* be broken. Alec Connell, whose streak lasted from November 29, 1924, to December 25, 1930, falls 245 starts short of Hall's record. No one from the modern era even approaches the top five. In fact, if you want to get technical, Hall also played in 49 consecutive playoff games, so the number is really 551.

"I didn't want to give up the net," he said. "In those days, there was always that fear of losing your job. And, yes, I was aware of the streak."

Only 81 active players have more than 100 consecutive games played. Not one of them is a goalie.

Hall's streak began on October 6, 1955, and lasted until November 4, 1962. The Blackhawks acquired Hall, along with hockey legend Ted Lindsay, in the middle of the streak, in 1957.

"He got traded to Chicago with me. For the next 15 years, he was the best goaltender in the National Hockey League," Lindsay recalls. "Those 15 years, the Red Wings were looking for a goaltender. They had him...they let him go."

Remarkably, Hall did this all without wearing a helmet or mask. "You have to be lucky to have a run like I had, and I was," Hall said. "Of course, you have to be a little bit crazy to play where I played, and I plead guilty on that count too."

Understandably, the legend's nerves would sometimes get the best of him. Hall famously vomited before every game he played in.

"Glenn Hall sat right across the dressing room from me," recalls former Hawks captain Ed Litzenberger. "Before every game, he would get up, he would stagger across the dressing room right past me, and go into the bathroom and throw up...every game before the game started."

"I did get nervous. I loved to win, but goaltending was hell," Hall says. "Tell me, do you know a retired goalie who says he misses it? I don't."

At one point during his time in Chicago, Hall almost ended the streak on his own. Blackhawks GM Tommy Ivan issued $100 fines for "indifferent play." Ivan fined Hall for, in his mind, not playing as well as he could have.

"The GM said, 'If you don't like the fine, quit.' So, I contemplated that. I really, really did," Hall said. "I went back to my wife and we talked about it. The problem was, I didn't know how to do anything else. The only thing I knew how to do is play goalie. So I paid the ransom and continued to play. That was the closest I came to stopping the streak."

The concept that Hall wasn't prepared seems ridiculous when considering the praise he gets from his former teammates.

"Hall used to win 10 or 12 games for us all by himself, until we got the refreshments out of our knees. Glenn stood on his head," recalls Bobby Hull.

Hall's streak officially came to an end on November 7, 1962. "My back started bothering me a few days before," recalled Hal. "I started a [November 4] game and figured the adrenaline would carry me through as it had in the past. This time, it would not."

Hall's time with the Blackhawks ended when they left him unprotected in the 1967 expansion draft. The St. Louis Blues selected the Hall of Famer and Hall led the Blues to their third consecutive

Stanley Cup Final appearance. Despite losing the series 4–0 to Montreal, he won the Conn Smythe Trophy as playoff MVP.

During those playoffs, Hall, at the age of 36, stopped 490 of 535 shots. He registered a 2.44 goals-against average and a .916 save percentage. In the Final against the Habs, he posted a .927 save percentage. Only four other players in the history of the game—Roger Crozier (1966), Reggie Leach (1976), Ron Hextall (1987), and Jean-Sébastien Giguère (2003)—have won the Conn Smythe without capturing the Stanley Cup. The next season, Hall won his third Vezina Trophy.

"He was the [Blues] franchise, and he was 36 years of age," said former Blues coach Scotty Bowman.

The goalie called it a career after the 1971 season and got the call from the Hall of Fame in 1975.

"I'm proud of what I did on the ice. I really am," said Hall. "I would have loved to have won more Stanley Cups. I was only on one Stanley Cup team, and yet, I feel very, very good about the one."

19

JR

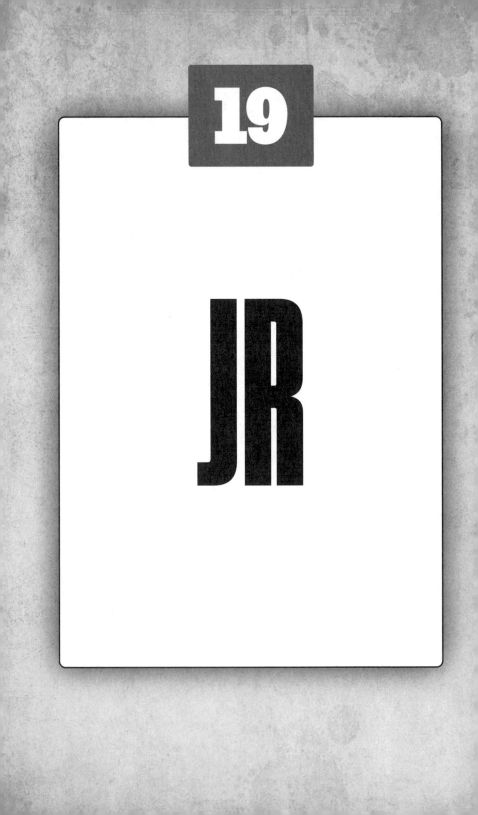

When I was thinking about writing this book, I knew there was one place I wanted to start. If I could credit one player with my love of hockey, it would be Jeremy Roenick. For me and thousands of other hockey fans who grew their fandom in the 1990s, there is no player who defines "what it means to be a Blackhawk" more than JR. Few players in the team's history have embodied the idealized Blackhawk quite like Roenick.

An electrifying talent with a penchant for dazzling goals and bone-crushing hits, Roenick forced Chicago to fall in love with him almost immediately. His career in Chicago coincided with the hair metal scene of the late 1980s and early 1990s, and it's easy to make comparisons between those bands and the players of that era. While Mario Lemieux, Wayne Gretzky, and Jaromir Jagr had the polish and innate, superior ability like Van Halen, Roenick had the rawness and grit of Mötley Crüe. Maybe not the best, but perhaps the most memorable, entertaining, and controversial.

"He'd rather run over you to score a goal than go around you. He was the face of the franchise. It was something special to watch Jeremy play," said former teammate and current radio broadcaster Troy Murray.

Roenick is one of two Blackhawks to record back-to-back 50-goal seasons (Bobby Hull is the other), but fans remember his physicality and his willingness to play through injury as much as his goal-scoring. During a 1989 playoff series with the St. Louis Blues, Roenick lost a few teeth after a high hit from Glen Featherstone.

"He went to go cross-check me in the chest. He's a lot taller than me and cross-checked me in the middle of my face," Roenick said. "Now, I'd gotten hit with Steve Larmer's skate, cut me for 15 stitches in the first period, and then I got hit in the mouth. And I think up to that point I never had stitches and I never lost a tooth, and I said I never wanted to lose teeth. I lost three in my first playoff game. The referee,

Kerry Fraser, came up to me and said, 'Nothing happened to you.' I said, 'Really?' And then I opened my mouth and all the pieces of my teeth fell out in front of him. He ended up giving [Featherstone] a five-minute major. I got a two-minute minor. I think I did set up a reputation for myself. I think I proved to myself that I can withstand a lot."

Roenick went on to score the game-winning goal, sending the Blackhawks to the conference final. He was 19 years old. After the game, head coach Mike Keenan, who often clashed with Roenick during his career, called the performance Roenick's best of the playoffs. When told of his coach's comments, Roenick responded, "I just want to show him I have the guts and the heart to do what it takes."

Roenick displayed those guts and that heart over his entire 20-year NHL career.

"I love to hit, I love to hit hard, and when I played, I didn't hit within the rules that they have now," Roenick said in an interview with the *Chicago Tribune*'s Steve Rosenbloom. "I would jump off my feet. I would go high. A lot of times I'd head-hunt. I would not fit very well in the rules today at all. At all."

That reckless abandon, on and sometimes off the ice, defined JR's hockey career.

In 1996, the Blackhawks faced off with the Colorado Avalanche in a thrilling six-game series. Many believed the winner of this series would go on to capture the Stanley Cup. Turns out, they were right.

With the series tied 1–1 (Roenick scored the overtime winner in Game 1), the teams returned to Chicago for Game 3. Down 3–2, Roenick received a perfect pass at the blue line from Eric Daze, sending him on a breakaway. Roenick undressed Colorado goalie Patrick Roy with a beautiful backhand-to-forehand deke, tying the game. The contest went to overtime but ended quickly, thanks to Hawks winger Sergei Krivokrasov, who wristed a shot that was deflected over Roy's shoulder.

Game 4, again in Chicago at the United Center, saw the two teams battle back and forth, forcing overtime for the third time in the series. Roenick gathered a loose puck at center ice with nothing between him and Roy. After he went to make his move on the legendary goaltender, Avalanche defenseman Sandis Ozolinsh pulled Roenick down. No

A PIXELATED STAR IS BORN

In 1991, video gaming company EA Sports began publishing its still-thriving annual NHL series. While it took a couple of seasons to catch fire, the games *NHLPA Hockey '93*, *NHL '94*, and *NHL '95* are still regarded by many as the finest in the series' long history. For young hockey fans at the time, myself included, the games were a way to learn about the players around the league and the rules of the game. I played hours and hours of those games and I still do.

Since the series began, there has been one digitized player synonymous with the game: Jeremy Roenick. This mid-1990s pixelated version of JR is as close to a perfect video game athlete as has ever been created. The speed and scoring ability, combined with the ability to lay devastating hits, made him unmatched on the virtual ice.

In one scene from the 1996 Jon Favreau film *Swingers*, Trent, portrayed by Chicago actor and Blackhawks fan Vince Vaughn, and Sue, played actor Patrick Van Horn, are engaged in an intense and profane game of *NHLPA Hockey '93*. We see that Trent's Blackhawks are beating Sue's Los Angeles Kings 9–5 when Roenick lays out Wayne Gretzky with a vicious hit. As Trent himself points out, "It's not even so much me as it's Roenick. He's good."

Trent then guides Roenick with the puck into the L.A. zone and quickly scores. Sue whines and complains that Trent is cheating and the goal was "bullshit." Then, as Sue is distracted taking money out of his wallet to pay for the food that's being delivered, Trent mischievously un-pauses the game and takes the opportunity to "make Gretzky's head bleed" via another Roenick hit. The result is a physical altercation between Trent and Sue.

The scene added to the legend of the pixelated Roenick, and the rest is history. The only video game athletes that can be mentioned in the same breath as Roenick's avatar would be Mike Tyson in *Punch-Out!!*, Bo Jackson in *Tecmo Bowl*, and Michael Vick in *Madden NFL 2004*, but certainly no hockey player has been close.

Even in their more recent releases, years after Roenick called it a career, EA Sports ensures that he is available as an unlockable legend every year. They know the series wouldn't be the same without him.

penalty shot was awarded. Looking back on the video of the play, you can see Roenick look up at the referee Andy Van Hellemond and ask, "What?" The Blackhawks would go on to lose the game 3–2 in triple overtime.

"We thought it was grounds for a penalty shot," said Blackhawks coach Craig Hartsburg. "Jeremy was wide open and in clean and got tripped."

He was right. It should have been a penalty shot.

Roy didn't seem to think the call would have mattered much either way. "I don't care if he got a penalty shot because I'd have stopped him anyway," he said.

The next day, Roenick offered an opinion of his own.

"It should have been a penalty shot...no doubt about it," Roenick said. "I liked Patrick's quote...that he would have stopped me. I just want to know where he was in Game 3. Probably getting his jock out of the rafters of the United Center."

Roy ultimately won the war of words, adding, "I can't really hear what Jeremy says because I have my two Stanley Cup rings plugging my ears."

The Avalanche won the next two games and eventually captured the Stanley Cup.

It's easy to speculate what could have happened had the shot been awarded, but had the Hawks won that game, it's hard to imagine them losing the series. After the Avalanche won Game 4, you could feel the life get sucked out of the United Center. I think the team felt that as well.

Roenick was never shy about his opinions. Media members loved him because he was always good for a quote and was always available, but even they weren't always safe. Once, after a frustrating loss to the Red Wings, Roenick suggested a reporter should "go live in Detroit" because they were critical of the team's ability to keep up with their Original Six rival. In 2005, he even went so far as to lash out at fans upset about the NHL lockout.

"If people are going to sit and chastise professional athletes for making a lot of money and being spoiled and being cocky," he said, "they need to look at one thing and that's to look at the deal that we are probably going to end up signing in the next three weeks. And they better understand that pro athletes are not cocky. Pro athletes care about the game...Everybody out there who calls us spoiled because we play a game, they can all kiss my ass. They can all kiss my ass."

That didn't sit well with many hockey fans, but these days it seems most have forgotten about it. Roenick himself says fans tell him he's their favorite player "more often than you can possibly imagine."

Many around the league felt Roenick was too outspoken, too showy, too critical of other players and the league itself. Hockey is traditionally a sport where outspokenness is discouraged and seen as a selfish act, but that never stopped Roenick, and that's why so many teammates and observers outside the game loved him.

In a tribute video to Roenick, former teammate Chris Chelios said, "There hasn't been a better ambassador or personality for the NHL for the last 18 or 20 years."

However people felt about Roenick personally, there was no denying how great and complete a hockey player he was. Former teammate and current San Jose Sharks general manager Doug Wilson said of Roenick, "He played hard. He was fearless. I've had guys come up to me and say he was the greatest teammate they ever had."

When asked how he'd like to be remembered as a player, Roenick replied, "As a warrior. As a guy who gave everything on and off the ice. That I could hurt you on the scoreboard and in the corners."

Mission accomplished. Warrior is the perfect word to describe how I, and thousands like me, feel about Roenick.

20

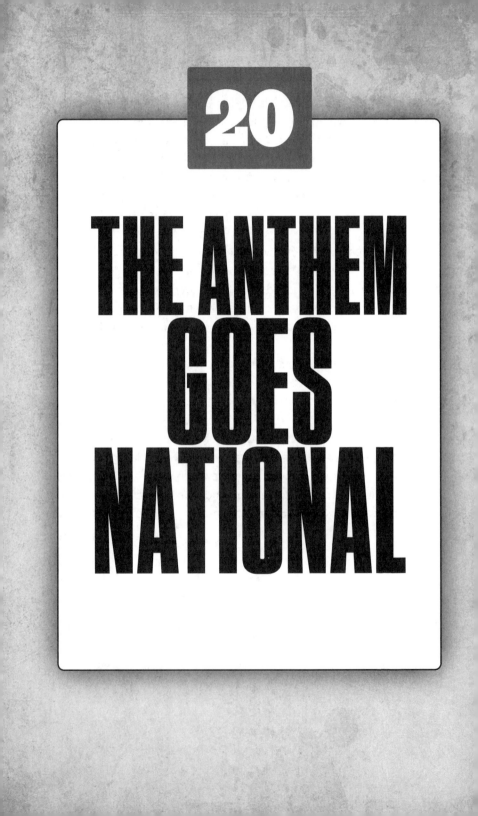

THE ANTHEM GOES NATIONAL

The origins of the Blackhawks' famous tradition of cheering loudly while the national anthem is performed remain in question. NHL.com's research department will tell you it began in 1985 during a Campbell Conference Final game against the Edmonton Oilers, though some longtime Blackhawks fans will dispute that fact.

Regardless of what you believe about the tradition's beginnings, there is no arguing that its biggest and most memorable performance came on January 19, 1991, at the Chicago Stadium during the NHL's annual All-Star Game.

Three days prior, President George H.W. Bush and the United States military began the Gulf War, launching a major airstrike on the Iraqi-occupied country of Kuwait. Because of the start of the conflict, there was some question whether the All-Star Game would even be held at all. The league, the players association, and NBC, the network broadcasting the game, all met and decided the game would go on.

"The United States government has had a policy going back to World War II that our citizens should carry on, and professional sports should carry on," NHL president John Ziegler said. "We take our guidance from the president of the United States and the prime minister of Canada. Up to now, there has been no indication that these policies should not continue."

And they did. Blackhawks fans knew it was their time to shine, and I was among them on that historic day.

I had just turned 13 years old. My dad surprised me with tickets to the game, something he did regularly despite not loving the game himself. Without him, I'm probably not the hockey fan I am today, so, thanks, Dad.

Describing the atmosphere as electrifying would be an understatement. Wayne Gretzky, Steve Yzerman, Ray Bourque, Mark Messier, and other NHL royalty would be joining local heroes Jeremy

Roenick, Steve Larmer, and Chris Chelios in the game, but the contest itself seemed secondary. In fact, without looking it up, I couldn't tell you who won the game, who scored, or anything else, but I can describe in great detail how I felt when the anthem was played.

My 20-year career in media has taken some of the magic out of sports for me. I've seen how the sausage is made and as it is in any industry, work is work. However, watching the videos of the anthem on YouTube, in all their grainy glory, raises the goosebumps to this day.

The building was shaking before the organ struck the first notes of the anthem. Singer Wayne Messmer was in perfect form. "I always refer to that as one of the rare opportunities of what you do, what you're gifted to do, what you've crafted doing, all come together at the right time," he said.

"I was standing next to Mark Messier during the anthem," Gretzky recalled. "I said to him, 'This is unbelievable.' The flags of both countries, the banners, the vibrations. You could tell that the fans, like us, were thinking of other things [aside from hockey]."

When the anthem began, every hair on my body stood up. I looked around, trying to take in the moment, knowing I was witnessing something special. I saw grown men with tears in their eyes. I saw women and children screaming and clapping with a fury I'd never witnessed in person before. Even now, my eyes are welling up just remembering the feeling.

I couldn't imagine a more powerful moment. I didn't think the crowd could get any louder, but then the final lines began: "Oh say does that star-spangled banner yet wave..." When Messmer delivered those lyrics, the crowd grew significantly louder. Even the shy wallflowers, like me, were joining in.

"It was tough to sing through that because you get this lump in your throat. But I made it through," Messmer recalls. "I finished and I stepped down off the platform and my hands were just shaking."

There was a sign in the stands that read, "GIs – the REAL All-Stars." General Norman Schwarzkopf, who led the coalition forces in the Gulf War, requested a video tape of the anthem to show the troops fighting overseas.

"Tears were streaming down my face because I think I understood the responsibility," Messmer remembered.

Everyone in that building understood their responsibility that day, and they delivered. All of the United States, all of Canada, and most of the world bore witness to what a united Chicago could do. It was one of the city's proudest and finest sports moments.

Oh, and the Campbell Conference beat the Wales Conference 11–5.

21

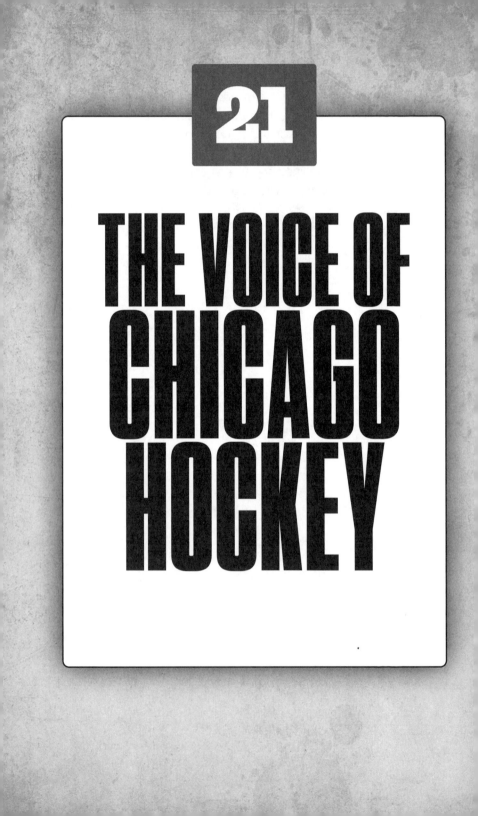

THE VOICE OF CHICAGO HOCKEY

Since 1980, one voice has been synonymous with Blackhawks hockey. That voice belongs to Pat Foley.

Foley's memorable calls of big saves over the years have become his trademark, from "Baaaaaaanerman," after a big save by Murray Bannerman, to "Belllll-foooour," after a great glove save from Eddie Belfour, to "Crawfoooooooord said no!" when two-time Cup champion Corey Crawford bailed out a defenseman. Foley's calls have been part of Chicago hockey for more than 30 years.

It all began for Foley when he was 10 years old. His father, Bob, owned a Buick dealership, and took him to a game at Wrigley Field, where he was able to sit in the radio booth and watch Jack Quinlan and Lou Boudreau call a game.

"I was completely enthralled," Foley told the *Chicago Tribune*. "That's the day the seed was planted."

During the broadcast, Quinlan asked Foley about his youth baseball team. That was the first time Foley's voice was heard on the air in Chicago.

From that moment forward, Foley committed to becoming a broadcaster. Even if it was emceeing local sports banquets, if there was a microphone, Foley wanted to be there.

He took that passion to Michigan State University, where he received his degree in telecommunications. After leaving the university, Foley began calling hockey games for the Grand Rapids Owls hockey team.

Foley's big break came two years later. Michael Wirtz, brother of Blackhawks owner Bill and the team's executive vice president, was often seen at Bob Foley's Buick dealership.

"If [Michael] hadn't been in hockey, [Pat] probably would have done something with automobiles," Foley's mother, Mary, recalls.

During one of Wirtz's visits, Bob handed an audio cassette to Wirtz and said, "Put it in your car, and maybe you can listen to it on your way downtown." It was a tape of Pat calling an Owls hockey game. The Hawks quickly hired Foley, and the rest is history.

"My first Hawks game was the night they retired Stan Mikita's No. 21. Tony Esposito is 200 feet away. I'm going, 'Good God, I'm doing an NHL game,'" Foley said. "I'll always be grateful [to the Wirtz family] for taking a chance on a young kid."

For the 1982–83 season, Foley was joined by former NHLer Dale Tallon. The two found immediate chemistry and would spend the next 16 years as one of the league's premier broadcast tandems.

Foley and Tallon played off each other brilliantly. Foley, who was then tasked with the simulcast of radio and television (for road games), handled the play-by-play with precision. When the action would stop, Tallon would offer an almost perfect balance of analysis and humor.

One moment in particular demonstrates their partnership perfectly. During a 1996 game against the Ottawa Senators, the Blackhawks trio of Bernie Nicholls, Murray Craven, and Eric Daze had an extended shift in the offensive zone. Here's the play-by-play:

> Foley: "The Hawks looking like the Harlem Globetrotters after that passing sequence, and [Senators defenseman] Shaun Hill blocked that in a bad spot. He's down."
>
> Tallon: "And Daze...we know he can really fire it."
>
> *Replay shows on screen.*
>
> Tallon: "Hill kicked out the right leg and was vulnerable in the right knee area and calf, and that's where he got it. There's not much protection there. He sticks out his leg like a goaltender and uh...well...from the second angle it doesn't look like it hit the knee."
>
> Foley: "I said he got it in a bad spot."
>
> Tallon: "Not his knee...maybe his wee-knee."
>
> Foley [after 19 seconds of background laughter pass]: "What passing on that sequence though, huh, Dale?"

Hilarity like this was commonplace with Foley and Tallon, especially because many of the Hawks teams they covered were not contenders. They were also tasked with doing a television and radio simulcast, which is very challenging for a play-by-play man, but Foley was always up for the task.

Another reason Foley is so beloved by Blackhawks fans, aside from the comedy and chemistry with Tallon and current partner Eddie Olczyk, is that he doesn't hold back. On March 10, 2004, the Blackhawks traded Russian defenseman Alexander Karpovtsev to the New York Islanders. The Blackhawks had acquired Karpovtsev in October of 2000 for defenseman Bryan McCabe. McCabe went on to be a four-time All-Star with Toronto, while Karpovtsev, when healthy, was a disaster for Chicago.

The day the trade was made, the broadcast was headed to a break after the second period ended. Without warning, Foley ignored all the cues to go to commercial break and let loose on the former Hawks defenseman.

"This is a very happy day for this Blackhawks fan because I never again am going to have to see Alexander Karpovtsev in a Blackhawks uniform," Foley began, as his partner, Troy Murray, chuckled awkwardly. "You know, Karpovtsev actually is a very good defenseman when he plays, and there's the rub. Because Alexander Karpovtsev looks for any reason not to play. In his time in Chicago he is the worst excuse for a teammate I've ever seen in over two decades doing this job."

But Foley wasn't done.

"A couple of examples? Ten minutes before a warm-up a few weeks ago, 'My shoulder hurts.' And a young defenseman who wasn't anticipating playing had to scurry...get into his uniform to dress for the game. He was coming back from an ankle injury earlier this season, almost ready to rejoin the lineup, had the collision in practice, 'I have a concussion.' Well, Dr. Karpovtsev always had an excuse. Always found a way to milk the system. He came to Chicago in exchange for Bryan McCabe, who has gone on to become an All-Star in Toronto, but even before that, Bryan McCabe was a player who cared and who tried.

TWO YEARS WITHOUT FOLEY

On May 19, 2006, the Chicago Blackhawks issued the following press release:

> For the 2006–07 hockey season, the Chicago Blackhawks and Comcast SportsNet agreed that, in the interest of better quality broadcasts on both radio and television, they would split the simulcast.
>
> Comcast SportsNet made the decision to hire its own broadcast team for the upcoming season.
>
> On May 9, the Chicago Blackhawks made a contract offer to Pat Foley to remain as their radio play-by-play broadcaster.
>
> However, due to recent circumstances, the Blackhawks today have withdrawn their contract offer to Mr. Foley.

Foley, who had been the team's broadcaster since 1980, was out of a job with little clarity as to why. The Blackhawks themselves were in a tailspin. They were coming off a 26–43–13 season and had failed to make the playoffs in three consecutive seasons; it may have well been four seasons had the league not canceled the 2004–05 campaign due to the lockout. The only press the Blackhawks were getting in those days was bad press. They had earned the reputation as "thrifty" to put it kindly and this release was another notch on the thrifty belt.

Blackhawks fans were livid that a legend would be let go over a minor contract dispute. Foley was just another beloved member of the Blackhawks family shown the door for penny pinching reasons. Just like Jeremy Roenick, Chris Chelios, Eddie Belfour, Tony Amonte, and countless others, it was another slap in the fan base's face.

Foley joined the Chicago Wolves broadcast that season, teaming with former Blackhawks broadcast partner Billy Gardner. "As far as professional organizations go, the Wolves are the top of the ladder," Foley said shortly after joining the AHL team. "I am really looking forward to this opportunity. I get to remain at home in Chicago and broadcast to fans I've had a relationship with for 25 years."

Later, Foley said, "I would have liked to be a fly on the wall the day the Blackhawks found out I was going to work for the Wolves." In those days, the Wolves (wisely) marketed themselves as the only winning hockey team in Chicago. That never sat well with the Blackhawks.

Foley's radio replacement with the Hawks, John Wiedeman, is still with the team today and does excellent work alongside color analyst and former Blackhawks star Troy Murray. On the television side, Foley was replaced by Dan Kelly. Kelly did a fine job but found himself in an impossible situation: replacing a legend while calling games for a terrible team. It was a toxic situation very few broadcasters could overcome.

After the passing of Bill Wirtz in 2007, his son Rocky and former Cubs executive John McDonough took over the Blackhawks organization and made bringing Foley back one of their top priorities. On June 16, 2008, the team made it official.

"We are thrilled to have Pat Foley back in our organization," McDonough said in the press release. "His voice is synonymous with Blackhawks hockey and it resonates loudly to our entire fan base."

Today, Pat Foley and Eddie Olczyk make up one of the finest home broadcast teams in all of sports, let alone hockey. Their on-air chemistry, clear genuine friendship, and selfless broadcast styles complement each other perfectly. I was never certain Foley would find a partner with whom he shared the kind of chemistry he did with Dale Tallon. He found it with Olczyk.

McDonough was right. Foley's voice does resonate with Blackhawks fans and it always will.

"The Toronto players, when that trade was made, said, 'We can't believe we got Bryan McCabe for Dean Martin.' Well, let me tell you, Alexander Karpovtsev doesn't sing. And, when you're trying to bring along a young team, this is not the kind of veteran that you want around young people in any way, shape, or form. That deal was one of the worst deals in the history of the Chicago Blackhawks, and when [former GM] Mike Smith writes his memoirs about his time in Chicago, I have the title for that chapter: Disaster! So, kudos to Bob Pulford and [new GM] Dale Tallon for being able to get anything more than a roll of tape for this overpaid underachiever. Alexander Karpovtsev is now the New York Islanders' problem. That will be his last National Hockey League stop. And he, basically, in my opinion, was a disgrace to the uniform when he was a member of the Chicago Blackhawks. As he leaves Chicago I have just one sentiment for Alexander Karpovtsev... good riddance. We are through two periods in New Jersey."

To this day, Foley remains the voice of the Chicago Blackhawks, and while his partners have changed over the years, his distinctive "Big save!" and "He shoots, he scooooooooores" calls are as familiar a sound as Harry Caray's "Holy cow" or Hawk Harrelson's "You can put it on the booooooard, yes!"

Foley is a Chicago icon and always will be.

22

THE FIRST TWO CUPS

When I set out to write this book, I didn't know much about the Blackhawks' first two Stanley Cups, the ones they won in 1934 and 1938. I'd heard some of the names, like Harold "Mush" March and Charlie Gardiner, but aside from the short clips shown during video montages at the United Center, I was quite out of touch. Sadly, there isn't a ton of information available about those teams, but the stuff I did find was very interesting.

Hockey's Original Six—the Boston Bruins, Chicago Blackhawks, Detroit Red Wings, Montreal Canadiens, New York Rangers, and Toronto Maple Leafs—are considered the league's flagship teams, with good reason, but in the 1930s, the league had nine teams. The other three were the Montreal Maroons, the New York Americans, and the Ottawa Senators.

In 1934, the playoff format of the league was also wildly different than it is today. The teams were divided into two divisions, the American and the Canadian. Boston, Chicago, Detroit, the New York Rangers, and (briefly) the Philadelphia Quakers made up the American Division. Toronto, the two Montreal teams, and the New York Americans made up the Canadian Division.

The playoff format was as follows:

Series A: Team #1 in Canadian Division vs. Team #1 in American Division (best-of-five)

Series B: Team #2 in Canadian Division vs. Team #2 in American Division (two-game, total goals)

Series C: Team #3 in Canadian Division vs. Team #3 in American Division (two-game, total goals)

Series D: Winner of Series B vs. Winner of Series C (two-game, total goals)

Series E: Winner of Series A vs. Winner of Series D (best-of-five) for Stanley Cup

When the 1934 playoffs began, expectations were low for the Blackhawks. They finished the regular season with a 20–17–11 record, only scoring 88 goals in those 48 games. They did, however, have Gardiner in goal. He played every game for the Blackhawks that season and only allowed 83 goals all year.

The Hawks beat the Montreal Canadiens in the first round, winning the series by scoring four goals to Montreal's three in their two games. From there, Chicago would face the Montreal Maroons in another two-game, total-goals series. They outscored the Maroons 6–2, advancing to the Stanley Cup Final against the Detroit Red Wings.

The Blackhawks entered the series against Detroit as big underdogs. *Tribune* writer Charles Bartlett didn't think much of the team's chances, either. "They will play the one team in the league which appeared to exercise some strange power over them," he said before the series started. In the regular season, the Red Wings had a 4–1–1 record against Chicago, outscoring their American Division rivals 13–9 in those six games.

The Stanley Cup Final began on April 3, 1934, at the Olympia in Detroit. The Blackhawks won the first game 2–1 in double overtime. Lionel Conacher put the Hawks on the board in the first period, while Paul Thompson put home the game-winner 1:10 into the second overtime.

Two days later, the teams would meet for Game 2. The second period ended tied 1–1, but the Blackhawks jumped all over the Red Wings and goalie Wilf Cude (what a name!) in the third, winning the game 4–1.

The Blackhawks were one win away from their first Stanley Cup, but the Red Wings wouldn't die easily, as they won Game 3 at Chicago Stadium 5–2.

Game 5, also at the Chicago Stadium, was a nail-biter. Gardiner and Cude didn't allow a goal for four full periods. Mush March finally broke the deadlock, giving the Hawks a 1–0 double-overtime win and the first Stanley Cup in the team's history.

After the win, Bartlett wrote, "March, a shrimp of a hockey player who matches his 140 pounds against all the heavyweights in the game, is going home with the most valuable puck in existence this morning.

He seized the little black disc out of the Detroit cage last night at the Chicago Stadium after having blazed past Wilfred Cude, the Red Wing goalie, to give Chicago the world's championship and the Stanley Cup for the first time in their eight-year career."

Chicago fell in love with their new champs, but tragedy struck shortly after the season ended. Gardiner, who had recorded five shutouts in the playoffs, had displayed some erratic behavior during the Cup run. He chalked the swings up to nerves. Shortly after returning home to Winnipeg after the season, Gardiner fell into a coma. A brain hemorrhage would claim Gardiner's life just two months after he led the Hawks to the Stanley Cup. He was 29.

The Hawks won their second Stanley Cup four years later, in 1938. Much like the 1934 team, the '38 champs weren't expected to win. In fact, they finished the regular season with a 14–25–9 record, and no team in the league scored fewer than the Blackhawks' 97 goals.

The playoff format had changed by 1936–37. The two-game, total-goals format was gone, and every series was decided in the best-of format:

Series A: Team #1 in Canadian Division vs. Team #1 in American Division (best-of-five)
Series B: Team #2 in Canadian Division vs. Team #2 in American Division (best-of-three)
Series C: Team #3 in Canadian Division vs. Team #3 in American Division (best-of-three)
Series D: Winner of Series B vs. Winner of Series C (best-of-three)
Series E: Winner of Series A vs. Winner of Series D (best-of-three) for Stanley Cup

In the first round, the Blackhawks eliminated the Montreal Canadiens in three games. In the semifinals, Chicago eliminated the New York Americans, also in three games. This time, their Stanley Cup Final opponent would be the Toronto Maple Leafs.

Chicago won Games 1 and 3, while Toronto took Game 2. Even with a 2–1 series lead, people didn't believe in the Hawks. In fact, the trophy wasn't even in the building after the Hawks won the game and the series after Game 4. Before the series began, NHL president Frank

Calder sent the Stanley Cup from Detroit—winners of the previous year's Cup—straight to Toronto.

As disrespectful as this sounds, it wasn't a bad assumption. The Blackhawks were a low-scoring, below-.500 team during the regular season. Their starting goalie, Mike Karakas, was unable to play in Game 1 because of a broken toe suffered in the final game of the series against the Americans. Karakas' backup, Paul Goodman, hadn't traveled with the team.

Desperate, the Hawks appealed the league, asking if they could use Rangers goalie Davey Kerr in the game. The league refused, so the Blackhawks were stuck with Alfie Moore, who had spent most of the season in the minor leagues, save for the two games he appeared in for the New York Americans. Moore, who years later would drink himself out of the game, wasn't exactly sober before Game 1, either. Hawks left winger Johnny Gottselig, who knew Moore, found him at a bar.

"He'd had about 10 or a dozen drinks," Gottselig said. "We put some coffee into him and put him under the shower. By game time, he was in pretty good shape."

Moore miraculously won the game for Chicago. Goodman was able to join the team for Game 2, while Karakas handled Games 3 and 4.

The Blackhawks were once again Stanley Cup champions. Their head coach, Bill Stewart, who also served as a major league umpire and NHL referee during his intriguing sports career, became the first American-born head coach to win the Stanley Cup.

23

THE HEART OF THE BLACKHAWKS

My Blackhawks fandom took shape in the mid-1990s. Growing up in the south suburbs of Chicago, the legends like Bobby Hull, Stan Mikita, and Glenn Hall were almost ingrained. I don't know how I learned about them, but it felt like I always knew them. Beyond those greats, I was sort of on my own when it came to the franchise's legendary players.

Going to Hawks games was always an exciting experience. The highlight videos they showed on screen were exhilarating. There was one clip that always stood out to me. There was a tall, skinny player with a white Blackhawks home sweater. His hair was as red as an inferno. In the highlight, this fiery redhead rips his gloves off and slams them to the ice, ready to fight whoever might come his way.

That player was Keith Magnuson.

I was immediately fascinated and had to know more. As kids are wont to do, I asked my parents first. My mother said, "Oh yeah. He was my favorite. We all loved him. He wasn't the best player, but he tried the hardest."

Now, Linda Zawaski is hardly a hockey aficionado, but "Maggie," as he was known to her and, well, pretty much everyone, stood out to her more than any others. "I think part of it was the fact that he seemed like one of us," she remembers.

This sentiment is shared by pretty much everyone in the hockey world. After Magnuson died in a car accident in 2003, the Blackhawks showed a video tribute before a game against New Jersey. Before Pat Foley began his emotional tribute, Devils broadcaster Glenn "Chico" Resch offered his memories of Magnuson: "He was tough. He played with a big heart. He was one of the greatest Hawks ever."

Foley, who is one of the finest wordsmiths in the game, summed up Magnuson the man and player so eloquently that night.

"His play with the Blackhawks showed his heart. Then he proceeded to steal our hearts," Foley, one of Magnuson's closest friends, began. "On the ice, he was a reflection of the city of Chicago. Big shoulders. Blue collar. Hard-nosed. Passionate. Loyal. Keith Magnuson stood up for what was right and he lived the way he played. He was everything a Chicago Blackhawk should be and he was everything you'd want your son to grow up to be."

Foley added during the speech that he considered Magnuson the greatest captain in Blackhawks history.

Magnuson played all 11 years of his NHL career with Chicago. During his rookie season, he and Hall of Famer and teammate Tony Esposito battled for the Calder Trophy as the league's top rookie; Esposito won the honor. When it was all said and done, Magnuson's career ended with 14 goals, 125 assists, and 1,440 penalty minutes. Only Chris Chelios amassed more penalty minutes than Magnuson in team history.

When his playing career ended, Magnuson made the jump to become the Blackhawks head coach. He spent parts of two seasons behind the bench, but found the role a challenge. When his teams struggled, Magnuson would find himself questioning his ability and his qualifications. Cliff Koroll, his longtime friend, teammate, and then assistant coach, would often join Magnuson for endless film sessions as Maggie tried to find answers for the struggling team. Terry Ruskowski, who played for the Hawks under Magnuson, recalls, "You kind of felt sorry for him. You could see the red in his eyes from the sleepless nights."

Magnuson also had trouble accepting that some players couldn't conjure the fire and passion like he could. "The thing about coaching," he said, "your character has to come out, but it can't come out so strong that you're forcing it on other people."

After a long losing streak at the end of January of 1982, Magnuson was relieved of his duties as head coach. Bob Pulford (who else?) took over as interim head coach. Magnuson never harbored hard feelings about the firing.

"It was killing me," he admitted years later. "Hockey is worth a lot to me, but it's not worth my family."

Magnuson's wife, Cindy, had noticed that while he was coaching, his mood would vary based on the team's results.

Though coaching didn't work out, Magnuson stayed involved with the Blackhawks until the day he tragically passed. In 1987, Magnuson, with several fellow former Blackhawks, founded the Blackhawks Alumni Association. Their mission was three-fold:

> To provide a scholarship fund for the "most deserving" high school hockey players in Illinois.
>
> To become involved in community affairs and charitable causes.
>
> To protect and take care of fellow alumni.

"What I think Maggie would most want to be known for is the Blackhawks Alumni Association, which is his greatest lasting legacy with the team," Koroll says. "Not all players were fortunate enough to have college degrees like we did, so our motto back then was 'players helping players.'"

"He gave everything he had, every minute of the day, to the logo, to the cause, to the players, to his friends, to his teammates," Dale Tallon said. "There was nothing he wouldn't do for them, nothing...I never heard him say 'no' to anybody. He was just so generous with his time, almost to a fault."

Since its inception in 1988, more than 100 Illinois hockey players have received scholarships from the Blackhawks Alumni Association. From the first time he donned the Chicago sweater until the day he passed, Keith Magnuson truly was the heart of the Blackhawks.

24

CROW

Full disclosure: when I set off to write this book, Corey Crawford wasn't on my list of the 50 most important players, moments, and key people in the history of the Blackhawks. In fact, Crawford wasn't added until 13 days before I finished writing the book. Not so coincidentally, 14 days earlier, Crawford picked up his 250th career win, a 2–1 shootout victory over the New Jersey Devils.

That sent me back, for the 15 millionth time since I started this book, to the Chicago Blackhawks' career leaders page on Hockey-Reference.com. I'd venture a bet that you, the reader, didn't know that Crawford's 260-plus wins are third all time in Blackhawks history after some guys named Tony Esposito (418) and Glenn Hall (276). Did you know that he is also first all time in goals-against average (2.45) and save percentage (.918) (min. 400 games)? He's also the only goaltender with two Stanley Cup championships.

Absorbing all this information, I asked myself why Crawford didn't come to mind when preparing this book, and I'm not sure I have a good answer for that question. The night Crawford picked up win number 250, I started a poll on Twitter: "Should Corey Crawford have his number retired?" Seventy percent of the voters said he did, which to me was surprising, considering how much flak he's gotten from Hawks fans over the years.

As a hockey writer, podcaster, and sometimes radio host, I took a lot of heat for being a Crawford "apologist." It seemed that during the Hawks' recent heyday, when the fans were looking for someone to blame when things occasionally went sideways, Crawford would be the punching bag. Backup after backup came to town and won the hearts of Hawks fans, who would root for Crawford to be replaced. Oddly enough, Crawford's continued solid play after the team's late-2010s defensive drop-off may have ultimately been the eye-opener his detractors needed.

I've tried to figure out where the doubting of Crawford came from. As best as I can tell, the "Crawford isn't elite" narrative ironically began during one of the most dominant stretches of his career. During the 2013 Stanley Cup run, Crawford posted a .932 save percentage and a goals-against average of 1.94. However, during Game 4 of the Final against the Boston Bruins, a game the Blackhawks won 6–5 in overtime, Crawford surrendered five goals, all on the glove side. From there, the narrative was born. Somehow, Tuukka Rask, who lost the game and surrendered six goals of his own, came out of the game with his reputation untarnished. It's amazing how broadcast comments on a nationally televised game can affect the reputation of a player, regardless of all facts and statistical information to the contrary.

Patrick Kane went on to capture the Conn Smythe Trophy as playoff MVP that season. After winning the award, the winger admitted that Crawford should have won the honor. "I think [Crawford] might have gotten snubbed, to be honest with you," Kane said.

In 2015, en route to Crawford's second Cup win, the netminder had another stellar playoff performance, recording a 2.31 goals-against average and an excellent .924 save percentage. This time, it was Barry Melrose declaring Crawford should have won the Conn Smythe that Duncan Keith took home.

The other argument against Crawford is that he was the beneficiary of an incredible defense and was simply the right guy in the right place at the right time. Yes, the Blackhawks had a stellar defensive corps during their championship run. That can't be denied, but Crawford's save percentage remained consistent, even when the team's defensive regression began in 2017–18. That year, he had a .929 save percentage, the best of his career. In 2018–19, despite playing behind a horrible team defense, he managed a .908 save percentage. In 2019–20, with only a slightly less porous defense in front of him, Crawford maintained a .917 save percentage.

Not convinced? There's a hockey statistic called Goals Saved Above Average. This is a cumulative stat that represents the number of goals allowed by a goaltender compared to the number of goals that would have been allowed by a league-average goalie. Simple right? Well, not really, but it's a good way to compare his performance regardless of what kind of team was playing in front of him.

In this category, Crawford ranks fourth in Blackhawks history behind Esposito, Hall, and Ed Belfour. Esposito and Hall have their numbers retired. Had Belfour won two Stanley Cups, his number would be hanging in the rafters as well.

To me, the Stanley Cups are what put Crawford over the top. Had the Hawks not won two Cups with Crawford in net, should his number be retired? Probably not, but he did win them. Bottom line. That's the purpose of playing in the NHL in the first place, and Crawford won more of them than any goalie in team history.

"He's been great for us, game in, game out," Joel Quenneville said in 2017. "His consistency early in games, when the games are on the line late, he finds a way to make big saves, timely saves, but really consistent in the net finding pucks, handling the puck well. I think that he's been instrumental in us getting points, being in the position that we're in."

Crawford's career is defined by consistency over flash. Night after night, he gave the Blackhawks an opportunity to win. Nearly as often, Crawford was the reason the Blackhawks won. His No. 50 deserves to hang in the United Center rafters one day along with the other heroes of the 2010s dynasty.

25

THE GREATEST FREE-AGENT SIGNING IN CHICAGO SPORTS HISTORY

For decades, Chicago Blackhawks fans felt the pain of settling when it came to free agency. Typically, because of the financial limitations ownership put on general managers, the Blackhawks would find themselves shopping in the bargain bin, hoping a free agent like defenseman Jon Klemm would elevate his game, or that an aged Doug Gilmour would find the fountain of youth. These deals rarely if ever worked out for the Hawks.

In the few cases where they did pursue top free agents, like Brett Hull or Mike Modano, they were often left with nothing, falling well short of the financial expectations and only providing leverage for better deals for those star players. Losing at free agency was just part of being a Blackhawks fan.

That all changed in the summer of 2009.

The Hawks were coming off an unexpected run to the Western Conference Final. They beat a tough Calgary team in the first round and dispatched their new rivals, the Vancouver Canucks, in six games in the second round. Lacking that one final piece to the championship puzzle, they fell short of the Red Wings in five games in the conference final.

"They were a great team that year," Dave Bolland recalls. "Off of that year, we knew we were just missing one piece."

Detroit winger Marian Hossa, who had signed a one-year deal with the Wings the previous summer, had a front-row seat to the Blackhawks' ascent and could tell where the team was headed. The Wings eventually lost in the Stanley Cup Final to the Pittsburgh Penguins, and Hossa became an unrestricted free agent.

On July 1, 2009, Blackhawks GM Dale Tallon got his man. The team signed Hossa to a 12-year, $62.8 million deal.

"To add Marian, an elite and world-class player, to our exciting young core reinforces our commitment to try to win the Stanley Cup," Tallon said. "He's a horse out there. He can play defense and offense

SOUPY SOLD

While the signing of Marian Hossa will likely go down as the best in Blackhawks history, if not Chicago sports history, it may not have happened if Dale Tallon hadn't gotten his man the previous summer.

The 2007–08 Blackhawks were a team on the rise. Despite missing the playoffs, the team finished the season with 88 points, just three points out of a playoff spot, and a 40–34–8 record under head coach Denis Savard. Patrick Kane and Jonathan Toews were rookies and finished first and third on the team in scoring, respectively.

The city of Chicago was certainly taking notice of the Blackhawks, but were players around the league?

Ahead of the opening of free agency on July 1, 2008, the worst-kept secret in hockey was the Blackhawks' desire to sign defenseman Brian Campbell. He was one of the game's premier offensive defensemen and one of the top free agents available.

Historically, the Blackhawks only seemed to pursue big-name free agents at the end of their careers, such as Doug Gilmour, Theoren Fleury, and Wendel Clark. When they did occasionally set their sights higher, they'd inevitably lowball the player and then tell fans, "Well, we tried. The guy didn't want to play here." More commonly, the team overpaid higher-tier role players and count on them to deliver more than they ever had in their careers. Players like Jon Klemm, Adrian Aucoin, and Martin Lapointe were solid players on other teams, but the Blackhawks wanted them to become star players. It never worked.

By 2008, however, this was no longer your father's Blackhawks front office. Rocky Wirtz and John McDonough had taken over in 2007 and the financial reigns were taken off GM Dale Tallon.

When July 1 hit, the Hawks wasted no time and signed Campbell to an eight-year, $56.8 million contract.

"We decided we'd try to make an impact today to give our fans something to get excited about," Tallon said. "When you do that, you're going to overpay, but now we have the resources and the ability to do that."

"I believed they were a team on the cusp of greatness, and, boy, was I smart at knowing that," Campbell said at his retirement press conference in 2017.

Campbell's signing signified a new era of Blackhawks hockey. Chicago was suddenly a legitimate free-agent destination. The 2008–09 Blackhawks reached the Western Conference Final, where they lost to Marian Hossa's Red Wings in six games. Had Campbell chosen another team, it's unlikely the Blackhawks would have reached that series. If they hadn't, would Hossa have had an in-person look at the Hawks, insight that may have led to him choosing to sign with Chicago that summer? We'll never know, but it certainly didn't hurt.

On November 21, 2019, the Blackhawks honored Campbell during their "One More Shift" presentation. It was a fitting tribute to a player who doesn't get enough recognition for his impact on the Blackhawks organization.

and score 40 goals. He's a hard guy to slow down and to stop. He's durable. He's a game-breaker."

"When I became a free agent, they asked me what's my goal. I said to win the Stanley Cup," Hossa said. "So, to go to the team where there's potential. I wanted a long term with a good city with a great base and a future to win."

"When he came in, he brought a force. He was that next big step that we needed," Bolland says.

Hossa played eight seasons with the Blackhawks before a skin condition forced him to call it a career after the 2016–17 season. When it was all said and done, Hossa had played 534 regular season games with Chicago, scoring 186 goals and adding 229 assists. He played another 107 playoff games, tallying 21 goals and 52 assists. Oh yeah, he also won three Stanley Cups.

If free-agent success is measured in championships won (and what else should it be measured in?), Hossa is the greatest signing in Chicago sports history. Sure, Carlton Fisk was a four-time All-Star and hit 214 homers when he was catching for the White Sox, and Cubs ace Jon Lester has a World Series and two All-Star appearances (so far), but until he wins another pair of World Series, Hossa has the edge.

Chicago sports media member Ben Finfer tweeted of Hossa after his retirement, "...he has been the best free-agent signing in Chicago sports history and yet still underrated."

Hossa's impact on the ice was so much more than numbers on a score sheet. Yes, he was a top-level scorer, but his defensive game was as solid as anyone's in the NHL. His ability to puck-handle with one hand while fending off a defender with the other was incredible. The Frank J. Selke Trophy, given annually to the league's best defensive forward, could have gone to Hossa every single year he was in Chicago, but in recent history, it's been an award that has gone exclusively to centermen. The last winger to win the award was Dallas' Jere Lehtinen, in 2003.

There were many great moments in Hossa's career in Chicago, but say the words "Nashville, Game 5" to any Hawks fan, and a smile will come across his or her face.

The Blackhawks were coming off a solid 2009–10 season (Hossa's first with the team) but locked in a frustrating and tough first-round series with the Nashville Predators. Nashville had taken Games 1 and 3 while the Hawks won Games 2 and 4. Game 5 in Chicago seemed like the pivot point for the rest of the playoffs.

Nashville struck first on a goal from David Legwand, but the Hawks answered with three consecutive goals of their own, one each from Andrew Ladd, Niklas Hjalmarsson, and Tomas Kopecky. The Hawks were dominating, but a shorthanded goal late in the second period from Nashville winger Joel Ward gave the Preds the spark they needed. Despite getting outshot 24–8 over the first 40 minutes, the Predators came out flying in the third period.

Ninety-four seconds into the final frame, Nashville took the lead on a Martin Erat goal. The Predators now had three goals on just nine shots, and Erat wasn't done. Just over 10 minutes later, he scored again to give Nashville a 4–3 lead. With 8:21 to go, the Hawks were down a goal, and you could feel the life sucked out of the United Center.

The teams battled back and forth, exchanging chances to score. Then, with just over a minute left, Hossa boarded Preds defenseman Dan Hamhuis and was called for a five-minute major penalty. Down a goal, shorthanded, with one of their best penalty-killers in the box, the Blackhawks needed a miracle.

They got two.

The first came with just 13.8 seconds to go. With the Blackhawks net empty, Jonathan Toews put a shot on Preds goalie Pekka Rinne. Patrick Kane found the puck on the doorstep and buried it, tying the game. But the Hawks would still have 3:56 of Hossa's penalty to kill in overtime.

As overtime began, Nashville got their chances, but Antti Niemi held down the fort until Hossa's penalty expired. When it did, Hossa exited the box and went directly to the front of the Predators net, miraculously just in time to find the rebounded puck from Brent Sopel's point shot. The Hawks won and history was made.

The images following Hossa's historic goal will be burned in the mind of Hawks fans forever. Hossa leapt with his hands in the air then slid to his knees, spinning in a circle as he pumped his fists. It has been shown in every Blackhawks and Hossa highlight video since, and is one of the iconic moments in Chicago sports history.

To me, there is no better free-agent signing in Chicago history. As a hockey fan, I considered it an honor to watch Hossa play the game I love. He was a complete player. He was a class act. He was respected by teammates and opponents alike. Marian Hossa is today enshrined in the Hockey Hall of Fame as a Chicago Blackhawk.

26

DOUG WILSON

With the sixth pick in the 1977 NHL draft, the Chicago Blackhawks selected defenseman Doug Wilson, and he made an immediate impact. That fall, Wilson began the season with the Blackhawks and never looked back. A premier offensive defenseman, Wilson bridged the gap between two of the best eras of Blackhawks hockey.

When he entered the league for the 1977–78 season, Wilson manned the blue line with Dale Tallon, Bob Murray, Phil Russell, and Blackhawks legend Keith Magnuson. Stan Mikita still had three years left in his career. Other Blackhawks greats such as Pit Martin and Cliff Koroll were still around, as well. When Wilson's Blackhawks career ended after the 1990–91 season, he was teammates with Chris Chelios, Ed Belfour, Jeremy Roenick, Michel Goulet, and Steve Larmer.

During the 14 years in between, all Wilson managed to do was win a Norris Trophy, make the All-Star team seven times, and become the Blackhawks' all-time leading scorer for a defenseman, with 779 points. That point total puts him ahead of Dennis Hull, Pit Martin, and Jeremy Roenick. Jonathan Toews passed Wilson during the 2019–20 campaign, the 13th season of his NHL career. Wilson is currently 15th all time for NHL defensemen with 827 points between Chicago and San Jose.

"He was one of the best defensemen in the NHL," former Red Wings captain Steve Yzerman remembers. "He was extremely well respected around the league and an elite player."

Former teammate and Hall of Famer Denis Savard agrees.

"He was a great teammate," Savard told ESPN.com. "He was a guy that was awesome for all of us to have on the team. Just a great person...He had 39 goals one year, was a Norris Trophy winner. I don't know how many have ever won the Norris and not been elected to the Hockey Hall of Fame, do you?

"Willy was an all-around great player. He played well defensively, he played in all situations. It was no fluke he scored all those goals. And defensively, he played against top lines every night...The way he handled himself on and off the ice throughout his whole career, he's not just a Hall of Fame player but a Hall of Fame person."

At the time of his retirement, the only defensemen with more career points than Wilson were Bobby Orr, Denis Potvin, Ray Bourque, and Paul Coffey. All four of those players are in the Hall of Fame. The only one of them who can claim to be as defensively competent as Wilson is Orr, who may be the best player in the history of the game not named Gretzky.

In November of 2019, Barry Rozner wrote in the *Daily Herald* about why Wilson was still waiting for his call to the Hall of Fame:

> The league was really run by Bill Wirtz, and Wirtz was closely aligned with Alan Eagleson and Bob Pulford, all of them sticking by one another until the end.
>
> As the president of the NHLPA, it was Wilson who led the charge to remove Eagleson, the man with massive conflicts of interest as players association director, who stole from players, got in bed with owners, and was eventually jailed for fraud and embezzlement.
>
> But in the process of trying to form a legitimate NHLPA, Wilson was blackballed. There's no other explanation for his exclusion from the Hall of Fame.

Since his retirement as a player, Wilson has become one of the game's best general managers. As the man in charge of the San Jose Sharks, he is the second-longest-tenured GM in the league, behind only Nashville's David Poile. The Sharks have made the playoffs every year but one under Wilson's watch and have reached the conference final five times.

Wilson once used a very savvy free-agency maneuver *against* the Blackhawks. In the summer of 2010, weeks after the Blackhawks won their first Stanley Cup since 1961, Wilson knew the team needed to make several roster moves because of the salary cap. The Hawks had just dealt seven players from the roster and still had work to do.

Wilson signed defenseman Niklas Hjalmarsson, a restricted free agent, to a four-year, $14 million offer sheet. Wilson's move forced the Hawks to choose between re-signing Hjalmarsson or Cup-winning goalie Antti Niemi. The Hawks matched the offer, signing Hjalmarsson. Wilson then signed Niemi to a one-year, $2 million deal. The next summer, the Sharks locked him up for four years with a $15.2 million contract.

Blackhawks historian Bob Verdi praises Wilson's tenure as San Jose GM.

"The Sharks are a contender every year," Verdi says. "That's the hardest thing to do in this league—to stay consistently competitive—but he and his staff have managed to do it. It really is a model franchise."

"I've known Doug for 30 years now," Yzerman said. "When I retired and began working with the Red Wings and when I was involved with Hockey Canada, he was a guy I talked to a lot. I picked his brain on things. He's been a [general] manager for a long time, so when I became a [GM] it was very helpful for me, guys like Doug, who really reached out and were there to give you advice."

Given his accomplishments, there was no way the Hall of Fame could keep him out forever. In 2020, Wilson finally got the call. He was typically humble in acknowledging the honor, showing no animosity about having to wait for so long.

"This was very unexpected," Wilson told the *Mercury News*. "I look at it and I truly believe this, that just for me to have been considered and mentioned in this category, is beyond any of the dreams that I had when I started playing this game."

27

1961

Bobby Hull. Stan Mikita. Pierre Pilote. Glenn Hall. With so many stars, it seems impossible that the Blackhawks teams of that era would only win one Stanley Cup, but it's true.

In 1961, the league was still in its Original Six phase, with teams in Chicago, Detroit, Boston, New York, Toronto, and, of course, Montreal. The Canadiens won five consecutive Stanley Cups from 1956 to 1960. They also appeared in 10 straight Stanley Cup Finals from 1950 to 60. The Blackhawks knew any road they had to a championship went through Montreal.

"Some people still consider that group as the best team of all time," says sports reporter Tim Cronin.

The 1961 Hawks, coached by Rudy Pilous, had a great collection of depth players who complemented their gallery of stars wonderfully. Defensemen included Elmer "Moose" Vasko, Jack "Tex" Evans, Dollard St. Laurent, Wayne Hillman, and Al Arbour, along with Pilote. On offense, the Blackhawks had a trio of famous lines: The Scooter Line, with Stan Mikita, Ken Wharram, and Ab McDonald; The Million Dollar Line, centered by Bill Hay with Bobby Hull and Murray Balfour on the wings; and The Line, centered by Ed Litzenberger.

"Everybody's style seemed to marry with the guy that he was playing with," Litzenberger says. "You have to be family before you can win."

Family was a recurring theme among the players on the team.

"The guys that had come from other teams were guys with good heads and with good hearts. It was a joy to come to the rink every night, knowing you had that supporting cast," Bobby Hull recalls. "You had a strong family tie. That's why we had such a successful franchise."

Stan Mikita called the collection of Blackhawks players "characters with character."

When the regular season ended, the Blackhawks finished in third place, 23 points behind the Canadiens, their first playoff opponent.

"We felt that we could beat them," Litzenberger recalled. "I said, 'They're just a bunch of guys, the same as we are. All you have to do each and every shift is win your shift. If you don't lose your shift, you can't lose the game.'"

The Hawks apparently lost a lot of shifts in Game 1, losing 6–2 in Montreal, but bounced back with a 4–3 comeback victory in Game 2.

The series shifted to Chicago for Game 3. The Hawks protected a 1–0 lead until Henri Richard scored with 31 seconds left in regulation. In the second overtime, it looked as if the Canadiens had won the game, but a Don Marshall goal was overturned due to a high stick. In the third overtime, Murray Balfour scored, giving the Hawks a 2–1 win and a 2–1 series lead.

"To work that long...then to have to go through another almost three periods to win at the end, that was likely the most memorable moment of the '61 playoffs," Hull recalls.

The Canadiens took Game 4 in Chicago, winning 5–2. The series shifted back to Montreal, but the Blackhawks weren't intimidated. They had won there before and they knew they could do it again.

"Everybody said to play in Montreal was bad. I said, 'It's just another rink. You don't look at the fans, you don't hear the fans, all you do is play your game,'" Litzenberger said. "After we got that first goal [in Game 5], you could feel it. The guys knew that we were as good as [the Canadiens] were."

The Blackhawks won Games 5 and 6 by the same score, 3–0, on the shoulders of goaltender Glenn Hall. They advanced to their first Stanley Cup Final since 1944.

Hull credits Hall's goaltending and the veteran Blackhawks defense with their success over Montreal. "There was a sense of urgency in that group that said, 'Hey, this might be the only chance we're going to get to win the Stanley Cup,'" he said.

Their opponent in the Final was the rival Detroit Red Wings, who had beaten the Toronto Maple Leafs in five games in their semifinal matchup. It was the first time since 1950 that two American teams would battle for the Cup.

"During the Original Six, the rivalries were very intense," remembered Litzenberger. "Sometimes you'd be on the same train together, but you wouldn't speak. They were the enemy. If they didn't have the same sweater on as you, they were the bad guys...on and off the ice."

In Game 1, the Blackhawks got out to a 3–0 lead before the Wings scored a pair of goals, both assisted by Gordie Howe, but Glenn Hall, as he had done the series prior, made several key saves down the stretch. The Hawks won the game 3–2.

The series didn't follow today's typical 2-2-1-1-1 format. Because of an ice show scheduled at the Chicago Stadium, Game 2 took place in Detroit at the Olympia.

In that contest, a pair of Detroit legends, goaltender Terry Sawchuk and forward Alex Delvecchio, starred as the Wings topped the Hawks 3–1. Delvecchio scored the game-winner and the late empty-netter to put the win on ice. Pilote scored the lone goal for the Blackhawks, with a backhander in the second period.

Game 3 saw the series back at the Chicago Stadium. The Blackhawks coasted to a 3–1 win after a fruitful second period, as Mikita, Ron Murphy, and Balfour scored for Chicago. Hull and Pilote assisted on a pair of goals each.

Game 4 in Detroit began with a 1–0 Chicago lead on a goal from Bill Hay. Alex Delvecchio tied things up until Bruce MacGregor broke the tie for his first NHL goal. The series was tied 2–2 and would once again shift to Chicago.

In Game 5, the teams headed into the third period tied 3–3. The Hawks then scored three unanswered goals—two from Mikita and one from Pilote—en route to a 6–3 win. The victory gave the Hawks a higher level of confidence.

"We felt that, all things being equal, we were ready to go," Hull says. "We could sense right from the beginning with Stan's line and with our Million Dollar Line, we were up to the task of beating the Detroit Red Wings."

Terry Sawchuk was injured in Game 5, so the Red Wings leaned on backup goaltender Hank Bassen for Game 6. Detroit took the lead on a Parker MacDonald goal. During the first period, Hawks coach Rudy Pilous found some motivating words for the team.

"I just told them, 'Tonight's game was worth $1,000 to the winner, and the loser gets nothing,'" he said.

Apparently, his message got through. In the second frame, Hawks penalty-killer Reggie Fleming beat Bassen for a shorthanded goal, tying the game and scoring what may have been the biggest goal in Blackhawks history up to that point.

"They were ahead of us, they were on the power play, but Reggie, stealing the puck and scoring, neutralized the power play. The momentum came back to our club. Detroit...you could just see them sag after that," Hull says. "We played the rest of the game outskating them at every turn."

Ab McDonald put home a Hull rebound, giving the Hawks a 2–1 lead heading into the third period. In the final frame, Eric Nesterenko gave Chicago a 3–1 lead with a wrist shot past Bassen and the Hawks were on their way. The Red Wings appeared to be out of gas and out of fight. Evans made it 4–1, scoring an empty-netter for his first goal of the entire season. A late breakaway goal from Wharram made it 5–1. The Hawks had won their first Stanley Cup championship since 1938.

"You can't believe how happy the guys were. This is a hockey club that's been in the bottom of the league for 100 years, and now we're Stanley Cup champs," Litzenberger said.

Hull gives all credit for the win to the veteran players on the club. "We were basking in it, but those veterans, those were the guys that won the game for us," he said.

"I'm very fortunate and very lucky to be associated with such a fine bunch of fellas," said Pilous during the postgame celebration. "Really good hockey players with a thoroughbred heart to win."

"[The next day] I had to meet Mayor Daley after being on an all-night party with my guys," Litzenberger said. "That was kind of difficult."

Despite the feeling of organizational confidence and a roster loaded with stars, this Blackhawks group never won another Stanley Cup. In fact, the franchise wouldn't hoist the Cup until a new group of stars including Patrick Kane, Jonathan Toews, and Duncan Keith broke through in 2010.

On January 9, 2011, the Blackhawks honored the 1961 champions with a pregame ceremony.

"It's been 50 years and they still love us," Hull said. "It's a tribute not only to the Chicago Blackhawks, a tribute not only to our hockey club, but these wonderful hockey fans here in Chicago."

"It's a great gesture on their part to allow this to happen for us," Mikita said of the reunion. "Now I know how Michael [Jordan] felt out there."

"It's just amazing," Pilote said. "Just amazing, and you really feel proud of the organization, that you were a Blackhawk."

28

SECORD'S SCORING PUNCH

In the history of hockey, there are hundreds of players who could put up big goal totals. An even larger group could put up big penalty minutes and punch the opponent about the head, face, and neck.

Al Secord may have been the finest example of someone from both groups.

Secord, who was traded to Chicago from Boston in December of 1980, scored 40-plus goals three times, including a 54-goal campaign in 1982–83. He's 18th all time in franchise history with 213 goals and sixth all time with .457 goals per game.

Impressive, right?

Secord also ranks third all time in Blackhawks history in penalty minutes (1,426) behind only Chris Chelios (1,495) and Keith Magnuson (1,440).

To Secord, scoring and protecting teammates were both equally important parts of his job.

"I was playing with Denis Savard regularly," Secord says. "My presence gave him more time to operate on the ice and I got more ice time than ever before."

Secord was businesslike on and off the ice. While many players on opposing teams are friendly during and after games, that thought never crossed Secord's mind.

"I never wanted to get to know the opposing side and I remember hearing that from Gordie Howe, actually, watching him as a kid," Secord said. "It's true. I'm the type of guy, if I become your friend, it's much more difficult to do [my] job."

Former teammate and current Blackhawks radio analyst Troy Murray describes Secord perfectly: "If he wasn't scoring a goal and someone was cross-checking him, he was getting into a fight with that guy. That was the mentality: 'If I'm going to the front of the net and if you want to try and move me out, I'm going to fight you. I'll show you

you're not going to be able to do that.' And for the defenseman who didn't want to try and move him out, that's why he scored 40, 50 goals on a regular basis for a couple of years."

As Secord became a reliable scorer in his career, his coaches didn't want him in the penalty box as often. He brought more to the team on the ice than in the sin bin. In fact, during his 54-goal campaign in 1982–83, Blackhawks head coach Orval Tessier instructed Secord to take fewer penalties and fight less often. Obviously, it worked, as Secord recorded a career high in goals and points, but it never sat well with him.

"Even though I scored well, I felt like I didn't play the way I was supposed to play," he said. "I was told not to hit guys so often. I needed to play physical, and I didn't. It's a big part of my game, to be on the other guy's skin. When I hit a guy and the crowd starts chanting, it brings energy to me and to my teammates. And I was missing that element. It felt strange."

Here's a fun, interactive experiment you can play at home whilst reading this book: Google "Al Secord" and let the autofill do the rest. It will inevitably fill in the word "fights." The search will produce dozens of results.

The first two I found came from the same game. On January 10, 1986, the Blackhawks were in Detroit to face the Red Wings. Detroit had a pair of the most feared fighters in the National Hockey League, Joey Kocur and the reigning heavyweight champ, Bob Probert. Secord fought them both to a draw. In fact, Probert grew so frustrated with his inability to get an upper hand on Secord that he headbutted the Hawks winger, who was one of the last players in the league to play without a helmet. When that didn't work, Probert lifted his knee to the head of Secord, who was tied up with the linesman. Probert was thrown out of the game and given 21 minutes in penalties. The Hawks would go on to win the game 9–4, with Secord adding a goal and two assists.

Right there, that's Al Secord in a nutshell. A mundane, regular season game in January tells you all you need to know.

"He was the prototypical forward you wanted to have who could score goals and would do anything he needed to do to defend his team," Murray said. "I loved him as a teammate. To me, Al will go down as one of the toughest guys the Blackhawks had in the history of their franchise and one of the best goal-scorers too."

When his playing days were over, Secord began his second career as a pilot with American Airlines. Secord has now reached the rank of captain with the company. His love of flying traces back to his younger days fighting forest fires in Ontario, often via airplane.

"Not that I'm a control freak but you are in more control and you can control the atmosphere," Secord said of his flying career. "I work with so many enjoyable people and there are 50 ways to do the same job. We just have a serious attitude as far as getting the job done but we make it a pleasant atmosphere. So I really like it."

Al Secord, the consummate professional. Always just doing his job. (But if I were a pilot invading his airspace, I'd watch my back.)

29

BIG BUFF

The Blackhawks of the 2010s were a team full of huge personalities, but none were bigger, literally or figuratively, than Dustin Byfuglien. "Big Buff" was everything Chicago embraces in a folk hero: he was big, he was mean, and he "didn't give a fuck" what people thought about him.

Selected in the eighth round (245th overall) of the 2003 NHL draft, Byfuglien remained a bit of a mystery until his permanent arrival in 2007–08. At the time, few fans even watched or cared about the Blackhawks. For those of us who were paying attention, we knew the Hawks had drafted this heavyset kid with a name that was tough to pronounce. Now and again he'd show up at prospects camp and in the preseason, but he never seemed destined for the NHL. Stories of his struggles with weight would come out every year, and it didn't seem like anyone was sold on whether he would ever be an NHL player, let alone an All-Star and Stanley Cup hero.

Turns out, it didn't matter.

Byfuglien played major roles for the Blackhawks at defense and forward, but it was his performance in the 2010 Stanley Cup playoffs that fans will remember for a lifetime. We'll get to that in a second, because it would be an injustice to not give you a bit of Byfuglien's backstory.

Years ago, before the 2010 Stanley Cup championship, 670 The Score and Budweiser hosted a series of bar events with Byfuglien and then Score host Jesse Rogers. Rogers and Byfuglien would go town-to-town, bar-to-bar, and do an hour or so on the air, then hang with the locals. In radio, it's an understood rule to hold off (or at least take it easy) on the booze until the on-air portion of the event was over. Byfuglien was never taught this rule of radio. Beer after beer, shot after shot, Byfuglien was there for a good time. To his credit, he was able to keep it (mostly) together on the air, but stories would begin to pour out after every event. The amounts of alcohol he allegedly consumed at these events (he had a driver) have become the stuff of legend. The promotion, in that form, was short-lived. The next season, a different crop of Blackhawks players did these appearances. They were off-the-air only and suddenly the Hawks found it wise to send a "representative" from the team to babysit...err...supervise the players at these events.

The stories don't end there. Byfuglien once "borrowed" a police officer's gun at a bar for a laugh. Another time he rode a motorcycle from one bar into another. These are the stories we know about. I can't imagine what stories dare not be told.

Fast-forward to 2010. The Blackhawks had stolen Chicago's heart with an incredible and dramatic playoff run. They dispatched Nashville in round one, then began their rivalry with the Vancouver Canucks in the Western Conference semifinal. In that series, Byfuglien recorded four goals and two assists and was integral in the Hawks' advance to the conference final.

While the series against Nashville and Vancouver proved challenging, the Hawks buzzsawed their way through the Sharks, sweeping them in four games. Byfuglien led the way, scoring in all four games of the series. The most memorable came in overtime of Game 3. After a dominant shift in the Sharks zone, Dave Bolland found the puck behind the San Jose net. Byfuglien saw his chance and broke from the left point straight into the slot. Byfuglien didn't miss, sniping the puck over the shoulder of Sharks goaltender Evgeni Nabokov. The Hawks went on to clinch the series with their 4–2 win, with Byfuglien scoring the fourth goal of the game.

The Philadelphia Flyers and Stanley Cup Final were next.

While the 2010 Blackhawks weren't an overly physical team, they needed to adapt for the playoffs and especially the Final. The Flyers had players like Daniel Carcillo, Scott Hartnell, and, of course, Chris Pronger. Pronger became Public Enemy No. 1 in the series. His combination of dominant defense, physical prowess, and cheap-shot artistry made him a prime candidate for the role.

Early in the series, Pronger speared and slashed Byfuglien in the torso and throat. Byfuglien retaliated and got called for a penalty. It felt like Pronger was getting away with murder the whole series. I guess 16 years and a Hall of Fame career get you that sort of pass.

The Hawks were clearly frustrated with Pronger's antics, as were Blackhawks fans. The *Chicago Tribune*, trying to capitalize on the fans' venom, published a regrettable poster of Pronger wearing a figure skater's skirt with the headline "Chrissy Pronger: Looks like Tarzan, Skates like Jane."

During Game 5, Byfuglien found the opportunity to exact his revenge on the Flyers defenseman. Lined up at left wing in the Philadelphia zone, the Flyers won the faceoff into the right corner. Pronger went to play the puck and Byfuglien put him in the crosshairs. The two came together in the corner, but only Byfuglien came out. The United Center crowed erupted. That hit was another snapshot in a season and playoff run full of great moments. Byfuglien ended Game 5 with two goals, two assists, and that unforgettable hit on his score sheet. The Hawks went on to win the Stanley Cup in Game 6.

During the Stanley Cup championship parade in downtown Chicago, Byfuglien took to the stage wearing the WWE championship belt the team had given him after Game 5. He hadn't had the opportunity to pass it on to Kane after the Cup-winning goal in the clincher, so he took the chance to do it at the lectern. In typical Byfuglien fashion, he said, "All you cab drivers better be careful, because this guy's taking [the belt] home this summer." He was, of course, referencing Patrick Kane's assault of a Buffalo cab driver from the summer before. That was Byfuglien. Unpredictable and unafraid.

Sadly, the Blackhawks were forced to ship Byfuglien to the Atlanta Thrashers (now the Winnipeg Jets) after the 2010 Cup season. He was one of many cap casualties for the Blackhawks that summer. Byfuglien has gone on to appear in three All-Star games for the Jets and has become one of hockey's most beloved characters.

Of all the Blackhawks who have left the organization since their 2010 Stanley Cup, Byfuglien is probably the player the fans miss the most. The organization has not been able to find a power forward or big, physical defenseman since his departure. Two of their 2019 draft picks, 6-foot-4 center Kirby Dach and 6-foot-6 defenseman Alex Vlasic, are the best candidates to finally fill Byfuglien's shoes. But they'll have a hard time doing so in the hearts and memories of Blackhawks fans.

30

BILLY REAY

The winningest coach in Blackhawks history might not be who you think it is.

Yes, Joel Quenneville won three Stanley Cups with Chicago and is the second-winningest coach in NHL history, behind only Scott Bowman, but his 452 wins with the Blackhawks fall well short of Billy Reay's franchise record of 516.

While Reay never captured the Stanley Cup during his 14 years as Blackhawks head coach, he reached the Final three times. He only missed the playoffs once and is still praised by some of the legendary players for whom he coached.

"Billy Reay was a terrific coach, and I'm sure I'm not alone when I say I consider myself fortunate to have played under him for so many years with the Blackhawks," Stan Mikita said. "Beyond that, though, he was a good man. I guess it's unusual to call your coach or your boss a friend, but that's how I felt about Billy."

"Billy was great," recalled Tony Esposito. "Billy left you alone to do your job, and if you did your job, that was all he expected of you. And as a result, guys wanted to play for him."

Many consider Reay a "players' coach," which was rare in the 1960s and 1970s, in any sport.

"Billy dealt with us like men," said Jim Pappin. "He communicated one-on-one and to a group, whatever it took. I never heard a bad word about him from the guys. We knew we were lucky to play for him."

Reay's trust in his players, like many modern sports coaches and managers, allowed his players to compete to the fullest of their abilities. Instead of looking over their shoulders, fearing his wrath after any mistake, they knew they had the confidence of their coach.

Former Cubs skipper Joe Maddon uses this philosophy in his management. Maddon says, "I tell the players, 'You have my respect, and I have to earn yours.' If I ever coach instinct out of a player, shame on me."

That's not to say that Reay didn't occasionally let the team know he was unhappy.

"Billy had the knack of knowing when to come down on a team and when to let up," Esposito says.

In 1976, the Blackhawks were on a long winning streak and decided to spend a night at a Philadelphia watering hole. While the players were reveling in their success, Reay, in a suit and tie, walked into the bar, stared at the team, and walked out. He didn't say a word. He didn't have to. The message was received loud and clear.

"He just wanted us to know that he knew where we were and what we were doing," Esposito joked. "And, of course, after he leaves, we're all wondering the same thing: 'What if he comes back in another hour?'"

The team didn't stick around to find out.

"Billy never socialized with us, but he helped encourage our attitude of togetherness," Mikita recalled. "Today, they call it 'chemistry.' Billy was good at stressing the team concept and having us play for one another. We wanted to play hard for him. Not only because we didn't like going into his office where he looked at us with that glare of his—we called him 'X-Reay'—but we didn't want to let him down, either. He let players play and demanded only that you give your best. Ask the guys who played for him: Billy Reay was a terrific coach and a good man. A real good man."

While his players loved him, Reay wasn't exactly beloved by the media. Despite his dapper hats and fancy suits, Reay wasn't a flashy character. He offered very little to the media in terms of colorful quotes or inside information. Some feel that reputation explains why he's not a member of the Hall of Fame.

Reay's tenure as Blackhawks head coach came to an end right before Christmas of 1976. The team returned home from a tough road trip on December 22. As Reay arrived at his home around dawn, he found an envelope under his door. Reay's wife, Clare, thought it was just a Christmas card and left if for her husband, but it wasn't a card. It was a pink slip.

The winningest coach in Blackhawks history had been fired.

Fourteen seasons, three Stanley Cup Final appearances, 516 regular season wins, and all he got was a lousy note under the door. A classic Bill Wirtz move.

Reay didn't have much to say about the firing and took it in stride.

"It's all part of the hockey business," he told Mikita.

Reay's son, Bill, wrote a chapter on his father's life philosophies in the book *Chicken Soup for the Soul - Hooked on Hockey*:

> My dad operated with five guiding principles, as a coach and as a father and husband:
>
> Be a good example. It's not what you say; it's what you do!
>
> Take full responsibility for yourself.
>
> Never ask another person to do something you are not willing to do yourself.
>
> Be fair, firm, and consistent.
>
> Praise in public, criticize in private...the rest will take care of itself.

The timing of Reay's firing is ironic. In the book, Reay's son tells an anecdote of his father's love of the holiday season

"Early on in his tenure he convinced the Blackhawks ownership to have a Christmas party for the players and their families," Reay wrote. "Santa would come, everyone would receive a gift, and it would be a day to gather together as a family. The Christmas party became a tradition. For the young players, Dad did something very special on his own. He gave them a new pair of skates for Christmas as a surprise."

One can only imagine how painful it was for Reay to be fired at a time so special to him.

"I just wish we could have won a Cup for him," Mikita recalled. "We had some really good teams, but it wasn't meant to be. The worst was in 1971, when we led Montreal 2–0 in the Final and 2–0 in the seventh game. Bobby Hull hit the post. It could have been 3–0.

The Canadiens turned around, Jacques Lemaire scored, and they beat us 3–2. That hurt. Still hurts."

"Billy took some heat for not winning a Cup in Chicago with a lot of good players and good teams," Mikita continued. "He won more games than any coach in Blackhawks history, and I wish before he passed away in 2004 that he'd have gotten into the Hall of Fame. He belongs there. Billy Reay was class...all class."

31

HOCKEY AT WRIGLEY FIELD

Over the years, the Friendly Confines known as Wrigley Field has hosted a number of unique events. The stadium, located in Chicago's Lakeview neighborhood, opened in 1914 and has been the home of the Chicago Cubs ever since. The Chicago Bears used Wrigley for their home games from 1921 to 1970. The Chicago Sting, of the North American Soccer League, used Wrigley for select home games in the 1970s and 1980s. Musical acts Jimmy Buffett and the Police were the first to use the venue for concerts.

But never had Wrigley been host to a hockey game until the Blackhawks and Red Wings strapped on the skates on January 1, 2009.

The NHL debuted its outdoor hockey series, the Winter Classic, on New Year's Day of 2008 at Ralph Wilson Stadium, home of the NFL's Buffalo Bills. The Pittsburgh Penguins and Buffalo Sabres skated to a shootout on a cold and snowy day. The game gained the attention of hockey and non-hockey fans alike. The sight of some of hockey's biggest stars skating outside, in the snow, was a spectacle too appealing to ignore.

The league officially announced the event at Wrigley Field on July 22, 2008. Select members of the Blackhawks, along with legends Bobby Hull and Stan Mikita, were in attendance.

"The NHL is delighted to bring its most historic rivalry to one of the most historic venues in sports," NHL commissioner Gary Bettman said. Cubs chairman Crane Kenney predicted the Winter Classic would "be one of the events most memorable when people look back at the history of Wrigley Field."

The 2009 Winter Classic was the NHL's first at a marquee, legendary sports venue and featured one of the league's oldest rivalries. The Blackhawks were a young team on the rise, while the Red Wings were coming off their 2008 Stanley Cup win.

Blackhawks president John McDonough, the man Rocky Wirtz had handpicked from the Chicago Cubs to spearhead the team's new direction, was an integral part in getting the event off the ground. His connections in both leagues and experience with high-level sporting events proved invaluable in the pursuit of the game.

"I think the hockey gods really wanted this game to happen here," McDonough remarked.

The Blackhawks were excited for the opportunity, not only because of the once-in-a-lifetime nature of the game, but for the chance to announce their arrival to fans and the league.

"We're certainly excited about it. It's going to be a great opportunity for the Hawks to show people on national TV and everyone watching that we've come a long way," Patrick Sharp said.

Demand for the Winter Classic was huge. The game sold out in under an hour. The league, according to a spokesman, received 240,000 ticket requests.

Before the game could be played, however, Wrigley Field had to be converted from a baseball venue to a hockey venue. The NHL brought in a crew, led by Dan Craig, the NHL's facilities operations manager. Craig and his crew began preparations on December 16, working tirelessly to prepare the field, coping with the elements a Chicago winter provides. Along the way, the crew dealt with six inches of snow, a one-week temperature shift from 34 to 56 degrees, and a tornado warning. Each issue created a new and unique challenge, as did getting the needed equipment into Wrigley Field.

The Zambonis used in the game were delivered from Detroit and Minnesota. As the crew was trying to back one of the Zambonis off the truck bed, the driver realized the brakes were frozen. It was too late, and the Zamboni fell to the ground with the driver still in the seat. The Zamboni and driver were fine, but it was just an example of the many challenges, aside from keeping the ice playable, that the crew had to contend with.

Back in July, Jonathan Toews said, "It's called the Winter Classic, so it would be cool if we have to deal with the elements a little bit." The captain would get his wish. The puck drop temperature was 27 degrees, perfect for maintaining ice integrity, not as fun for those in the stands.

OUTDOOR WOES

Including their debut in the 2009 NHL Winter Classic at Wrigley Field, a 6–4 loss to the Red Wings, the Chicago Blackhawks have played six outdoor games as part of the Winter Classic or Stadium Series. Their record in those games is 1–5 and they've been outscored 24–15.

Let's look at the franchise's outdoor game history:

Game	Date	Opponent	Venue	Result
WC	1/1/2009	v Detroit	Wrigley Field	6–4 L
SS	3/1/2014	v Pittsburgh	Soldier Field	5–1 W
WC	1/1/2015	@ Washington	Nationals Park	3–2 L
SS	2/21/2016	@ Minnesota	TCF Bank Stadium	6–1 L
WC	1/2/2017	@ St Louis	Busch Stadium	4–1 L
WC	1/1/2019	v Boston	Notre Dame Stadium	4–2 L

For rosters as loaded with talent as those Blackhawks teams were, their struggles are almost inexplicable. Chicago's winning percentage from 2009 to 2019 was .614, compared to the comical .166 in outdoor games.

"For whatever reason, we haven't come out on top and haven't played too well in them," Patrick Kane recalls. "It's frustrating because it's on a national stage, there's a lot of hype, and you want to put a good show on for your fans. Maybe sometimes we're thinking too much about that rather than going out and playing a simple game. It's a little frustrating."

Perhaps Kane is right, or maybe less-than-ideal ice conditions have proved troublesome for more highly skilled teams, which most of those Blackhawks teams surely were. Whatever the reasons, even after six outdoor games, the Blackhawks and their captain still find joy in the experience.

"It's unfortunate," Jonathan Toews said after the 2019 Winter Classic loss to Boston at Notre Dame Stadium. "But it's a special opportunity to be able to play in this building. I think it even exceeded my expectations. So much excitement to be out there. I think we all really enjoyed it."

I attended the game as a spectator from a rooftop across the street from Wrigley. At the time I bought the tickets, it felt like an awesome idea. I got up there an hour before puck drop, then watched the 60-minute game and two full intermissions; by that time, I had trouble feeling any part of my body. But I wouldn't have traded the experience for anything. There was a feeling of arrival for the Blackhawks organization. Win or lose, the team was back on the map.

The game got off to a promising start. Just under two minutes into the game, Brent Seabrook sent Detroit winger (and former Blackhawk) Dan Cleary into the Blackhawks bench with a crushing check. Then, 3:24 into the game, Kris Versteeg buried a Martin Havlat rebound to give the Blackhawks a 1–0 lead. Six minutes later, Mikael Samuelsson tied the game for the Red Wings, but Havlat and Ben Eager each added goals to make it 3–1 Chicago after the first period.

The second period was all Red Wings. Jiri Hudler scored a pair of goals, tying the game at 3–3, then Pavel Datsyuk rushed through the Blackhawks defense and gave the Wings a 4–3 lead.

The Wings began the third period in similar fashion. Brian Rafalski scored 3:07 into the frame, then 17 seconds later, Brett Lebda scored the Wings' sixth goal of the game. The Blackhawks pulled starting goalie Cristobal Huet for Nikolai Khabibulin, but it was too late. Duncan Keith added a late goal to make it 6–4, and that's how the game would end.

Despite the final result, the game was full of memorable moments, from Jim Cornelison's performance of the national anthem before the game, to Seabrook's big hit, to the "Seventh-Inning Stretch" featuring Blackhawks greats Bobby Hull, Stan Mikita, Denis Savard, and Tony Esposito, accompanied by Cubs legends Ryne Sandberg, Fergie Jenkins, and Billy Williams.

"It was great to be a part of it," Joel Quenneville said after the loss. "The fans were great. It was a special place to be and play in. Certainly we're not happy with the way it ended up, but it was a privilege to be here today."

The Blackhawks and Red Wings would meet in the 2009 Western Conference Final. The Red Wings beat the Hawks in six games, only to lose the Cup to the Pittsburgh Penguins in a Stanley Cup rematch.

The Blackhawks, despite the Winter Classic loss, showed the NHL how passionate and committed their fans are, and the league took note. The Blackhawks have since appeared in five other outdoor games, including three more Winter Classic games. As of the 2019–20 season, the Blackhawks' record in outdoor games is 1–5; they've been outscored 24–15 in those games. Has what started out as a blessing become a curse? Probably not.

32

PIERRE PILOTE

Throughout their history, the Chicago Blackhawks have had dozens of offensive or two-way defensemen, but before Chris Chelios, Gary Suter, Duncan Keith, or Brian Campbell, there was Pierre Pilote.

"I always believed that if I had the puck, the other team didn't have it," Pilote told the Hockey Hall of Fame in 2006.

Pilote's offensive instincts came from his days of playing forward as a teenager. He didn't play organized hockey until he was 17 years old. The year before, he tried out for the Niagara Falls Junior B team, but as a center. The team was full at that position, so Pilote didn't make the team. From there, he focused on being a defenseman, and made the team the following season.

"I had to learn the position, but I was always thinking offensively," Pilote recalls.

After one year with Niagara, Pilote was recruited by Rudy Pilous, who was the coach of the St. Catharines Teepees of the Ontario Hockey League. In 52 games, Pilote picked up 53 points, including 21 goals. Pilote spent the next four seasons with the Buffalo Bisons of the American Hockey League before joining the Blackhawks for the 1955–56 season.

"My first game in Chicago was great," Pilote remembers. "I looked around, the organist was playing. It was just amazing. Fabulous."

The same adjectives could be used to describe Pilote's career with the Blackhawks. Chicago wasn't exactly a hockey dynasty when Pilote arrived, but two years into his career, Bobby Hull joined the team, while his St. Catharines coach, Pilous, was named head man of the Blackhawks. The next season, Stan Mikita jumped on board.

The influx of offensive talent propelled Pilote's scoring game as well. "I was always thinking offensively," Pilote said. "It evolved when the Blackhawks started getting guys like Hull and Mikita. We became more offensive minded."

Hall of Famer Glenn Hall joined the Blackhawks in 1957–58 after he was acquired, with Ted Lindsay, in a trade with the rival Red Wings. Pilote credits Hall's goaltending with his ability to focus on moving the puck.

"Another important thing about being an offensive defenseman, you have to have a good goalie back there. We had Glenn Hall, the best," Pilote said.

In 1961, Pilote, Hull, Mikita, and Hall captured the Stanley Cup, beating the Montreal Canadiens, who had won the previous five Stanley Cups, in six games. The Hawks met the Red Wings in the Cup Final, winning that series in six games, as well. In those playoffs, Pilote recorded 15 points in 12 games. Had the Conn Smythe Trophy existed at the time, Pilote would have won it easily.

Pilote was named the Blackhawks captain the following season, a title he held for seven seasons. Of his captaincy, Pilote said, "You have to be a good leader and a good politician. We had three or four superstars and you had to know how to handle these guys. No matter how good a captain you are, it's just like politics—you have to win a majority. You have to have the guys on your side, but there's always a little bit of dissension and you're always trying to fix it before it gets too far and gets into the office. If a guy had a beef, we'd talk about it. If it was reasonable, I'd go to the management. I just tried to lead by example."

Even during his captaincy, Pilote often found himself in the huge shadows of Hull, Mikita, and Hall, and while he may not have been the "face of the Blackhawks," he might have been the actual "face" of the Blackhawks; it's hard to not notice how much Pilote resembles the logo on the Blackhawks sweater.

"We used to laugh about the crest," Bobby Hull recalls. "The older Pierre got, the more he looked like Chief Blackhawk on our sweaters. He was proud of it, and so were we."

All told, Pilote played 821 games with the Blackhawks. He won three Norris Trophies in that time, winning the honor in 1963, 1964, and 1965. Perhaps more impressively, Pilote never finished lower than fourth in Norris voting from 1960 to 1967. He never finished lower than second in any season between 1962 and 1967.

"Pierre changed the game quite a bit," said Glenn Hall. "He was even pre–Bobby Orr with the defense moving in to be part of the offense, he was certainly influential."

"What Pierre Pilote did for me was show me that a defenseman had to have his head up and the puck in front of him so that he is always ready to move the puck," said New York Islanders legend Denis Potvin. "That's the way I tried to play: always ready to make a pass.

In typical Blackhawks fashion, things didn't end well when Pilote and the team parted ways. On May 24, 1968, Pilote got a phone call from Toronto reporter Red Burnett. Pilote, surprised to hear from the reporter, asked why he was calling. Burnett replied, "I'm calling to get your reaction to the trade." This was the first Pilote had heard of the deal. After asking Burnett if he was sure, all Pilote could muster was, "Holy shit." In the days and weeks following the trade, Pilote considered retiring. "I wasn't going to Toronto. I was going to quit," he said.

A friend of Pilote's, Albert Dick, gave him a collection of motivational LPs to listen to before making his decision.

"Perhaps he could tell I was torn up about staying in hockey, about going to Toronto, even though my mind was made up. After listening to those records, I had second thoughts," Pilote said.

He had trouble fitting in with the Leafs that next season, however, and called it a career despite overtures from the New York Rangers.

Pilote was elected to the Hockey Hall of Fame in 1975. The Blackhawks retired his No. 3 jersey, along with the late Keith Magnuson's, in 2008. He is one of seven Blackhawks, along with Hull, Mikita, Hall, Magnuson, Denis Savard, and Tony Esposito, to have the honor.

On September 9, 2017, Pilote passed away after battling cancer. He was 85 years old.

"Pierre was a man of humor and great dignity and a proud member of the Hockey Hall of Fame," said commissioner Gary Bettman. "The National Hockey League mourns Pierre's passing and sends heartfelt condolences to his family, teammates and many friends."

The Blackhawks had this to say about Pilote: "He will be remembered for his toughness, leadership, and reliability on the ice—as proven by his captaincy and streak of 376 consecutive games played. We will forever be grateful for his incredible contribution to the Blackhawks and the game of hockey."

33

MAJOR McLAUGHLIN

The founder of the Chicago Blackhawks, Frederic McLaughlin, was born in Chicago on June 28, 1877. He graduated from Harvard in 1901, then served for the United States Army during World War I, where he achieved the rank of Major.

Frederic's father, W.F. McLaughlin, who had founded the McLaughlin's Manor House coffee company in Chicago, passed away in 1905, leaving the company to his oldest son, George. Upon his return from war, Frederic would serve as the company's secretary and treasurer.

Even at the age of 42, the Major had quite the reputation around Chicago. His great granddaughter, Dr. Castle McLaughlin, an American history author and curator at Harvard's Peabody Museum of Archaeology and Ethnology, heard stories of the Major's playboy days.

"Frederic was the youngest of eight surviving children," Dr. McLaughlin says, "and he was considered one of the most eligible bachelors in Chicago. He had a famous apartment in the old brick coffee company warehouse along the river. It apparently had 25-foot ceilings and windows with velvet curtains."

McLaughlin was also a gambler.

In 1926, Lester and Frank Patrick of the Pacific Coast Hockey Association decided to sell six of their franchises. Despite a limited knowledge of the game, the potential of this particular gamble, combined with the appeal of a New York–Chicago rivalry, was too much for the Major to resist. McLaughlin rallied a group of Chicago businessmen, raised the $12,000 entry fee, then purchased the Portland Rosebuds franchise for $200,000.

The Chicago Blackhawks were born, and Major McLaughlin was their first president. The team's name stemmed from his days in World War I, having commanded the 333rd Machine Gun Battalion of the 85th Division of the Army. Members of the division called themselves the Blackhawks, in honor of the Sauk Chief.

In their first game, the team, coached by Pete Muldoon and led by the likes of Charles "Rabbit" McVeigh, George Hay, and Dick Irvin, defeated the Toronto St. Pats 4–1.

"When the opening whistle was blown, the Hawks dashed out and unloosed a sustained attack on the Toronto goal net," reported the *Chicago Tribune*.

"Oh, boy, I am glad I haven't got a weak heart," McLaughlin is reported to have said after the game.

McLaughlin was what some would call a meddler, constantly fiddling with the team's roster and coaches. He was once asked if his team was ready to compete for a championship. He said, "If it's not, we'll keep on buying players until it is."

The Blackhawks finished their inaugural season 19–22–3. The demanding McLaughlin thought he deserved better and relieved Muldoon of his coaching services. The "Curse of Muldoon" was born.

How fitting is it, by the way, that a Chicago team got hit with a curse after only one year in existence?

The next season (1927–28), the Hawks went 7–34–3, cycling through a pair of coaches, Barney Stanley (4–17–12) and Hugh Lehman (3–17–1). In 1928–29, the team went 7–29–8 with another pair of coaches, Herb Gardiner and Dick Irvin, both of whom were players on the team.

The team played their home games in the Chicago Coliseum, a converted Civil War prison. The Coliseum wasn't exactly a destination for Chicago fans. When stockholders and fans started losing interest in the franchise, McLaughlin took over the block of shares until he held the majority.

When the Chicago Stadium opened in 1929, the Blackhawks experienced a surge of popularity, but the Great Depression quickly began to take hold of the nation. In 1933, George McLaughlin was killed in an automobile accident, leaving the Major in charge of both the Blackhawks and the coffee company. Managing both took its toll on the team and on McLaughlin, but the Major was able to keep the franchise afloat by taking a loan from Montreal's Joseph Cattarinich.

That same year, the Major hired Tommy Gorman to coach and manage the team, admitting he wasn't qualified enough to do it himself.

"I'm sending myself to the cheering section," McLaughlin said. "I'm convinced that I'm just an amateur in hockey."

The Major was also a staunch patriot and did his best to fill his rosters with American players. "I think an all-American team would be a tremendous drawing card all over the league," McLaughlin said. The 1934 Blackhawks, which featured five American-born players, broke the Curse of Muldoon, winning the Stanley Cup over the Detroit Red Wings in four games. In 1938, the Blackhawks captured the Cup again, this time with eight American-born players on their roster. First-year head coach Bill Stewart was the first American-born coach to capture the trophy.

McLaughlin was famous for his feuds with other owners around the league. Red Wings owner James Norris, who was business partners with eventual Blackhawks owner Arthur Wirtz, set up a competing Chicago team in the American Hockey Association, locking McLaughlin out of the Chicago Stadium.

"Where hockey was concerned, Major McLaughlin was the strangest bird and, yes, perhaps the biggest nut I met in my entire life," Toronto's Conn Smythe said.

The Major also sparred with league president Frank Calder. The source for one of their many quarrels was McLaughlin's formal letter to the league's Board of Governors asking for Calder's removal. The board rejected the motion. Speculation at the time claimed that McLaughlin harbored strong feelings toward Canadians—some would call it envy, the Major would probably call it hatred—and felt that Calder, who was from Montreal, held a bias toward those teams.

When the Major passed away in 1944, Norris, who had attempted to get the Blackhawks from McLaughlin for years, finally had his opportunity, but there was a catch. Because he owned stakes in other NHL teams, he couldn't buy the Blackhawks outright. He put together a group led by Hawks owner Bill Tobin to take over as de facto owners.

Major Frederic McLaughlin was enshrined in the Hockey Hall of Fame in 1963.

34

EDDIE OLCZYK

Edward Walter Olczyk Jr. has been overcoming the odds for a long time.

When he tried to make the U.S. Olympic team as a 16-year-old in 1983, people told him he was too young. He made the 1984 team anyway and represented his country in Sarajevo. He must have done something right, because that summer the Blackhawks selected Olczyk third overall in the draft.

When he entered the NHL, some felt he'd have trouble staying in the league because of perceived weight management issues. "What's wrong with a hungry hockey player?" Olczyk joked.

At 18, just months after the draft, the hometown kid made the Blackhawks roster. Olczyk's impact was immediately felt, as he scored 20 goals and added 30 assists in his rookie season. He was a member of the Blackhawks' famed "Clydesdale Line," with teammates Troy Murray and Curt Fraser. Over the course of his 16 NHL seasons, he appeared in 1,031 games, netting 342 goals with 452 assists, including 77 goals and 132 assists with Chicago. He is a member of the U.S. Hockey Hall of Fame and a Stanley Cup champion, won with the New York Rangers.

When his career ended, people told him he couldn't be the first American-born lead television hockey analyst. Yep, he proved them wrong too.

Shortly after a two-year head coaching stint with the rebuilding Pittsburgh Penguins, Olczyk joined the Blackhawks booth alongside living legend Pat Foley. They've been the television team ever since. He's also the top analyst on NBC Sports Group's NHL broadcasts, where he shares the booth with the brilliant Mike "Doc" Emrick. He's called Stanley Cup Finals, Winter Classics, and countless NHL contests. Olczyk is considered one of the best in-game analysts in all of sports, let alone hockey.

In August of 2017, Olczyk faced his biggest challenge: stage 3 colon cancer. "My first thought was, how long do I have to live?" Olczyk remembers. "I knew cancer has four stages, from one to four, with four being the most severe.

"You can think you have everything in life, but it doesn't matter if you don't have your health—and at that moment I didn't know what to think."

In my 20-plus years covering sports at 670 The Score, I've been around for hundreds of sports stories. Some of them wonderful, some of them heartbreaking; deaths, births, trades, signings, and everything in between. I've heard some stunning takes. No one agrees on everything. People can find something negative to say about anything and anyone, with two exceptions: Walter Payton and Eddie Olczyk. That's right, not even Michael Jordan had a 100 percent approval rating.

Olczyk was a frequent contributor at the station at the time. He was on several times a week as the Blackhawks were competing for Stanley Cups. He was on before every stage of Thoroughbred racing's Triple Crown (he's a fantastic handicapper, if you didn't know). Hell, we'd even put him on in the summer just to get his friendly voice on the air again. Any excuse we could find, we used it to book Eddie Olczyk as a guest, and he was always willing.

When news of Olczyk's diagnosis became public, the outpouring from our listening audience was overwhelming. In the days after the news broke, I tried to illustrate to Olczyk just how incredible the outpouring had been. Listeners would call or text in and say, "When you talk to Eddie, please let him know I'm thinking about him." I'd respond, "I'll try to pass it on. Does he know you? What's your name?" They'd say, "No. I don't know him, but I just needed to express my thoughts to someone who does."

Two months after his diagnosis, Olczyk got to experience the fans' love firsthand. Here's an excerpt from his book, *Eddie Olczyk: Beating the Odds in Hockey and in Life*:

> On October 7, I attended the Blackhawks game against the Columbus Blue Jackets to do a first-period interview

> with Pat. It was my first time out publicly and I wanted to talk about my cancer and just lay what was happening out for people. The Hawks showed an image of me on the giant scoreboard while I was sitting in the Blackhawks suite for the game and the crowd went wild, giving me a standing ovation and shouting, "Edd-ie, Edd-ie, Edd-ie." Pat said it was like I was back playing with the Hawks wearing my No. 16 jersey. I was touched by the reaction. The players on both benches stood and acknowledged me and the coaches were clapping. I felt everybody was with me. My attitude all along was this was a team effort, and to get that type of reception made me feel really good. I felt right at home.

Olczyk deserved all the ovations, thoughts, and prayers. From the moment he was well enough to speak about his condition, he used his platform to educate others on how to identify potential signs of cancer and to inspire those dealing with the deadly disease.

"That is truly my inspiration and my goal," Olczyk told 670 The Score's *Spiegel and Parkins* show (the show I produced at the time). "I know that I'm reaching out to people I don't know. The only reason I want to share my story is to help people. I'm trying to inspire one person to stay away from it or beat it themselves and hopefully it can be a domino effect down the road."

In the moments before he made those comments, Olczyk took the phone number of a caller who was desperate for advice. A total stranger. That's the kind of guy Eddie Olczyk is—a major celebrity willing to help a total stranger.

Shortly after Olczyk's final chemo treatment, Illinois congressman Mike Quigley, a huge Blackhawks fan, discussed Eddie's situation on the house floor. With Olczyk's No. 16 jersey at his side, Quigley said, "Like many others who have faced cancer, he was concerned that he was letting people down and he began to question his mortality, but as he went through treatment and reflected on this ordeal, Eddie started to recognize that it was OK to be scared. He knows it's important to emphasize that there's nothing wrong with people getting colonoscopies at an earlier age. He knows that if he can help just one individual get a checkup sooner, he will feel like his battle with cancer was worth it. To Eddie and to all fighting cancer, stay strong and know we're with you."

"I was very grateful for him doing that," Olczyk said. "What an honor."

On March 8, 2018, Olczyk got the image of his final scan and showed it to Blackhawks physician Dr. Michael Terry, who had been with Olczyk through the entire ordeal.

"Edzo, from what I can see, it looks really clean," Terry said.

It was over. Olczyk had once again beaten the odds.

"I don't think I'll have enough time on this earth to thank everybody, but hopefully everybody knows how important it's been to me and my family," Olczyk said. "Forever is a long time, but I'll be thanking people forever."

There's no way to quantify how many people Olczyk inspired, but I know at least two. One was the caller who reached out to Eddie in desperation, and the second was me, who took Olczyk's advice and got my skin looked at after years of avoiding a trip to the doctor. My skin issues came back negative, but who knows what would have happened had I waited? I'm glad I had Olczyk, indirectly, in my ear to inspire me the way he has so many others.

35

A RIVAL FOR A NEW ERA

Every great hero needs a villain, just like every great team needs a rival. For the 2010s-era Blackhawks, they found that rival in the Vancouver Canucks.

For three straight seasons, the Hawks and Canucks battled each other in memorable and heated playoff series, and nothing breeds contempt like familiarity.

The whole thing began in 2009. While no one knew it yet, the Blackhawks were on their way to winning three Stanley Cups. The summer prior, they succeeded in adding top free agents for the first time in recent memory. Defenseman Brian Campbell and goaltender Cristobal Huet were considered two of the best free agents on the market, and both chose to sign with Chicago. While Huet's signing didn't pan out, adding Campbell to the quickly developing core of Jonathan Toews, Patrick Kane, Duncan Keith, and Brent Seabrook made the Hawks one of the best teams in the Western Conference. The Blackhawks were also starting to get some national attention, as they competed in their first Winter Classic, against the Red Wings at Wrigley Field.

For all the talent the Blackhawks had in that era, the Canucks roster was stacked in its own right. Identical twins Daniel and Henrik Sedin were in their primes, and All-Star goaltender Roberto Luongo was between the pipes. But the real Villains of Vancouver were defensemen Kevin Bieksa and Willie Mitchell and forwards Ryan Kesler and Alex Burrows. The foils to these Canucks were typically Dustin Byfuglien and Dave Bolland, though Ben Eager, Duncan Keith, and others would add to the fun as the rivalry went on.

In March of 2009, the Blackhawks and Canucks were in a tight race in the Western Conference standings. The Hawks entered the game with 91 points, the Canucks with 89. A win for Vancouver would tie them with the Hawks. Early in the third period, the Hawks found themselves down 3–0 and getting frustrated. Byfuglien, who was playing forward for the Hawks at the time, had an in-close chance against Luongo. After the save, the puck jumped in the air. Byfuglien cross-checked Luongo in the face. After an initial gathering, it seemed as if common sense would prevail, but after several moments, multiple fights broke out. Eager locked up with Bieksa and they began throwing punches. Then Burrows and Keith dropped the gloves. This may be the flashpoint for the entire rivalry.

"I think after the big brawl, that's sort of when that rivalry came together," says Bolland. "We hated each other. We hated them and they hated us. We wanted a piece of them."

Keith got the upper hand in the fight early, so Burrows started pulling Keith's hair. The confrontations continued as the referees tried to gain some semblance of control.

"There are too many altercations and too few officials here," Pat Foley commented on the broadcast.

The Canucks won 4–0. After the game, Duncan Keith was asked about the tussle with Burrows.

"That's not something I've ever had happen to me," Keith said. "My little sister never even pulled my hair when I was a kid. It's kind of comical when you have a grown man trying to pull your hair on the ice."

The Blackhawks finished the regular season with a 46–24–12 record, good for 104 points and fourth in the conference, while the Canucks finished with 100 points and in fifth place.

Chicago squared off against the Calgary Flames in the first round, winning the series in six games. In their first-round series, the Canucks swept the St. Louis Blues. The collision course was set for these two new rivals. Nothing cements a rivalry like a playoff series, and the Hawks and Canucks were about to begin an epic run of games.

Game 1 went to the Canucks 5–3, but only after the Hawks had stormed back from a 3–0 deficit with a trio of third-period goals. Kane scored twice and Bolland added the third Hawks goal, but Sami Salo put Vancouver up for good with 73 seconds to play in the game. Ryan Johnson added an empty-netter.

In Game 2, the Blackhawks overcame an early 2–0 deficit to win 6–3. Bolland scored a pair of goals and his role as Public Enemy No. 1 in

Vancouver was developing nicely. He'd be a thorn in the Canucks' sides for years to come. In the final seven minutes of the game, the teams combined for 10 penalties and four 10-minute misconducts as tempers started to flare. Toews, Byfuglien, Burrows, and Rick Rypien all found early ends to the evening, and it was only Game 2.

Game 3 was relatively uneventful, at least compared to most Chicago-Vancouver games of the era. Aside from offsetting roughing penalties to Kesler and Troy Brouwer, the game stayed under control for the most part. The Canucks won 3–1, with the only Hawks goal coming from defenseman Brian Campbell. After the puck went past Luongo, Byfuglien stood in front of the Canucks netminder and shared a few choice words. Luongo responded by swatting Byfuglien in the face.

Trailing 2–1 in the series, the Blackhawks needed to win Game 4, especially with the action set to shift back to Vancouver for Game 5. Both Nikolai Khabibulin and Luongo were tremendous in goal. Vancouver took the 1–0 lead nearly nine minutes into the second period after Darcy Hordichuk picked up a loose puck and put it behind the "Bulin Wall." The Hawks battled for the rest of the game, finally getting rewarded with just under three minutes to go. Martin Havlat found a loose puck in the slot and didn't miss, despite falling down on the shot attempt. The game was tied.

With 20 seconds left in the third, Bolland got a breakaway and was pulled down, but the referees opted to not reward a penalty shot. The game was headed to overtime, and it felt as if the entire series hung in the balance.

The Canucks missed on a pair of prime scoring opportunities. With just over two and a half minutes played in OT, the Hawks controlled the puck for a furious shift. Bolland found the puck near the point and let go a blind slapshot toward the net. Andrew Ladd was parked in front of Luongo, and the puck hit his stick and deflected in behind the Canucks goalie. The Blackhawks had won and the series was tied.

This marked the beginning of a theme: the Blackhawks had a knack for beating Vancouver in the most ruthless and heartbreaking ways possible. The man at the heart of many of those moments was Dave Bolland.

In Game 5 of the 2009 series, the two teams went back and forth. The Hawks took a 1–0 lead. Then the Canucks went up 2–1. The Blackhawks tied it on Byfuglien's second goal of the game. Then, with just over five minutes to go in the game, Bolland struck with the game-winning goal. It was his fourth of the five-game series and it spelled the beginning of the end for the Canucks.

In Game 6, however, Bolland would not be the hero. Instead, it was someone far better known for scoring goals.

It was a wild scene at the United Center that night, as 22,687 fans stuffed the building to watch the Blackhawks eliminate their new rivals. They wouldn't leave disappointed, but they surely lost a few years off their lives.

Mason Raymond started the scoring, giving the Canucks a 1–0 lead in the first period. Patrick Kane tied the game exactly two minutes later, then the Hawks scored two more goals, one from Kris Versteeg, the other from Jonathan Toews. Less than a minute after Toews put the Hawks up 3–1, Daniel Sedin pulled the Canucks within one. Three-plus minutes later, Shane O'Brien tied the game for Vancouver.

The teams continued to seesaw in the third period. Three minutes in, Mats Sundin gave the Canucks a 4–3 lead. Less than two minutes later, Hawks winger Adam Burish tied the game at 4–4. Six and a half minutes later, Daniel Sedin scored his second goal of the game, putting the Canucks up 5–4. Forty-five seconds later, Kane scored his second goal of the game, tying things up at 5–5 with exactly seven minutes to go in the game. Forty-nine seconds later, Jonathan Toews scored a power-play goal, putting the Hawks up 6–5. With 3:49 left, Kane wrestled a puck away from Steve Bernier and streaked up the left-wing boards. He cut into the slot and was met by Shane O'Brien. Shifting to his backhand, Kane roofed a shot over Luongo, giving the Hawks a 7–5 lead. Hats littered the United Center ice, and the Hawks were on their way to the Western Conference Final, where they would ultimately fall to the Detroit Red Wings.

In 2010, the Blackhawks had a whole new level of expectations. The off-season acquisition of Marian Hossa put the team into a different stratosphere. They were not only a Cup contender, but a Cup favorite. The Hawks would finish the season with 112 points, second overall in the Western Conference. The Canucks finished nine points behind Chicago, winners of the Northwest Division.

Both teams won their opening-round series in six games. The Hawks beat the Nashville Predators, while the Canucks dispatched the Los Angeles Kings. For the second consecutive playoffs, the Blackhawks and Canucks would meet for a chance to make the Western Conference Final.

Earlier in the season, a pair of memorable incidents helped keep the rivalry alive between playoff series. In an October game, Canucks defenseman Willie Mitchell, who was headed back on the ice after a penalty, saw Toews entering the neutral zone with his head down. Mitchell made a beeline toward Toews, lowered his shoulder, and unloaded. Toews was knocked out immediately, falling to the ice. He struggled to regain his feet and tumbled on his hands and knees to the Hawks bench. He missed six games with a concussion.

Later in the season, Hawks winger Andrew Ladd and Canucks forward Ryan Kesler dropped the gloves during a game in Vancouver. Ladd punched Kesler quickly in the face, cutting him on his cheek. Kesler wrangled Ladd and tossed him to the ice. Ladd then slammed Kesler to the ice for good measure. After the scrap, Ladd could be seen pointing at his cheek, taunting Kesler for getting the worst of the bout.

"He's a coward, he'll always be a coward," Kesler told the *Vancouver Sun* after the game.

"He is a little punk. That's what it is," Byfuglien said after hearing Kesler's comments. "Ladd obviously got the better part of that thing. He can say what he wants, and Ladd can take care of himself."

The two teams met again in March. Thirty-seven seconds into the game, Ladd went after Kesler. The two tussled a bit before Shane O'Brien came to help. O'Brien was given the extra penalty.

Mitchell would miss the playoff series, but the hit from early in the season was fresh in Toews' mind before the series began.

"You kind of want to get revenge a little bit when you play against the player who put you in that situation," Toews said. "There's definitely no hard feelings. I got a call from Willie Mitchell [after the hit], and he explained that he's had some trouble with concussions. I definitely appreciate when a player does something like that and shows the respect he has. He was just playing his game."

Toews' reasoned reaction aside, the Hawks and Canucks were about to embark on another memorable and emotional playoff series.

The Canucks took Game 1 at the United Center easily, winning 5–1. The Hawks were a disaster in their own end and never really had a chance. Game 2 was a much tighter affair, despite the Canucks getting out to an early 2–0 lead just over five minutes into the game. A lesser team, coming off a 5–1 loss and facing an early deficit, might have folded, but this was Joel Quenneville's Blackhawks we're talking about. Brent Seabrook answered a few minutes later, and the Hawks took over the game. Roberto Luongo was stellar in net, but finally broke early in the third when Patrick Sharp tied things up for Chicago. Then, with 1:31 remaining in the third, Kris Versteeg, who had been one of the best Blackhawks that night, broke the tie. The Hawks won 4–2.

As I mentioned earlier, the Blackhawks always seemed to find a way to make losing as painful as possible for the Canucks. Game 2 was another example. Take a 2–0 lead, blow 2–0 lead, lose in the last two minutes.

The Hawks won the next game 5–2 and would produce one of the iconic images of the series. Early in the game, the Canucks were taking runs at Dustin Byfuglien. With 8:36 to go in the second frame, Byfuglien poked the puck behind Luongo for the second time in the game to make it 3–1 Chicago. In celebration, Byfuglien skated along the boards, taunting the Vancouver crowd. It's one of those moments that will be etched in the minds of Blackhawks fans—and probably Canucks fans—for years to come. As a cherry on top of the sundae, Byfuglien added a hat-trick goal in the third period. As the final horn blew, Byfuglien battled with a group of Canucks led by Kevin Bieksa. The Hawks had a 2–1 series lead and were finally feeling like the Cup contender everyone knew they were.

In Game 4, it took Brent Seabrook all of 18 seconds to open the scoring, but Vancouver answered moments later. When the smoke cleared, the Blackhawks won 7–4 on the back of a Jonathan Toews hat trick and were one win away from advancing to the Western Conference Final.

The celebration would have to wait, as the Canucks won Game 5 in Chicago 4–1. But the Hawks took Game 6 in Vancouver easily, winning the game 5–1 and earning a trip to the Western Conference Final for the second time in as many years. This time, the Blackhawks would skate away with their first Stanley Cup since 1961.

In 2011, the teams met for the third consecutive season and the Canucks would finally get some measure of revenge, but it wasn't without moments of doubt. During the regular season, while the Canucks were on their way to earning 117 points and the Presidents' Trophy, the Blackhawks were dealing with the post-Cup salary cap fallout. Gone were Dustin Byfuglien, Brent Sopel, Colin Fraser, Kris Versteeg, Ben Eager, Andrew Ladd, and Adam Burish. The Canucks were primed for a Cup run while the Hawks were looking to reload.

The Canucks got out to a 3–0 series lead after 2–0, 4–3, and 3–2 wins over the Hawks, but nothing comes easy for Vancouver against Chicago. The Hawks battled back and tied the series after a wild and memorable Game 6 in Chicago.

Cory Schneider got the start in goal over Luongo, who had struggled after the Canucks allowed 12 combined goals in Games 4 and 5. The Canucks scored early and held the lead until Bryan Bickell tied the game with 5:03 left in the first. Alex Burrows answered, giving the Canucks a 2–1 lead with just over a minute left in the first. The Hawks tied the game 2–2 after Schneider turned the puck over.

Kevin Bieksa gave Vancouver a 3–2 lead early in the third period, but moments later, winger Michael Frolik was awarded a penalty shot after being pulled down on a breakaway. Not only did Frolik score to tie the game, but Schneider, who did the splits in an attempt to make the save, was injured on the play. Luongo entered the game to the deafening jeers of the United Center crowd. It was a wild atmosphere and Luongo was clearly rattled by the moment. Despite that, Luongo played well, but not well enough, as Ben Smith poked a rebound past him for the overtime winner. It was Smith's third goal of the playoff series.

Game 7 shifted to Vancouver. The atmosphere was tense as Canucks fans braced for another heartbreak at the hands of the Blackhawks. The Canucks held a 1–0 lead after the first 58:04 of the game. With 1:56 left, Jonathan Toews found a Marian Hossa rebound and put it behind Luongo. You can imagine how the Canucks were feeling in this moment.

The Blackhawks started overtime with a power play. Patrick Sharp had a one-on-one shot at Luongo but the Canucks netminder made the save. Minutes later, Blackhawks defenseman Chris Campoli, who the Blackhawks had acquired at the trade deadline, attempted to clear a puck from the defensive zone. His attempt failed and bounced right to Burrows, who blew a shot past the glove hand of Corey Crawford. The Canucks celebrated as though they'd won the Stanley Cup, but considering their history of heartbreak at the hands of the Blackhawks, it was certainly understandable.

"It's a good feeling," said Canucks coach Alain Vigneault after the win. "The Cup champions pushed us to the limit but at the end we found a way to win."

The Canucks would go on to lose to the Boston Bruins in the Stanley Cup Final in seven games. As a stark contrast to the celebration over the series win over the Blackhawks, Canucks fans took to the streets and rioted after the loss in the Final. It was an ugly end to what could have been a memorable season for the Canucks.

The Blackhawks would go on to win two more Stanley Cups. The Canucks are still searching for their first in franchise history.

"It was always a blast to play against Vancouver," Bolland says.

36

IRON MIKE

Every era of hockey has a few iconic figures who represent the game at that point in time. In the 1950s and 1960s, it was "Mr. Hockey," Gordie Howe. No helmet. No nonsense. Howe was a physical specimen who represented America's idealized athlete at the time. In the 1970s, players like Bobby Clarke, Tiger Williams, and, for the Blackhawks, Keith Magnuson represented an era of individuality and self-expression.

The 1980s and 1990s combined the feel of those earlier eras. The arrival of megastars like Wayne Gretzky and Mario Lemieux ushered in a new era of popularity and attention for the league. At the same time, the culture of the United States (and Canada) in the late '80s and early '90s represented vanity, partying, and a rock-'n'-roll lifestyle. Athletes from other sports, such as the NFL's Brian Bosworth and Jim McMahon and MLB's Jose Canseco, became representative of the era.

The Blackhawks of that era were no exception. It started with Jeremy Roenick, the team's flashy centerman. Roenick later called himself "Styles" and would often talk about himself in the third person. Hot-headed goalie Eddie Belfour and defensive stalwart/Chicago party captain Chris Chelios were the faces of one of the hippest franchises of the era.

At the head of it all was head coach Mike Keenan, a product of his era as much as any of the players. Unpredictable. Out of control. Impossible. Asshole. These are just a few of the words players used to describe his coaching methods.

Keenan coached the Blackhawks from 1988 to 1992. "Iron Mike," as he was called, even while coaching in the shadow of Bears coach Mike Ditka, was a classic hardass. He was hated by his players and was the opposite of a "players' coach."

"Playing for coach Mike Keenan in Chicago was like camping on the side of an active volcano," Roenick wrote in a 2012 Deadspin piece entitled, "Mike Keenan, the NHL's Last Great Asshole Coach." "You had to accept the reality that he erupted regularly and that there was always a danger of being caught in his lava flow," Roenick continued. "He was a tyrant, a schoolyard bully, an old-school coach who tried to motivate players through intimidation, belittlement, and fear."

And that was only the first paragraph.

Roenick says Keenan's intimidation methods worked on him: "I was afraid of him. As a rookie, I felt as if my future depended on pleasing Keenan. I believed he was capable of murdering my career before it began. I believed he could do that with no sense of remorse."

"I'm not afraid to say it...the word that comes to mind is 'psychotic.' You never knew what to expect," Chris Chelios said in a 2019 interview. "I could tell you stories of players chasing him in the dressing room trying to get at him to beat him up. He did terrorize a lot of players."

Chicago defenseman Dave Manson was one of the players who went after Keenan. The coach would berate Manson between periods, blaming him for the team's struggles. Roenick recalls the incident vividly:

> Keenan had determined that Manson was responsible for everything wrong with the Blackhawks that night. Manson had his skates unlaced and his jersey off when Keenan began unloading on him with this verbal barrage. Manson snapped. He stood, yanked off his shoulder pads, and flung them across the locker room, just missing Keenan as he ducked out of the way. That was merely the first salvo of Manson's attack. As the pads were launched, Manson began running, in his skates, directly at Keenan. Keenan fled out the door with Manson on his tail. We all scurried to the door to witness the outcome. You can imagine how fucking comical it was to see Keenan sprinting down a hallway, in the bowels of Chicago Stadium, with Manson in determined pursuit. As he chased Keenan, sparks were leaping off Manson's skates as the blades scraped across the cement. If Manson hadn't lost his balance while trying to run on skates, he might have pummeled Keenan.

Chelios referenced a few other incidents between Keenan and teammates but wouldn't name names: "Another guy choking him... another guy kicking him in the nuts. We had more fights in pregame skates amongst each other than we did against the other team. It was a crazy few years with Keenan."

Even Chelios, despite his status as one of the game's premier players and best defensemen (he did win the Norris Trophy three times, after all), wasn't safe from Keenan.

"The one story that stands out, we played the Kings," he said. "The second or third shift into the game, I hit the puck out of the air and it was going into the net, and Larry Robinson comes across and takes a baseball swing at the puck and knocks it out of the air to save a goal. We get back to the bench, and Larry was laughing at me, so I started laughing back. Keenan saw me laugh...I didn't know it at the time. He benched me the rest of the game, and people were mother-effing Keenan the rest of the game—'Why aren't you putting him out there?' blah, blah blah. Then he throws me out there in the last minute of the game to try to embarrass me. The game's over, as fast as I can I get down those stairs at the old stadium, I got into his office and break everything possible. I then stuck my stick into the ceiling so he knew it was me."

Belfour has a similar story.

It happened in 1990 as the Blackhawks were hosting Philadelphia in a December matchup. With 10:08 left in the first period, the Flyers scored a goal, giving them a 2–1 lead. Keenan, in a bizarre move, pulled Belfour.

When the goalie got to the bench, he was visibly agitated. He turned, shouting toward Keenan. Keenan quickly moved down the bench toward Belfour, but the goaltender had stopped listening. Keenan then grabbed Belfour by his jersey and pulled back, hard. Then the coach got face to face with Belfour, who was still wearing his mask.

"Eddie didn't hear a thing I said," Keenan recalled. "He was too mad."

The Stadium fans weren't having it, either. Belfour was the league's winningest goalie at the time. Chants of "Eddie, Eddie" rained down from the rafters. Fifty seconds later, Keenan put Belfour back in the game.

At the time, some felt Keenan buckled under the pressure of the fans' negative response, but Keenan denies that claim: "I didn't even consider it. What am I supposed to do, let the crowd coach?"

Keenan justified the move by saying the Blackhawks weren't ready to play, and he didn't want to subject Belfour to that kind of effort.

"A player on our bench made a behind-the-back comment to Belfour when he let in the second goal," Keenan said. "It was about Eddie's lack of preparation for playing the game. I said, 'To hell with you, if that's what you think about a guy who's taken you this far this year. If you think he's that bad, I'll put someone else in net.' Why subject Eddie to that [poor team play] two nights in a row? It was no reflection on Eddie."

Despite his unconventional methods, Keenan got results. He won three conference championships, including with the Blackhawks in 1992. Two years later, he won the Stanley Cup as head coach of the New York Rangers.

"The truth is that Keenan scared me into being a better NHL player," Roenick says.

"I'm a risk-taker," Keenan said. "Taking risks makes me more vulnerable [to criticism]. It doesn't mean I'm wrong."

37

STEVE LARMER, HALL OF FAMER

Halls of Fame are often difficult to figure out. Seemingly obvious inductees are held out while unworthy candidates seem to find their way in, often because of politics, self-promotion, and valuing personality over performance. In hockey, there may not be a more obvious exclusion than that of Steve Larmer.

In recognition of his excellent 90-point rookie season (a Blackhawks record) in 1982–83, he was awarded the Calder Trophy. During his 15-year, 1,006-game NHL career, Larmer recorded 441 goals and 571 assists, good for 1,012 points. His teams never missed the playoffs once during his career. Larmer appeared in 140 postseason games, tallying 56 goals and 75 assists for 131 points. He has nine career hat tricks, all with Chicago. He is third all time with 884 consecutive games played, behind only Doug Jarvis (964) and Garry Unger (914). His streak was only broken because he chose to hold out when he wanted out of Chicago.

"It was time for a change," Larmer told the *Chicago Tribune* during the 1994 Stanley Cup Final. "I spent a long time there, and I just felt it was time to take a different road."

Had he not held out at the start of the 1993–94 season, he would be the league's all-time Iron Man.

While his career numbers speak for themselves, Larmer has had many hockey voices speak up on his behalf as well. Blackhawks announcer Pat Foley used his 2014 Hall of Fame speech to make his case for Larmer (and teammate Doug Wilson, who gained induction in 2020).

"I've been fortunate enough to call Blackhawks hockey for over a third of the games they've ever played, and I've never seen a better two-way player come through there," Foley began. "When Steve Larmer left Chicago and went to New York, it is no coincidence that shortly thereafter [the Rangers] won the Stanley Cup. And who was on the ice in the final minute of Game 7 trying to protect a one-goal lead? Steve Larmer would be a worthy recipient of the Hall of Fame induction."

While it's difficult to find a justification as to why Larmer hasn't made the Hall of Fame—considering several players of his caliber, like Cam Neely, Lanny McDonald, Joe Mullen, and more recently Martin St. Louis have been inducted with similar career accomplishments—there are a few factors that could play a role. They're unfair and nonsensical, but they could offer a bit of an explanation.

During his time in Chicago, Larmer was often overshadowed by his linemate, Hall of Famer Denis Savard. Savard was one of the most electrifying talents in the NHL, mastering his Spin-O-Rama maneuver and bringing thousands out of their seats with his dazzling play night after night. Meanwhile, Larmer just went about his business, racking up points, playing shutdown defensive hockey, and doing his job.

"When I left Chicago for Montreal, for the rest of my career I was never the same player," Savard remembers. "I missed [Larmer] more than he missed me."

One might also wonder if Larmer's quiet demeanor—his nickname was "Gramps"—and no-nonsense attitude on and off the ice have anything to do with his exclusion. It's ironic that a sport that constantly promotes itself as the "we, not I" game, that promotes "doing things the right way," would punish one of its best players for doing just that. The *Chicago Tribune*'s Steve Rosenbloom stated it well: "Back in the 1980s and '90s, you watched, you saw what he did, you knew he was as important as he was quiet."

While it's clear Larmer will probably never speak up for himself when it comes to his Hall of Fame chances, those who watched him and played beside him can do the speaking for him.

When the Blackhawks honored Larmer during their "One More Shift" presentation in December of 2016, the team produced a video montage of his career, featuring comments from several broadcasters and teammates.

"Steve Larmer was probably one of the most underrated players in his day in the National Hockey League," said Troy Murray.

"He was smooth. He picked up the puck off the boards better than any player I've ever seen" said Eddie Olczyk.

"He'd rather talk about the team. He'd rather talk about somebody else who had a good game. It was never about him. It was always about the team," said Steve Konroyd.

"Steve Larmer was as good as there was in his own end as a winger. I can tell you a bunch of defensemen who played with Steve Larmer, they all knew...if you're in trouble in your own end, when he's on the ice, get it over on the right side...it's getting out," said Pat Foley.

"Larms represents what the Hall of Fame is all about on the ice and off the ice, and I think he'll get there. I believe that sooner or later he'll be in there, for sure," said Denis Savard.

Even today, well after his career has ended, Larmer chooses to defer praise to his teammates.

"Being able to play with those guys...none of that would have ever happened without the opportunity to play with Denis Savard and Al Secord," he said. "It gave me a lot of confidence. Al was great at driving to the net and Denis was probably one of the better playmakers, so it was just finding open space. A lot of those goals were easy tap-ins or wide-open nets."

Watching highlights of Larmer's career clearly demonstrates the lengths Larmer will go to take the spotlight off himself. Sure, there were a few tap-ins and wide-open nets, but more often than not, Larmer was blasting a slapper past a goalie or scoring dirty goals in front of the opposing net.

"Steve Larmer never wanted any attention on himself, ever," Foley said.

Hopefully, with enough of these voices speaking up for him, Gramps will finally end up where he belongs: enshrined in the Hockey Hall of Fame.

38

SLAYING THE DRAGON

Blackhawks fans of a certain age still feel a bit uneasy when they see the Detroit Red Wings logo. Not only does it represent the Blackhawks' longest-running, Original Six rival, it also represents years and years of tormenting losses. It represents years of Blackhawks failures paired with Detroit successes.

Hawks fans of the 1990s and 2000s remember the Red Wings as their biggest and most hated rival. At the same time, the Red Wings and their fans barely even noticed the existence of the Hawks. Detroit fans would fill an otherwise empty United Center when the Wings came to Chicago. Chants of "Let's-Go-Red-Wings" would echo through the rafters. More often than not, Steve Yzerman, Sergei Fedorov, and Nicklas Lidstrom would toy with the lesser Blackhawks, skating to an easy victory. On nights the Blackhawks did happen to keep the game close, the Wings would always seem to find a way to win in the most crushing way possible.

That Winged Wheel was an icon of dread for Blackhawks fans. Even after the Blackhawks had won two of their three Stanley Cups, I visited Joe Louis Arena and felt uneasy. It was a *Hockey Night in Canada* game between the Wings and the Maple Leafs. Intensity was high, but I didn't have a rooting interest. Still, seeing those hallways, that entryway, and that center ice logo with "Hockeytown" written around it gave me that familiar feeling of nausea. The memories associated with that logo and that building are all negative for me.

Well, almost.

In 2009, when the Blackhawks unexpectedly reached the conference final, the Red Wings were not ready to hand over the torch. The Blackhawks' inexperience was evident, and the Wings dispatched the Hawks in five games. Detroit eventually fell to the Penguins in the Stanley Cup Final. The Blackhawks would pluck Marian Hossa away from the Wings that summer and go on to win the Stanley Cup with Hossa's help in 2010.

Of course, winning the Cup is all that matters, but to me and a lot of Hawks fans like me, there was one hurdle the team hadn't cleared. They needed to beat the Red Wings in a playoff series.

That chance would come in 2013.

The Blackhawks were coming off a dominant but shortened regular season. Because of the lockout, Chicago played just 48 games and posted a mind-boggling 36–7–5 record. The team set an NHL record by picking up at least one point in the first 17 games of the regular season. They were the best team in the league, and it wasn't particularly close. They faced the Minnesota Wild in the first round, and predictably beat them in five games.

In the conference semifinal, the Blackhawks drew their longtime rival, the Red Wings. The Hawks took Game 1 easily, winning 4–1. A trip to the Stanley Cup Final seemed like a foregone conclusion, but of course, the Red Wings never go away easily. Detroit won the next three games by a combined score of 9–2. The Blackhawks were reeling and searching for answers.

"It takes something like this to slap you in the face to really understand what adversity is and how tough the playoffs can be," Hawks captain Jonathan Toews said after Game 3. "A lot of guys in this room have been in tough positions before in the playoffs and that's never stopped us. We know this is a long series and we're going to be fighting until the end."

Facing elimination, it was difficult to find a path to victory for the Blackhawks. Only 22 times in NHL playoff history had a team gone on to win the series facing that kind of deficit, but Chicago's coaches and players never wavered.

"We talk about momentum and how important it is come playoff time," coach Joel Quenneville said. "They obviously got it right now, but one game could turn everything around. That's what we're looking for. The big picture looks bleak, but I think, at the same time, we've got two home games here and you've got one at a time."

Brent Seabrook added his own wisdom ahead of Game 5.

"Everybody's counting us out now except us in here. There have been a few guys in this room who have come back from 3–0 and given them a chance to win. We look back at the Vancouver series [in 2011] and being down 3–0 we gave ourselves a chance and had a hard-fought game in Game 7 and just missed out by one goal."

Game 5 of the series took place at the United Center, and the Blackhawks took full advantage of the home-ice atmosphere. The teams exchanged scoring chances in the first period, with both goalies fighting off shot after shot. With 14 minutes gone in the first period, Hawks winger Bryan Bickell found a Patrick Kane rebound and put the puck behind Jimmy Howard, giving the Hawks a 1–0 lead. The United Center crowd was deafening. The first goal of that game felt like it could dictate how the rest of the series would go. Had the Hawks found themselves trailing, one wonders if they would have been able to pull off the unlikely series comeback. Instead, Bickell's goal started the whole thing.

The Hawks won that game 4–1, outshooting Detroit 45–26 along the way. Hope was reborn, but it was on to Detroit for Game 6. The Hawks were going to have to win a road game at the House of Horrors known as the Joe Louis Arena.

It only took Hossa 3:53 to open the scoring after a mad power-play scramble in front of the Wings net. Jonathan Toews took the puck into the crease when Hossa found it on Howard's pad. Hossa pulled it to his backhand and put it behind the Wings goalie for the 1–0 lead, but with one minute to go in the first period, the Wings answered. A poor clearing attempt from Dave Bolland was intercepted at the line by winger Drew Miller. His point shot created a rebound that landed right on the tape of Patrick Eaves and the game was tied.

In the second period, the Blackhawks failed to score on a pair of power plays despite a number of quality chances. When things got back to even, the Red Wings started to pull the momentum in their favor. Henrik Zetterberg and Justin Abdelkader traded a couple of good scoring chances, but Crawford stood tall. Brent Seabrook barely blocked another great scoring chance from Daniel Cleary. Moments later, though, Crawford would let a long shot from Joakim Andersson flutter past his glove hand and the Hawks were down 2–1 after two periods. The Red Wings were 20 minutes away from advancing to the Western Conference Final.

But the Hawks weren't done.

Less than a minute into the third period, unsung Hawks defenseman Niklas Hjalmarsson wrestled a puck away from Valtteri Filppula. Waiting on the doorstep was Michal Handzus. Handzus had so much time, he was able to stick-handle twice and pick his spot. Suddenly, the game was tied at 2–2.

Tension suddenly engulfed the Joe Louis Arena crowd. To me, it was a familiar tension—the kind I had felt dozens of times over the years during these games, but this time it was the Detroit fans feeling uneasy. They knew the kind of team they were up against and now all the momentum belonged to Chicago.

The Hawks would not give it back.

Five minutes later, Toews centered a pass right in front of Howard. Bickell was standing there, as if on cue. He gave the Hawks the 3–2 lead and they never looked back.

At the 9:43 mark of the third period, Hawks winger Michael Frolik had a breakaway. Wings defenseman Carlo Colaiacovo disrupted his attempt enough for the referees to call a penalty shot. Frolik roofed a backhand goal over Howard and the Hawks led 4–2.

As is tradition, however, the Red Wings can never just go away. Defenseman Damien Brunner put a point shot behind Crawford with under a minute to go, but the Hawks held on and forced Game 7.

The story of Game 7 I'm about to tell you might not sound real. It might sound as if it's pulled from a fairy tale or one of those 1980s Matt Christopher sports books, but in the immortal words of Han Solo, "It's true. All of it."

I recall how stressful that day was for me personally. It was my duty to be on the air at 670 The Score when the game ended. Would I be previewing a trip to the Western Conference Final, or recapping a disappointing end for a historically great team? I paced the city. I couldn't eat or sleep. The strange fan/media space I live in was only doubling my stress. I don't think I sat down the entire game.

The Madhouse on Madison was indeed a Madhouse that night. The crowd had much more confidence than I did. It turned out the fans in attendance were right.

The Blackhawks killed off an early Detroit power play, then Detroit returned the favor. The first period was scoreless. The mayhem was still to come.

With just over one minute gone in the second period, Patrick Sharp, Marian Hossa, and Michal Handzus worked a beautiful give-and-go passing play. Sharp, from a difficult angle, was able to lift the puck over the outstretched leg of Howard. The Hawks had the lead.

Both teams played tremendous defense, limiting scoring chances. When chances did come, Crawford and Howard stool tall. The Wings finally evened things up early in the third period, when Zetterberg buried a Gustav Nyquist rebound shot. Remember—it's never easy when it comes to the Red Wings.

With 1:47 to go in the third period, Andrew Shaw found a wide-open Hjalmarsson at the point. The Swedish defenseman reared back and blasted a shot past Howard. The Blackhawks had seemingly taken the lead. The United Center crowd was in a frenzy, but behind the play, a whistle had been drowned out by the crowd. Near the Red Wings bench, Brandon Saad and Kyle Quincy had been mixing things up when referee Stephen Walkom, one of the most respected and experienced officials in the NHL, called both players for roughing. Instead of the Blackhawks taking the lead, a confrontation away from the play had potentially taken victory away from Chicago.

Hjalmarsson, who rarely showed emotion on the ice, was livid. After nearly throwing his stick the length of the ice, Hjalmarsson collected himself. Boos reigned down over the United Center ice. The third period expired.

Overtime was next. Against the Red Wings. What could possibly go wrong?

I didn't sit for the entire intermission. When your favorite team suffers a devastating loss, it's hard enough to take. I was on the precipice of not only having my heart ripped out but having to talk about it for three hours on a 50,000-watt radio station without swearing once. Thank goodness it only took the Blackhawks 3:35 to let my heart and soul off the hook.

Brent Seabrook, who I will always love for this moment, corralled a loose puck in the neutral zone. He waltzed into the slot and fluttered a puck over Howard's glove hand. In the celebration scrum, Seabrook can be seen shouting "Yes!" to the heavens. He was speaking for all Blackhawks fans in that moment.

The Blackhawks had done it. The Red Winged dragon had finally been slayed.

39

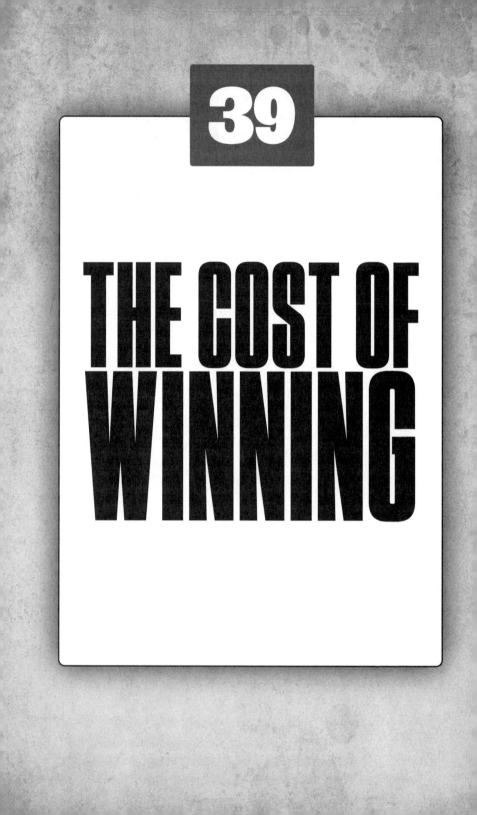

THE COST OF WINNING

It's no secret that the late Blackhawks owner Bill Wirtz was frugal. Most would call him flat-out cheap. He was a proponent for an NHL salary cap for years. When the league locked out the players and canceled the 2004–05 season, he finally got his wish. The league implemented a strict cap system, with a $39 million salary cap for the 2005–06 season.

Wirtz and the Blackhawks filled out the roster for that season predictably, signing big-name but aging free agents well past their primes. Defensemen Adrian Aucoin and Jassen Cullimore, forwards Martin Lapointe and Curtis Brown, and goaltender Nikolai Khabibulin looked good on paper. They had experienced a lot of success in their careers. Cullimore and Khabibulin were just coming off a Stanley Cup victory with Tampa Bay.

The only signing that worked out was Khabibulin. He played four seasons in his first go-around with the team. He was...fine.

The other pickups could only be qualified as disasters. The Blackhawks finished the season with 26 wins, good for only 65 points. As a result, they landed the third overall pick in the draft. That pick was Jonathan Toews.

The next season wasn't much better. Toews returned to play another season at North Dakota, and the Hawks finished last in the Central Division with 71 points. They won the draft lottery and selected Patrick Kane.

While the NHL rosters were nothing to write home about, there was some buzz around some of the Hawks prospects. Names like Dave Bolland, Corey Crawford, Brent Seabrook, Duncan Keith, and others were close to becoming full-time NHL contributors. The team had also just traded for Patrick Sharp, who was emerging as a legitimate top-six forward. Add Toews and Kane into that mix, and the Blackhawks had a very exciting future.

Bill Wirtz passed away on September 26, 2007. His son Rocky took over and the Blackhawks were immediately ready and committed to spending money, televising games, and, most importantly, winning.

There's the irony.

As soon as the Hawks were ready to throw around some real money, they had a new salary cap to deal with.

The first casualties of the salary cap came after the 2010 Stanley Cup victory. The summer prior, then GM Dale Tallon made a paperwork error. A handful of Blackhawks free agents were due qualifying offers, but the offers didn't arrive in time for the league's mandated deadline. The result was a pair of richer-than-probably-necessary deals for winger Kris Versteeg and defenseman Cam Barker, each of whom got three-year, $3 million contracts. When the 2010 season ended, the Hawks found themselves with some tough decisions to make.

With forward Marian Hossa and defenseman Brian Campbell well into rich deals signed seasons prior, the Blackhawks needed every penny available. The blunder cost Dale Tallon his job and Stan Bowman was left to clean up the mess.

The Blackhawks had to dump salary. They traded Stanley Cup hero Dustin Byfuglien, bottom-six forward Ben Eager, and defenseman Brent Sopel to the Atlanta Thrashers (now the Winnipeg Jets). Bowman admitted the trade was "simply a salary cap move."

The San Jose Sharks made the mess worse. They threw a four-year, $14 million offer sheet contract at restricted free-agent defenseman Niklas Hjalmarsson. The Blackhawks had to match the deal or let the defenseman walk. They matched, but it cost them the ability to re-sign Cup-winning goalie Antti Niemi, who ended up signing with the Sharks.

Fourth-liner Colin Fraser was dealt to the Edmonton Oilers the same day.

Days later, the Blackhawks shipped Versteeg to the Toronto Maple Leafs for Viktor Stalberg (who would later contribute to the Blackhawks' 2013 Cup win).

On July 1, the Blackhawks made another trade, sending winger Andrew Ladd to the Thrashers for defenseman Ivan Vishnevskiy and the second-round pick that became journeyman defenseman Adam Clendening.

All told, the team was forced to ship out seven of its regular roster players from a Stanley Cup championship team.

The cap woes would continue for years to come, and while no teams were as affected as the 2010 roster, some big-name players were moved in the name of cap space or in the name of ridding a bad contract from the team.

In the summer of 2011, the Blackhawks were forced to move on from defenseman Brian Campbell, who was their biggest signing in the summer of 2008. His $7 million salary was too much to afford, despite his effectiveness. The team was also forced to deal winger Troy Brouwer to the Capitals that summer.

The sacrifices continued year after year. In 2013, Dave Bolland, who had scored the Stanley Cup–winning goal in Boston weeks earlier, departed. Versatile wingers Michael Frolik and Daniel Carcillo were also shipped out.

Before the 2014 season, the Hawks dealt offensive-minded defenseman Nick Leddy to the New York Islanders.

In the summer of 2015, after another Stanley Cup win, the Hawks dealt two major pieces. First, they shipped Brandon Saad and a pair of prospects to Columbus for Artem Anisimov, Marko Dano, Alex Broadhurst, and Mike Paliotta. Patrick Sharp, who had scored 239 goals for the Blackhawks since joining the team in 2005, was shipped to Dallas along with the Blackhawks' top defensive prospect at the time, Stephen Johns.

The biggest sacrifices were yet to come.

During the Blackhawks' 2013 Cup run, up-and-coming forward Bryan Bickell scored nine goals and picked up eight assists. The postseason performance came right on time for Bickell, who was becoming an unrestricted free agent. Consistency had always been an issue with Bickell, but it seemed he was finally poised to break out. The Blackhawks signed him to a four-year, $16 million deal.

If Bickell's career had continued on the trajectory of that playoff run, the contract would have been a bargain. Unfortunately, Bickell's consistency became an issue again, and the Hawks found themselves with an undesirable deal. On November 11, 2016, Bickell revealed he had been diagnosed with multiple sclerosis. The disease would cut his career short.

That summer, the Blackhawks found themselves with cap issues again and needed to move Bickell's contract. Unfortunately, it also necessitated losing one of their top young players, Teuvo Teravainen. The Blackhawks shipped the duo to Carolina for a 2016 second-round pick (Artur Kayumov) and a 2017 third-round pick (later traded to Detroit for winger Tomas Jurco). Since the deal, Kayumov has not played a single game in the NHL. Jurco contributed a whopping 11 points in 42 games over two years for the Blackhawks. Teravainen, on the other hand, has scored 245 points in his 313 games with the Hurricanes.

Nine days later, the team traded gritty forward and fan favorite Andrew Shaw to the Montreal Canadiens for two second-round picks. One of those picks became star winger Alex DeBrincat, so it wasn't a total loss. In the summer of 2019, the Blackhawks brought Shaw back to the team, to the delight of his teammates and many Hawks fans.

Things didn't get much better in the summer of 2017.

After the team was swept by Nashville in the first round of the playoffs, Stan Bowman promised big changes were needed and were coming. Shockingly, he traded stalwart defenseman Niklas Hjalmarsson to the Arizona Coyotes for defenseman Connor Murphy and center Laurent Dauphin. Hjalmarsson was one of the unsung heroes of the three Stanley Cup teams. He was also a favorite of Joel Quenneville's. Murphy struggled to gain Quenneville's trust, and it wasn't until Quenneville's firing that the Blackhawks got to witness Murphy's upside.

Later that day, the big bombshell dropped.

Artemi Panarin, who the Hawks had signed as an international free agent two summers earlier, was coming off a 74-point season. He was, aside from Patrick Kane, the team's most dynamic forward. Assuming that Panarin would need a big-money deal, Bowman preemptively dealt the winger to Columbus. In return, the Blackhawks regained Saad, who was coming off back-to-back, career-high 53-point seasons.

At the time, it seemed like a reasonable deal to make. Saad was under contract for $6 million, but he only mustered 35 points in

2017–18. Meanwhile, Panarin recorded 82 points in 81 games for the Blue Jackets and became one of the game's premier forwards. In the summer of 2019, he signed a huge, 7-year, $81.5 million deal with the New York Rangers. Saad, on the other hand, found himself bouncing from line to line, often spending time with the Blackhawks' bottom six.

It's rare that a team benefits when making deals forced by the salary cap, but it seems like no one has been hurt as much as the Blackhawks.

40

THE DARK AGES

Before there were Jonathan Toews and Patrick Kane, there were Tyler Arnason and Mark Bell. Before there were Duncan Keith and Brent Seabrook, there were Jim Vandermeer and Jaroslav Spacek. I could go on listing the names of Blackhawks long forgotten, like Josef Marha, James Black, Brad Brown, and Jim Cummins, until the cows come home, but I'd prefer you not throw up on your book, Kindle, or iPad.

The era of Blackhawks hockey from the 1996–97 season to the 2006–07 season were some of the most forgettable years of hockey Chicago has ever seen. The teams, aside from a blip on the radar in 2002 (a first-round playoff exit), were high on hope but low on talent. As we recap these seasons, as painful as they were, it's important to understand just how the Blackhawks were able to draft players like Toews and Kane. Years of bad play will get you some potentially franchise-changing picks, and that's what happened to the Blackhawks. Fortunately for them, as their new stars were arriving, the group of men who had held them back all those years were on their way out.

The 1996–97 Blackhawks entered the season having just traded the face of their franchise, Jeremy Roenick, to Phoenix in the off-season in exchange for a package headlined by Alexei Zhamnov. Zhamnov was a good-not-great player tasked with having to prove his worth to an angry fan base. That would never work. The other "name" players on the 1996 roster were all well past their primes; Denis Savard was 35, Brent Sutter was 34, Gary Suter and Murray Craven were 32. The young players, aside from 21-year-olds Eric Daze and Ethan Moreau, didn't provide much to the team. The bulk of the roster would be best described as filler. Sure, there was some NHL talent, but the Blackhawks had a robust collection of third- and fourth-liners while their top players were ideally second-liners. That is not the way to build a competitive team. Toward the end of the 1996 season, the

Blackhawks traded goalie Eddie Belfour to the San Jose Sharks for journeyman winger Ulf Dahlen, young defenseman Michal Sykora, and backup goalie Chris Terreri. Tony Amonte and Chris Chelios were now the only remnants of the great Blackhawks teams of the 1990s, and they had very little help.

As the years went along, Blackhawks fans would hear about the latest kid coming to save the franchise.

The 1997–98 season marked the debuts of forwards Daniel Cleary, who the Blackhawks had chosen 13th overall in the 1997 draft, and Dmitri Nabokov, the Hawks' first-round selection in 1995. Defenseman Christian Laflamme, who the Hawks had selected 45th overall in 1995, also debuted that season. Cleary, who recorded nine points in only 41 games with the Blackhawks, went on to have a solid NHL career, but only after the Detroit Red Wings took a flyer on him after some so-so seasons with Edmonton and Phoenix. Laflamme had an eight-year NHL career, but was never more than a bottom-pair defenseman. Nabokov played only 25 games in Chicago and another 30 with the New York Islanders. He returned to play in Russia after bouncing around the AHL for a few years. Even back in his home country, Nabokov was hardly the star player the Blackhawks thought he would be.

After finishing fifth in the Central Division in 1997–98, the Blackhawks thought it would be a good time for one of their classic "cheap reloads." They signed aged NHL stars Doug Gilmour (35) and Paul Coffey (37) as free agents. They also signed Eddie Olczyk (32) and traded for enforcers Mark Janssens and Doug Zmolek. Former Blackhawks captain Dirk Graham was named head coach, replacing Craig Hartsburg, who was known to clash with Chelios from time to time. The result of these moves was so disastrous, not even the biggest Blackhawks pessimist could have predicted it would go this poorly.

Gilmour put up 56 points in 72 games with the Hawks but was a shadow of his former self. Coffey was even worse. He was a minus six in only 10 games with Chicago before the Hawks shipped him to Carolina for winger Nelson Emerson. Olczyk was at the end of his career and wasn't much of a scorer anymore, while Zmolek and Janssens were bottom-tier players on a bottom-tier roster. The result was a terrible team with horrible chemistry. The 1999 team finished

29–41–12, but not before they traded captain Chris Chelios to the rival Red Wings for defenseman Anders Eriksson and a pair of first-round picks.

Having not learned their lesson in the 1999 season, the Blackhawks doubled down by signing an aged veteran before the 2000 season. This time, it was 33-year-old Wendel Clark. That experiment lasted all of 13 games, in which Clark recorded a pair of assists before the Blackhawks released him. The team would miss the playoffs again, but a young, scrappy winger named Kyle Calder made his NHL debut, and while we didn't know it at the time, he was ready to be an important Blackhawk going forward. The 2000–01 season offered another hopeful prospect, as 6-foot-3, 220lb center Mark Bell would make his debut.

The 2001–02 Blackhawks, with the emergence of Bell and Calder as—well as the continued development of winger Steve Sullivan, who the Hawks picked up off waivers in October of 1999—were a playoff team after a 96-point regular season. Young center Tyler Arnason appeared in 21 games that season as well. The Hawks didn't know it, but they were about to find some relevance again.

The 2002–03 season should have been full of hope. Three young potential star players were ready for full-time NHL action, but in typical Blackhawks fashion, they reached another contract impasse, this time with Tony Amonte, who had carried the Hawks since the Roenick trade. The Hawks, failing to sign their star captain, got nothing in return for his services and he signed with Phoenix as a free agent. The Hawks' answer to Amonte leaving came in the form of former Calgary Flames star Theo Fleury. Fleury, who had struggled with drug abuse and off-the-ice antics, signed a two-year, $8.5 million deal with Chicago in August of 2002.

"We've gone through this process with Theo with our eyes open and we know what his personal situation is," Hawks GM Mike Smith said on the day of the signing. "We believe Theo can help our team and we can help Theo."

On October 9, just two days before the regular season was set to begin, the NHL suspended Fleury indefinitely for violating his substance-abuse aftercare program. Fleury returned to play 54 games for the Blackhawks, adding 33 points. During his time in Chicago he looked slow, disinterested, and often out of it. Years later, he'd reveal the depths of his personal issues in his autobiography.

After the signing, Bill Wirtz pointed to Bob Probert's personal reformation after he had joined the Hawks in 1995: "Since signing with the Blackhawks as a free agent, Bob Probert has established himself as a husband and father of four children as well as a model citizen in the community." But that summer, the Blackhawks forced Probert to retire and join the radio broadcast booth. I was the producer of those Blackhawks games on the radio and I witnessed firsthand Probert's decline back into substance abuse. It was sad to see, because Probert was one of my favorite players. I could see the systems in place were failing him, and he was failing himself.

Despite Fleury's struggles and negative influence on the team, Arnason, Bell, and Calder started to thrive. The trio combined for 110 points in the clutch-and-grab era of the NHL. The team once again failed to make the playoffs, but the A-B-C Line was on its way to stardom, and more help was on the way.

In 2001, the Blackhawks drafted Finnish forward Tuomo Ruutu ninth overall. Ruutu was hyped as "the best player in the world not in the NHL," and with good reason. He was a rare mix of skill and physicality. After two years of negotiation issues, the Blackhawks finally agreed to a contract and the Finnish star was on his way. He arrived for training camp and laid out fellow prospect Igor Radulov with a massive hit on his first shift. Taking a run at a teammate was a bit of an odd move, but Ruutu was announcing his presence with authority. Unfortunately, Ruutu found himself injured shortly after the hit was made. This would be a theme of his career in Chicago, but he played all 82 games during the 2003–04 NHL season, adding 44 points.

You'd think things would be hunky dory for the team with a young core in place, but Blackhawks coach Brian Sutter was as old school as they came. He loved the way Bell, Calder, and Ruutu played; gritty scorers with skill, physicality, everything a hockey player should be in the eyes of a Sutter. Arnason, on the other hand, was a bit of a floater. His game was a little too lackadaisical for Sutter. In February of 2004, things came to a head at a Nashville honky tonk. Sutter got in Arnason's face, threatening to beat up the Hawks' young star. Eventually, Sutter would let him go and punch the wall at Tootsie's Orchid Lounge instead. Arnason called it "an exchange of views that got a little heated."

Once again, the team failed to make the playoffs, and once again, the Blackhawks decided that veteran leadership and a coaching change would fix things. The Blackhawks signed free agents Martin Lapointe, Adrian Aucoin, and Curtis Brown, and made former Hawk Trent Yawney the coach. While those veteran signings (shockingly) didn't work out as planned, the 2005–06 season marked the arrivals of two pillars of the organization: Duncan Keith and Brent Seabrook.

Calder, Bell, and Arnason finished 1–2–3 in scoring for the team, while Keith and Seabrook combined for 53 points of their own. Their talent level was apparent, but both defensemen were incredibly raw and needed a few years to develop before they became the stalwarts they were for the future championship teams.

Their arrival timed out perfectly for the Blackhawks dynasty. In March of 2006, the team traded Arnason to Ottawa. In June, after landing the third overall pick in the draft, they selected Jonathan Toews. Then, in July of 2006, the Blackhawks traded Mark Bell to San Jose. The next month, they traded Kyle Calder to the Flyers for Michal Handzus. Toews would play another year at North Dakota and postpone joining Chicago by one year. As a result, the 2006–07 Blackhawks finished last in the Central Division and won the draft lottery. They selected Patrick Kane with the number one overall pick, and the rest is history.

It's amazing to wonder where the Hawks would have ended up if Toews had come out of college right away, or if they had re-signed Tony Amonte, or if Tuomo Ruutu didn't battle injuries his whole career. They absolutely wouldn't have had the opportunity to draft Patrick Kane. One must wonder if the failed signings were the plan all along!

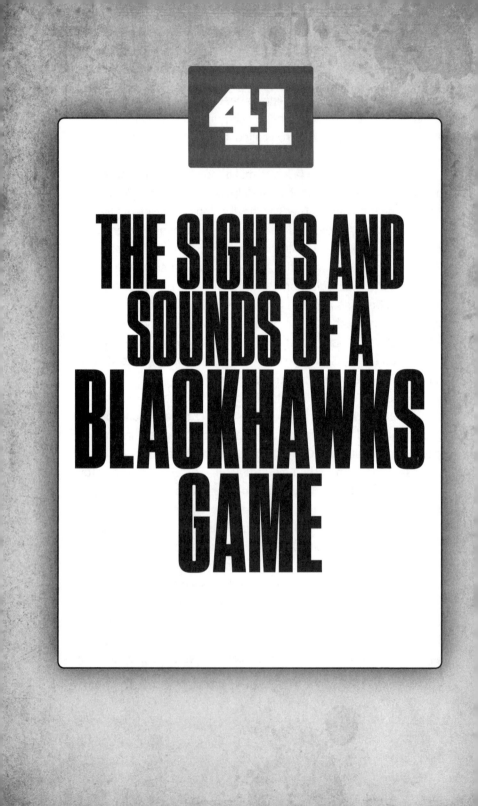

THE SIGHTS AND SOUNDS OF A BLACKHAWKS GAME

As a Blackhawks fan, going to a game was, and still is, an experience for the senses. The sights, the smells, and, more than anything, the sounds, are what define the Blackhawks hockey experience.

In my early days as a fan, taking the ride with my dad from Oak Lawn to Madison St. was an adventure. On game days, my dad would drive home from downtown, pick me up, and head right back to the city. Jim Zawaski, even in more leisurely situations, is not a patient driver. Mix in the headaches of a double commute and it was like being a passenger in the Millennium Falcon whilst escaping an Exogorth. Yes, that's a nerdy Star Wars reference.

The neighborhood surrounding the Chicago Stadium, and later the United Center, wasn't always the gentrified stretch of bars, clubs, and restaurants it is today. Stopping at a red light often felt like a risk. Police sirens blared, buildings were in disrepair, and there was a feeling of apprehension before you even entered the parking lot.

Once you began the trek from your car to the building, the sounds would begin to swell. This is where I fell in love with the experience. First, it was the sound of a distant saxophone, usually playing the theme to *The Flintstones*, *The Simpsons*, or whatever familiar ditty would get the player a couple of quarters for his efforts.

"Programs here! Get the program Dollar Bill doesn't want you to read!" Buying a copy of fan programs *Blue Line* or the *The Committed Indian* was a must.

As you got closer to the building, Blackhawks fans, almost all in red or white jerseys, would intersect at the various entrances. If the sidewalks were arteries, the Stadium was the heart. Fitting, I think.

Now and again, there'd be a Red Wings jersey mixed in with the Blackhawks jerseys. Every time, that guy would catch an earful... sometimes worse.

Then, the most glorious part of entering the building, the Stadium organ. To me, this is the quintessential part of a Blackhawks game. As soon as your ticket was torn or scanned, you could hear the music pulsing through the building. The lower notes would rattle the windows. The original Chicago Stadium Barton Organ boasted 3,663 pipes, and you could feel each one of them.

The original Blackhawks organist was Al Melgard, who first sat down at the Barton Organ in 1929, the year the Chicago Stadium opened. From 1958 to 1961, Melgard released a series of four LPs titled *Al Melgard at the Chicago Stadium Organ*. I'm proud to say I own a pair of them.

Melgard played the organ until his retirement in 1974. Ron Bogda took over, after serving as Melgard's assistant and backup since 1960. Famed White Sox organist Nancy Faust played at the Stadium for a spell until Frank Pellico took over full time, and he's been behind the keys ever since. Pellico has an album of his own, called *Fire and Ice*.

Every game, the organ takes center stage as the Blackhawks' famed rendition of the national anthem is sung. It's an unforgettable experience that is unique to Chicago Blackhawks games, especially if you were around to experience an anthem at the Chicago Stadium.

Another, lesser-known Blackhawks innovation is the goal horn. The Hawks were the first team to implement a horn to signify a goal. During the 1973 Stanley Cup Final against Montreal, Blackhawks owner Bill Wirtz decided to install the horn from his yacht for use in the Stadium. Since then, every NHL team has adopted some form of goal horn.

Of course, none of these features would mean much without the energy of a Chicago Blackhawks crowd, which gained fame after the 1991 NHL All-Star Game. The contest took place during the early stages of the first Gulf War. Chicago knew they'd have a national television audience to show their support, and they did.

The Chicago Stadium closed at the end of the 1993–94 season. On April 14, 1994, the Hawks played their last regular season game at the Old Barn, losing to Toronto 6–4. As the game ended, longtime Blackhawks PA announcer Harvey Wittenberg addressed the crowd:

Ladies and gentlemen, may I have your attention for one last message? This is a message to you, the Chicago Blackhawks fans. For 65 years here at the Chicago Stadium, ordinary, hardworking people known as Blackhawks fans have come together to create an extraordinary atmosphere. You have devoted your emotions to the Blackhawks and have become an important part of the team. Your loud and affectionate praise [has] given us an advantage that is unmatched in professional sports play. You have affected the lives and lifted the performances of every hockey player ever to skate on the Stadium ice. We look upon you as ideal fans: hardworking, devoted assets. And we thank you for this.

Here in the Chicago Stadium, performance is not just on the ice, the performance is everywhere: in the hallways, in the organ loft, that banners throughout the mezzanine, and the balconies. The Chicago Stadium experience has been truly special.

As you leave tonight, we ask that you:

Remember the great lady known as the Chicago Stadium.

Remember how it was built to happen.

Remember the championship banners swaying gently in the rafters.

Remember the people you sat next to 10 years ago that are your friends today.

Remember the organ loft and the press box and your favorite seat.

Remember the stairs leading all the way to the second balcony.

Remember your favorite great players, whether they are Bobby Hull, Jeremy Roenick, Tony Esposito, Eddie Belfour, Stan Mikita, Denis Savard, Keith Magnuson, and Chris Chelios.

Remember the feeling you have right now.

On behalf of the Chicago Blackhawks, thank you for making all of this possible, and Remember the Roar!

If you don't have chills after reading that, I can't help you.

When the wrecking ball struck the Chicago Stadium in February of 1995, about a hundred mourners gathered outside. Even Bill Wirtz wept.

"I came here as a boy," Wirtz recalled. "My father saved that building...It's a sad day, but economically it had to be done."

The United Center could never duplicate what the Chicago Stadium delivered so naturally, but everyone involved in the new stadium's design did their best to re-create the experience, and the

"CHELSEA, CHELSEA, I BELIEVE..."

It's the song that's been happily stuck in Blackhawks fans' heads since 2008.

"Da Da da-Da, Da da-Da, da Da-da-da-da-da."

"Chelsea Dagger" by the Scottish rock band The Fratellis is the song that plays after every goal the Blackhawks have scored at home since 2008. Spoiler alert: that's a lot of goals.

When a reporter from Global BC news in Vancouver took an iPod (remember those?) around the Canucks locker room and played the song, here are some of the responses they got:

Defenseman Shane O'Brien: "Nightmare. Turn it off...next song. That's awful, eh?"

Defenseman Kevin Bieksa: "Worst song in hockey."

Forward Ryan Kesler: "Yeah, heard that way too many times."

Forward Henrik Sedin: "Bad memories, bad memories, bad memories."

Sensing a theme there?

Yeah, opponents have heard that song a lot, but it almost wasn't the team's goal song. During the preseason in 2008, the Hawks tried out a number of tunes, including "Keep Your Head" by the Ting Tings, "Tick Tick Boom" by the Hives, and "Song 2" by Blur (you know...the "Woo-hoo! song). But "Chelsea Dagger" is the one that stuck.

In an interview with WGN Radio's Roe Conn, bassist Baz Fratelli discussed the phenomenon of the song.

"As long as they're paying the dough they're supposed to be paying, we'll get paid," he joked. "I'll have to get my accountant on that to make sure the Blackhawks are up to date with us."

Annoying, catchy, however you want to describe it, "Chelsea Dagger" means good things are happening for the Blackhawks.

fact that the building is generally well liked by Chicagoans is a good indicator of their success.

My father-in-law, Bill Lyons, worked as the United Center project manager for Morse Diesel, one of the companies that built the new stadium. "'Remember the Roar' was the Blackhawks' big thing," he tells me. "They wanted to make sure the crowd sound was equal to, or greater than, the old stadium." When developing the United Center, acoustic and sound system design technology was used to ensure the crowd noise levels were maintained based on the building's structure and surfaces. This was great for hockey and basketball games but became a problem when concerts would come to town.

In October of 1994, the year the United Center opened, Billy Joel was playing a concert at the new building. Sound reverberated through the cavernous building all night. At one point, Joel asked the audience, "So how's the sound now? Is it getting a little better?" The audience quickly informed Joel that the sound was definitely not getting better.

If you glance up at the United Center rafters today, you'll see a collection of black, rectangular blocks hanging from the ceiling, each roughly the size of a championship banner. Those were installed to fix the sound issues in the building, and while the United Center still isn't exactly the Chicago Theater acoustically, it's much improved from its first few concerts.

As far as the goal horn and organ go, the yacht horn made the trip over from the Stadium. The organ did not, but the Blackhawks spent $150,000 to build a new organ with the capability to record and play back the original Barton Organ tones.

"Here there are so many funky, computer-generated instrument sounds, like voice samples and distorted guitar, that I can play now with a flip of a switch," said Pellico. "There was only one sound in the old machine: pipe.

"It's just incredible. There is so much sound here."

While the United Center doesn't have the same overpowering feel the Stadium had, it still packs a punch, and that familiar "gut rumble" still happens now and again. Of course, that could be a week-old United Center hot dog too.

42

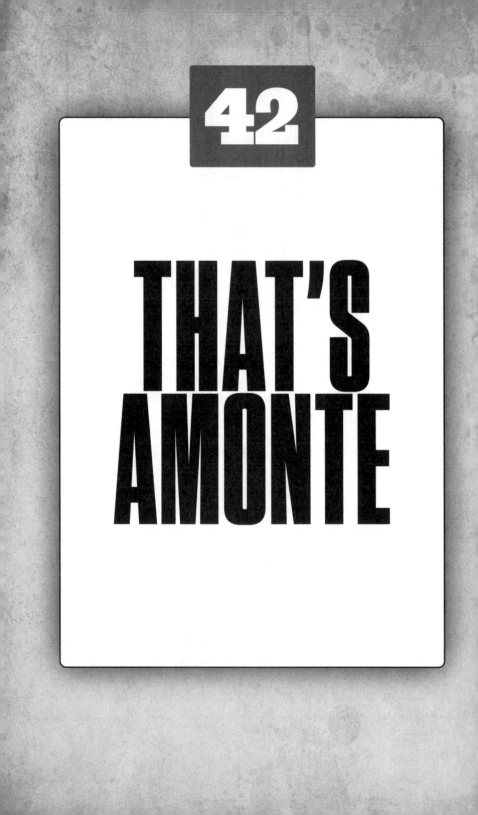

THAT'S AMONTE

Tony Amonte scored 268 goals as a Chicago Blackhawk. Only seven players have scored more for the organization: Bobby Hull, Stan Mikita, Steve Larmer, Denis Savard, Patrick Kane, Jonathan Toews, and Dennis Hull. That's it.

The reason he's often overlooked in Hawks history? Due to poor teammates and a regressive television policy, most of those 268 goals went unseen or simply didn't matter in the long run.

He was the lone superstar during an era of Blackhawks hockey that may have been the most ignored in history.

Amonte was acquired by the Blackhawks on March 21, 1994 (along with the rights to prospect Matt Oates), in the deal that shipped forwards Brian Noonan and eventual Stanley Cup playoff hero Stephane Matteau to the New York Rangers.

Former Rangers GM Neil Smith recalls the days and weeks leading up to the trade. Despite boasting the best record in the league, Smith knew the Rangers weren't a Cup-caliber team.

"There were a number of things that had to be done," Smith recalls. "We felt that the playoffs were different, that a different type of team would win the playoffs, as opposed to who would win in the regular season. I believed in deadline deals, to change your team, to tweak it for the playoffs. I don't believe that the same team that wins in an 82-game schedule wins in a 16-win schedule."

Rangers coach Mike Keenan, someone quite familiar to Blackhawks fans, had always been known as a coach who preferred physical and veteran players on his roster. While Amonte had shown scoring potential early in his career, scoring 84 goals in his three seasons in New York, he struggled to mesh with the often-salty Keenan and his style of play. Meanwhile, Keenan was openly pining to Smith about his desire to acquire Matteau.

"He said all year he wanted 'Matteau, Matteau, Matteau, Matteau,'" Smith said. "But I couldn't trade Tony Amonte even for Matteau; that's what [Blackhawks GM Bob] Pulford wanted. Mike didn't care, he would have traded Amonte straight up for Matteau."

Eventually, Smith was able to convince Pulford to add Noonan to the mix when he included Oates, and the rest is history. The Rangers went on to win the Cup after Matteau's overtime goal in the Eastern Conference Final and Amonte went to Chicago to begin the next chapter of his career.

Amonte was an electrifying player. He played, first and foremost, with speed. He was one of the league's fastest skaters and had the ability to blow by defenders with an ease few players in the league could duplicate. His flowing mullet only amplified the speedy look, with his locks blowing in the wind behind him.

Amonte also played with a swagger and reckless abandon that made Chicago fall in love. While he wasn't overly physical like Jeremy Roenick, he was always willing to go into a corner and win a puck. His stick-handling ability was elite. He mastered a move that I used to call, in my driveway in Oak Lawn, "The Amonte." It was a ridiculously difficult forehand-backhand-forehand switch that occurred so close to the goaltender it seemed almost impossible. Amonte mastered it, humiliating several goalies in the process.

His celebrations were top notch as well. After scoring a hat trick on the annual St. Patrick's "Green Hat Day," in 1997, Amonte gestured to the United Center crowd to let the hats rain down on the ice. They obliged, littering the ice with the emerald chapeaus. An angry but unidentifiable New York Islanders player went so far as to slap shot a hat back into the crowd.

Typical for Blackhawks of that era, Amonte's most memorable moment may not have even occurred in a Blackhawks sweater. In 1996, Amonte, along with his teammate Chris Chelios, represented the United States at the World Cup Tournament. In the deciding third game of the championship, the Americans were facing a Team Canada roster that boasted players such as Wayne Gretzky, Steve Yzerman, Mark Messier, Eric Lindros, and Paul Coffey. With 2:35 left in the third period of a 2–2 game, Amonte found a loose puck at the feet of Team Canada goalie Curtis Joseph and threw his hands up in celebration. Seconds later, Amonte jumped into the arms of U.S. defenseman Derian Hatcher and the legendary moment was born. The Americans would add a pair of empty-net goals and capture the gold medal in a thrilling 5–2 win.

Perhaps Amonte would have had more memorable moments as a Blackhawk if he had better players around him. When he arrived in Chicago, he was joining a pretty good team; Chris Chelios, Gary Suter, Ed Belfour, and his good friend (at the time) Jeremy Roenick were all on the roster. Unfortunately for Amonte, his arrival also occurred right before the core of the team was slowly disbanded. After the Roenick trade, Amonte found some chemistry with center Alexei Zhamnov, who was touted to Blackhawks fans as "Magic Johnson on skates." Zhamnov never lived up to that comparison. He was a solid and underrated player, but Hawks fans could never love him, having been acquired for the beloved Roenick.

After making the playoffs with Chicago for his first three plus seasons, the Blackhawks quickly fell off. Amonte would only have one more playoff opportunity in Chicago. The team had a surprising 96-point season in 2001–02, but lost to the St. Louis Blues in five games, a series in which the Blackhawks could only muster five total goals. In fact, they were shut out in Games 2, 3, and 4.

The playoff defeat was a disappointing and abrupt end to what should have been a celebrated Blackhawks career. Despite being named the captain before that season began, the Blackhawks couldn't come to terms with Amonte on a new deal, and he walked, signing with the Phoenix Coyotes. Just like Eddie Belfour, Jeremy Roenick, and Chris Chelios before him, it came down to the Blackhawks pinching pennies and not paying their top talent.

But Amonte was really all the Blackhawks had left at that time. They let their only truly dynamic player leave and got nothing in return. He was the franchise's last great player for a long time; the team went on to miss the playoffs the next five seasons.

After Amonte left, the organization pinned their hopes to prospects like Tyler Arnason, Mark Bell, and Kyle Calder, or washed-up veterans like Martin LaPointe, Adrian Aucoin, and Curtis Brown. They would not return to the postseason until 2008–09, Jonathan Toews and Patrick Kane's second season.

43

THE DISMANTLING

Despite never winning a Stanley Cup, most of the Blackhawks rosters in the 1990s were close to championship caliber. The team's core of center Jeremy Roenick, defenseman Chris Chelios, and goaltender Eddie Belfour was on par with several Cup winners at the time. Those teams often felt like they were a player or two away from a championship. Because of owner Bill Wirtz's famous frugality, the Blackhawks were unable, or maybe unwilling, to acquire the players who could have put them over the top. That Wirtz stinginess would ultimately destroy the existing core of stars.

Year after year, those Blackhawks teams would battle and fall short. One of their most memorable runs came in the summer of 1996, when they fell to the eventual Stanley Cup champion Colorado Avalanche in six games. Roenick was electrifying, Belfour was a brick wall, and Chelios was his typical, reliable self, but it wasn't enough. The Avalanche dynasty was born.

Meanwhile, things were starting to fall apart in Chicago.

That summer, Roenick was traded to the Phoenix Coyotes for center Alexei Zhamnov, winger Craig Mills, and a 1997 first-round pick that turned into prospect Ty Jones. As with most things with the Blackhawks in the '90s, it all came down to money. Roenick, who was a restricted free agent that summer, was looking for a fair market deal of $4.5 million per season after making $1.4 million the previous season.

"The situation with [Roenick's agent] Neil Abbott and the Blackhawks got to a situation where we basically had no choice," Blackhawks GM Bob Pulford said. "I didn't feel we were going to be able to make a deal, and I don't know if they even wanted to make a deal."

I remember where I was when I heard about that trade. I was working at Memorial Pool in Oak Lawn for the summer. There had been rumors about Roenick possibly being traded, and before the days of Twitter, fans had to sit around and wait for news. One of my friends approached me as if my dog had died, and I knew: JR, my favorite Blackhawk and the reason I love hockey, had been traded. It was the first real gut punch I took as a fan, and there would be many more to come.

Since his retirement, Roenick has expressed disappointment about how the situation played out. "Probably the one thing that's a downer in my career, or is one of my regrets, is that I didn't play my whole career in Chicago," he said. "I couldn't imagine what my life would be right now if that had happened."

The next domino to fall was goaltender Eddie Belfour. On January 25, 1997, the Blackhawks traded Belfour, a two-time Vezina Trophy winner, to San Jose for veteran forward Ulf Dahlen, defensive prospect Michal Sykora, and journeyman backup goaltender Chris Terreri. Belfour was scheduled to become an unrestricted free agent the next summer and was seeking a deal that would pay him $4 million a year.

"We didn't think we'd be able to sign him," Pulford said, repeating a familiar refrain. "We'd probably end up with nothing."

In the days after the trade, head coach Craig Hartsburg opined, "This whole thing was a contract, not Eddie not wanting to be a Blackhawk."

Belfour went on to win a Stanley Cup with the Dallas Stars in 1999. During that Cup run, he posted a 1.67 goals-against average and a .930 save percentage.

The third blow, and the final straw for many Hawks fans, came on March 23, 1999, when longtime captain, Chicago native, and face of the franchise Chris Chelios was traded to the rival Detroit Red Wings. To Blackhawks fans, this was the equivalent of Michael Jordan being traded to the Pistons, Walter Payton being traded to the Packers, Ryne Sandberg being traded to the Cardinals, or Frank Thomas being traded to the Cubs. It was a reality that only existed in nightmares, until it actually happened.

"Never in my life did I imagine I would leave the Blackhawks and play for another team," an emotional Chelios said the day of the trade. "It's not what I wanted."

Before the deal, Chelios had approached the Blackhawks several times looking for an extension. The first ask came in the summer of

1998. When the team denied that overture, Chelios tried again in January of 1999, only to be rejected again. That February, Chelios reached a handshake agreement with owner Bill Wirtz that he would not be traded without being asked. Chelios had one more contract request: a one-year extension for $3.72 million. This would be the Blackhawks' final denial. Chelios instructed his agent, Tom Reich, to begin negotiating a trade and a new deal with other teams. A few days later, Red Wings GM Ken Holland gave Bob Murray the deal he wanted and Chelios was a Red Wing. In return, the Blackhawks received defenseman Anders Eriksson and two first-round picks (defenseman Steve McCarthy and goaltender Adam Munro). The Red Wings quickly signed Chelios to a two-year deal.

The Blackhawks' former captain went on to play 10 seasons in Detroit, capturing two Stanley Cups along the way.

Of course, it would be one-sided to only tell the story from the traded players' perspectives, so let's review what the Blackhawks got in return in these franchise-altering moves.

First, the players acquired in the Roenick trade.

Alex Zhamnov had a solid if unspectacular career with the Blackhawks. He was a two-way centerman and top-level playmaker. In eight seasons with the team, he played 528 regular season games, registering 140 goals and 284 assists. He was named the captain in 2002 and was a major part in winger Tony Amonte's rise to prominence. Zhamnov had zero points in his five playoff games with Chicago.

Craig Mills played 31 games in his NHL career, 27 with the Blackhawks. In those games, he recorded a trio of assists and averaged 5:48 of ice time.

Ty Jones, who the Hawks chose with the 16th pick in the 1997 draft, played 14 NHL games in his career, eight with the Blackhawks in 1998–99. Jones failed to record a point and didn't resurface in the NHL until 2003, when the Florida Panthers gave him a look. He failed to record a point there, either.

Now, let's look at the Belfour trade.

Eddie the Eagle played for nine seasons after he was traded by Chicago. On top of winning the Stanley Cup with Dallas, he went 283–182–69 with 46 shutouts in that time.

Ulf Dahlen, a solid NHL veteran, was 30 at the time of the trade and never projected into the Blackhawks' long-term plans. He played all of 30 games with the Blackhawks, scoring six goals and dishing eight assists, before leaving the NHL for the Swedish Hockey League for the next two seasons. He returned to the NHL in 1999 to end his career with the Washington Capitals and Dallas Stars.

Michal Sykora, the centerpiece of the trade, played 56 games in Chicago. It would be unfair to use his offensive numbers as a piece of analysis, as he was a stay-at-home defenseman, but he finished his Blackhawks career with a minus-six rating. His career fizzled out after short stints with Tampa Bay and Philadelphia after that. He never materialized into the star defender the Blackhawks had envisioned.

Goaltender Chris Terreri performed capably as the backup to Jeff Hackett. In 28 games in Chicago, he went 12–11–4 with a 2.47 goals-against average and a .904 save percentage.

"I do know this was the best deal we could make," Pulford remarked in the days following the trade.

The Chelios deal might be the worst of all. While the former Hawks captain went on to play 578 regular season and 103 playoff games and win two Cups for Detroit, Anders Eriksson never quite got it done on the NHL level. He played 97 total games in Chicago, scoring five goals and adding 36 assists.

Steve McCarthy, who was chosen 23rd overall by the Blackhawks in 1999, struggled with injuries for most of his career. There were flashes of potential, but he just couldn't stay on the ice. He played 134 games over five seasons for Chicago. He had 16 points and a minus-18 rating in that time.

Goaltender Adam Munro, chosen with the 29th pick of the 2001 draft, played 17 NHL games, all with the Blackhawks. He finished with a 4–10–3 record, a 3.30 goals-against average, and an .887 save percentage.

After Chelios' departure, the Blackhawks made the playoffs only once in the next eight seasons. Chicago was among the league's worst teams in the standings and in attendance. They were among the worst franchises in professional sports, and these trades just added to their lowly status. Not only were Roenick, Belfour, and Chelios the team's best players, they were the faces of the franchise and defined that era of Blackhawks hockey. When they were all gone, the Blackhawks lacked any form of identity until Patrick Kane and Jonathan Toews arrived in 2007.

44

"IT WASN'T JUST A GAME... IT WAS A WAR."

Chicago and St. Louis. Perpetual rivals. The cities, separated by 300 miles of one of the most boring stretches of highway in the country, have always clashed in sports.

The Chicago Cubs and St. Louis Cardinals rivalry gets more attention, but the Blackhawks and Blues rivalry has more playoff matchups, more hatred, and more blood.

The Blackhawks and Blues have met in the playoffs 12 times; the Cubs and Cardinals have only played in three postseason series against each other. Their most recent meeting was in 2015, when the Cubs advanced to the NLDS. Before that series, the teams hadn't met since the 1886 World Series.

The most memorable moment of the Blackhawks and Blues rivalry took place during a regular season game at the Chicago Stadium.

The year was 1991, the date, March 17. You may know it as the St. Patrick's Day Massacre.

Before we get into the gory details, some context.

The Blackhawks and Blues had just played each other in three consecutive playoff series. The Blues beat the Hawks in five games in 1988, the Hawks returned the favor in 1989, then beat the Blues again, this time in seven games, in 1990. Nothing breeds contempt like repeated playoff series. Ask the 2010s Blackhawks and Canucks.

Entering this St. Patrick's Day game, the two teams were battling for playoff position and Campbell Conference supremacy. The Blackhawks held a 44–22–6 record (94 points), while the Blues were just three points behind with a 40–22–11 record. A win could give the Blackhawks some distance; a loss would close the gap. Everyone knew the significance of this game.

Funny thing is, no one really remembers the final score as much as the ultra-violence on the ice.

Reviewing the box score is pure comedy.

The antics began with a boarding call two minutes into the game, and the chaos ensued from there. All told, the teams combined for a staggering 278 penalty minutes. Included in that total are 24 two-minute minor penalties, 12 five-minute major penalties, and 17 misconduct penalties. The Blackhawks and Blues had a combined 13 players ejected, including seven Blackhawks, several of whom were fined and suspended.

Fourteen of those penalties occurred at the 6:31 mark of the second period, when Blackhawks winger Steve Larmer high-sticked Blues forward Gino Cavallini. Larmer was given a five-minute major and a game misconduct. The teams were gathered around the Blues goal, yapping at each other, when Blues defenseman Scott Stevens cross-checked Chicago winger Wayne Pressley. The referees didn't see the incident, but the Blackhawks did. Several fights broke out. Thomas locked up with Garth Butcher. Pressley engaged with Jeff Brown.

Then, it happened.

Blackhawks defenseman Dave Manson, one of the most feared players of his era, called Stevens to fight, one-on-one, at center ice.

Take it away, Pat Foley and Dale Tallon:

> Foley: "Now they come together, and they're standing toe-to-toe. Talking it out, now they wrestle. Big left hand by Stevens and a big right by Manson...and two of the toughest defensemen in the league are slugging it out...and now Manson...oh a big right hand by Manson! Stevens trying to hang in there with him. Still they slug away, and now down goes Stevens and here come the linesmen. Stevens and Manson in a slugfest and Stevens got the worst of that...Scott Stevens has been cut badly, it appears around the eye. Dave Manson really handed it to him."

> Tallon: "Stevens getting everything he deserved. He's been instigating all the altercations all night long. He finally got his due in that altercation with Manson. Manson made him pay."

"That was definitely a heavyweight battle," Jeremy Roenick remembers.

After Manson and Stevens' fight, the two head coaches, St. Louis' Brian Sutter—whose quote is the title of this entry—and Chicago's Mike Keenan, came together between the benches. To this day, it amazes me that the two didn't come to blows. Both were known as two of the more hot-headed coaches in the game. Somehow, the conversation remained calm. Then, Chicago tough guy Mike Peluso and Blues defenseman Glen Featherstone dropped the gloves.

Their fight was the final act in one of the most memorable and violent games in NHL history.

As the referees sorted out the chaos, Stadium organist Frank Pellico played the theme from *The Godfather*. It was a fitting tune for the moment.

Foley said, "Whoever is left on the benches better be ready for a lot of ice time. There aren't going to be any players left on the bench available to play after all the misconducts that are going to be handed out."

Foley was right. Seven of the 13 game-misconduct penalties were handed out after the fight.

"We carried that competitive edge right to the line...maybe over the line," Keenan recalled years later.

The Blackhawks won the game 6–2 and went on to win the division and Presidents' Trophy, finishing the season 49–23–8 for 106 points. The Blues fell one point short, ending the campaign 47–22–11 for 105 points.

In the moments following Stevens and Manson's battle, Foley, who was clearly disappointed with how the game had gone, laid a portion of the blame on the Blackhawks.

"We had about as ugly a game as you can have," Foley said in a somber tone. "A game between two of the top teams in the NHL should have been a showcase game. The Blackhawks, playing into their hands, retaliated...taking all sorts of unnecessary penalties and cheap shots."

"That's what rivalries bring out. They say they bring out the best in people...but they also bring out the worst in people," Sutter said.

45

SUPER MARIO SINKS CHICAGO

Once or twice in a generation, a player comes along who seems superhuman. In the 1980s and 1990s, Wayne Gretzky and Mario Lemieux were those players.

In 1991–92, Lemieux's team, the Pittsburgh Penguins, was loaded with Hall of Fame players, and the supporting cast was stacked with All-Stars. Lemieux, Ron Francis, Larry Murphy, Jaromir Jagr, Bryan Trottier, Rick Tocchet, Ulf Samuelsson, and Kevin Stevens made the Penguins one of the deepest teams in the league.

Their Stanley Cup Final opponent, the Chicago Blackhawks, were no slouches either. Jeremy Roenick, Ed Belfour, Chris Chelios, Dirk Graham, Michel Goulet, and Steve Larmer were Chicago's headliners.

The Penguins, who finished the regular season with 87 points, earned the third seed in the Patrick Division, drawing the Washington Capitals in the first round. They took care of the Caps in seven games, then eliminated the Presidents' Trophy–winning New York Rangers in six games. They then swept the Boston Bruins, securing their spot in the Stanley Cup Final.

The Blackhawks held the second seed in the Norris Division and faced the St. Louis Blues in their first-round matchup. They eliminated the Blues in six games after rattling off three straight wins to wrap up the series. The Hawks wouldn't lose another Campbell Conference playoff game, sweeping Detroit and Edmonton in back-to-back series.

Heading into the Final, the Blackhawks had won 11 straight games.

"We believed we were going to take down the defending Stanley Cup champion Pittsburgh Penguins," Chelios recalled in his book, *Made in America*. "We thought we could take them."

When Game 1 began, it looked like Chelios' feelings would be validated. Chicago got out to leads of 3–0 and 4–1, but a team as loaded as the Penguins doesn't go away easily, especially at home.

"I remember our slow start," former Penguins assistant coach Pierre McGuire said. "Our fans were getting a little bit nervous."

Rick Tocchet scored a goal late in the second period, cutting the Blackhawks' lead to 4–2. Then, about a minute later, Lemieux scored from along the goal line, banking the puck off Belfour's backside. A 4–1 lead had suddenly become a 4–3 lead.

"I remember that clear as day," McGuire says. "I remember Mario coming to the bench after he did that saying, 'OK, we're in a good spot,' and he was really energized by it."

Belfour and the Hawks were able to hold off the Penguins until the 15:05 mark of the third period, when 18-year-old Jaromir Jagr scored one of the most unbelievable goals in Stanley Cup history. Jagr found the puck near the left point, surrounded by Blackhawks. Dirk Graham was his first victim; Jagr left him in the dust. Brent Sutter was next. Jagr pulled the puck between his legs, turning the veteran forward into a puddle. Next up was defenseman Frantisek Kucera, who weakly and helplessly poked at the puck; Jagr pulled past him with ease. With all the space he had created, Jagr backhanded a puck over Belfour, and the game was tied at 4–4.

"The stick-handling moves that Jaromir had, I think he stick-handled around three of our guys and all their guys twice," Trottier recalled.

With 17 seconds left in the third, Hawks defenseman Steve Smith took a hooking call. The crucial faceoff, which was to Belfour's left, was won cleanly by Francis, who put it to Murphy at the point. Somehow, the Blackhawks forgot about Lemieux (honestly, how does that happen?). Murphy's rebound came right to Lemieux; Belfour never had a chance. The Hawks had blown two three-goal leads and lost the game.

"The shot from the point by Larry Murphy coming off [of Belfour], right to Mario, bang, empty net; the hockey gods were smiling on us," Trottier said. "You've got to make those kinds of breaks, but you need those things to happen for you."

That win crushed the Blackhawks.

"It was a devastating loss for our team," remembers Chelios. "To me, however, the turning point of the series was Game 2."

"Some of the veteran guys in the Blackhawks dressing room were reminding us not to let one game ruin our series, but I was so low after

[Game 1] that I couldn't dig myself out," Roenick remembers. "I didn't sleep the night before Game 2.

"I played so poorly that Mike Keenan benched me, along with my linemates Michel Goulet and Steve Larmer, in the second period. It was clearly my fault. I was ineffective to the point that I brought down the entire line. I remember Larmer yelling at me constantly because I was embarrassingly out of sync."

The Hawks lost that game 3–1.

"It was impossible for me to believe that benching Roenick's line at that point in the series was a good idea," Chelios said in defense of his friend Roenick. "To me, that was like quitting."

What was Keenan's justification? "Because our players were unable to penetrate their zone, our offensive players gave us very little offensive thrust," Keenan said. "Give full credit to Pittsburgh. They never gave us any room whatsoever. We were trying to wear them down a little."

It didn't work.

The Penguins won the next two games in Chicago, 1–0 and 6–5. The Blackhawks had lost the Cup at the Chicago Stadium.

"It was one of the two saddest days of my career...when we lost to Pittsburgh in the Finals. It was a heartbreaker," Belfour told 670 The Score in 2019. The other, Belfour says, is when he got traded from Chicago.

"It would have been the best thing to win a Cup in your hometown. It's just unfortunate we didn't put up a better fight...we lost four straight," laments Chelios. "I believe we could have won that series against Pittsburgh. However, after what happened in Game 2, I think we lost our swagger. We got swept instead."

46

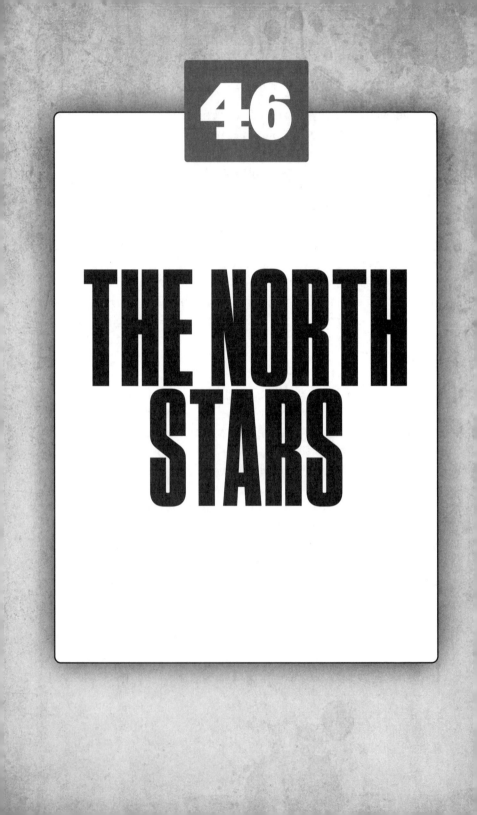

THE NORTH STARS

"Dino sucks! Dino sucks! Dino sucks!"

Yes, one of my first Blackhawks memories was hearing the "Dino Sucks" chant. I couldn't have been older than 11 years old at the time. I was at the Chicago Stadium with my uncle, but I wasn't a hockey fan. Not yet. Still, hearing that was something I'll never forget. I wasn't even allowed to use the word "sucks" at that age. I just remember how angry everyone seemed during that game. Not toward each other, but toward those ugly guys in the green jerseys.

"Those fans were crazy in Chicago," said Dino Ciccarelli, aka the guy the crowd thought sucked. "They ask me to compare the fans and I say [Detroit's] Joe Louis is a beer-drinking crowd. When you go to Chicago Stadium, they drink whiskey. So they're into it and that stadium had such passionate fans. If you weren't ready to play, they got you ready and they motivated me all the time with those dinosaurs and 'Dino sucks' and things like that."

The Chicago Blackhawks and Minnesota North Stars was arguably the best rivalry of the 1980s. In the stretch from 1982 to 1991, the teams met in the playoffs six times, including four consecutive from 1982 to 1985. Just like the Blackhawks and Canucks of the 2010s, nothing breeds contempt like a playoff rivalry.

"It was wicked, it was intense, and there was a true hatred between the two teams," remembered former Hawks center Troy Murray. "There was mutual respect but also a really true hatred. It was the 'Chuck Norris Division' and intimidation was a big part of it."

"Back then, in the old Norris Division, Chicago-Minnesota was the hottest rivalry in the league," Pat Foley said. "Virtually every game there was something amazing happening. There was great talent there, there was great intensity there, and there were some brawlers there, and so you had a little bit of everything."

According to hockeyfights.com, the Blackhawks and North Stars dropped the gloves 151 times over their 349-game history. Blackhawks winger Al Secord had 19 fights against the North Stars alone.

While the Blackhawks and Red Wings rivalry dates to 1926, it never got as violent and hate-fueled as the North Stars rivalry.

In 1989, Minnesota tough guy Shane Churla and Chicago's Wayne Van Dorp got in a pregame brawl. Every player in uniform got involved in one way or another. The melee went on for 12 minutes, as there were no referees on the ice to break up the fracas.

Often, the violence would spill into the crowd. During a 1982 playoff game, a brawl broke out amongst the fans at the Chicago Stadium. The fight was so intense, the game was delayed.

"I was on the ice when that happened and the linesmen would not drop the puck until the fight was under control," Murray recalled. "We just turned around and watched. That was crazy."

Violence aside, the teams played some exciting and memorable hockey. The Blackhawks enjoyed most of the playoff success, winning four of their first five postseason matchups, but the North Stars had the last laugh.

The 1990–91 Blackhawks season was one to remember. The team had hosted the NHL's annual All-Star Game in January and finished the regular season with the league's best point total (106 points). Say what you will about Mike Keenan's coaching, but thanks to the play of Jeremy Roenick, Chris Chelios, Ed Belfour, and others, hockey was back in Chicago, and the city was ready to chase its first Stanley Cup since 1961.

Because of their great record, the Blackhawks drew the highest seed in the Campbell Conference. Their first-round opponent was, you guessed it, the Minnesota North Stars.

Minnesota was not a strong team that season. They ended the regular season with a 27–39–14 record and 68 points, 38 points behind the Blackhawks. A series victory was all but assured for Chicago, a mere formality. The North Stars were nothing but a speed bump on the way to more worthy opponents like St. Louis or Los Angeles, or so everyone thought.

Minnesota eked out a 4–3 overtime road victory in Game 1, made possible by a trio of power-play goals. The North Stars had the man advantage 11 times in the game, and that was the difference.

"The reason we lost that [series] was because of our discipline," Chris Chelios remembers. "All the penalties we took...Keenan...that's how he coached. We got away with it [in the] regular season, but it stung us in the playoffs."

Game 2 went to the Blackhawks 5–2 in another penalty-filled contest. The teams combined for 146 penalty minutes and seven misconduct penalties.

The Blackhawks took a series lead after winning Game 3 by a score of 6–5. The game was much more under control, as the teams combined for "only" 53 penalty minutes and a measly six roughing calls. After the game, North Stars head coach Bob Gainey called out goaltender Jon Casey for allowing two soft goals.

Casey got the message.

Over the next three games, the North Stars dominated the Blackhawks, outscoring them 12–2 and outshooting them 222–159.

Belfour, who led the league during the regular season with 43 wins, a 2.47 goals-against average, and a .910 save percentage, went 2–4 with a 4.08 GAA in the playoffs.

Lifelong Blackhawks fan and 670 The Score radio host Dan McNeil recalls the loss with great detail.

"Reflecting on it makes me physically ill," he wrote in his book. "The Stars succeeded in getting under their skin. They coaxed Chelios and defenseman Dave Manson into dumb penalties. [That year] I was convinced the Hawks were going to be Stanley Cup champs. God damn those North Stars."

The North Stars got all the way to the Stanley Cup Final, ultimately losing to Mario Lemieux's Pittsburgh Penguins in six games.

The Blackhawks wouldn't have a chance to avenge the loss the next season, despite advancing to the Stanley Cup Final, where they were swept by the defending champion Penguins. The Hawks and North Stars never met in the playoffs again; after the 1992–93 season, the North Stars relocated to Dallas, rebranded as the Stars.

"I think [it was] the worst loss that I've ever had as a professional athlete," Roenick recalls. "As I'm walking off the ice, I get hit in the face with a hot dog by this little nine-year-old; talk about taking a beating off the ice and on the ice."

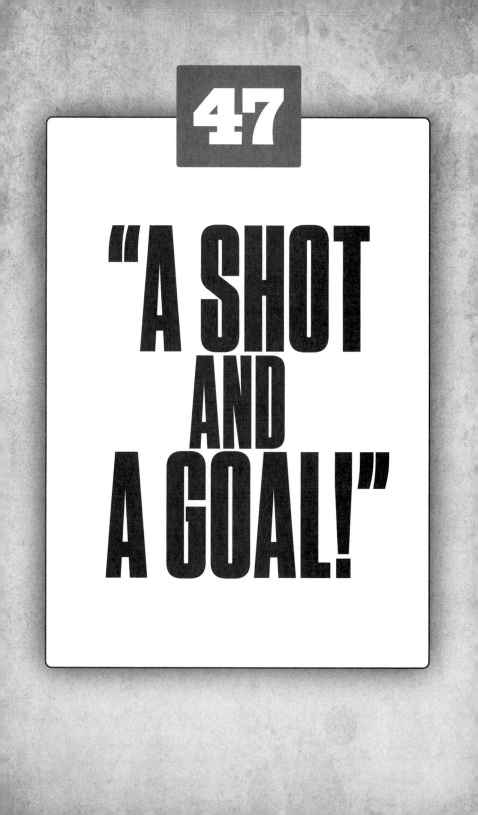

"A SHOT AND A GOAL!"

Before there was Blackhawks television play-by-play man Pat Foley or radio voice John Wiederman, there was Lloyd Pettit.

For a generation of fans, Pettit's "A shot and a goal!" was as famous and memorable as Jack Brickhouse's "Hey-hey!" or Harry Caray's "Holy cow!" Pettit had a premium seat for one of the best generations of Chicago hockey, and he made Blackhawks fans feel like they were sitting beside him the entire time.

"As much as Bobby and Stan brought the Hawks to the forefront, there was a third guy, and it was Lloyd," said Pat Foley.

Pettit's career began as an analyst for Blackhawks hockey before taking over the play-by-play duties in 1963, a job he held through the 1974–75 season.

My Blackhawks fandom began listening to Foley with the radio under my pillow, and from time to time I would hear Foley talk about Pettit on broadcasts. His adoration for Pettit piqued my interest, and I started looking for old tapes of Blackhawks games. We didn't have YouTube back then, but when I did hear them, I was immediately struck by Pettit's voice.

His voice was iconic, even though I had never actively listened to it before. It was somehow familiar, as if his old calls were created in a Hollywood studio. His voice is so pure, his calls are so concise, it would almost be foolish for Hollywood not to use his style as the standard.

Pettit had a gift for elevating the intensity of the moment as the game dictated. Radio listeners knew a scoring chance would be coming based on the level and speed of Pettit's voice. Those like me, who had only heard Foley call a game, quickly picked up on how much Pettit influenced his style.

"He had the gift to make the fastest game in the world come alive," Foley said. "He had the ability to read a play. You could tell by the rise in his voice that something exciting was going to happen before it did."

Foley has adopted and mastered this style of calling hockey himself, honing his skills on the television and radio simulcasts for years. Foley recalled, "One time, after I thanked [Pettit] for the interview, he said, 'You don't know this, but I was standing behind you for a while, and you're very good. You have a chance to make it to the NHL.' Wow, talk about a badge of honor. I felt like I had just been deputized. He'll never know how much that meant to me."

"In retrospect, Lloyd was one of the greatest broadcasters ever in Chicago, or anywhere," said Jack Rosenberg, the former head of WGN Sports, where Pettit called Blackhawks games for 14 years. Pettit also called Cubs games on WGN with Jack Brickhouse. Rosenberg recalls Pettit's versatility, noting he had the ability to read news, ad copy, and call other sports as well as anyone in the industry, but adds that hockey was his true passion.

"He studied the game and kept up on everything," Rosenberg said. "He could articulate it so well and he had such a great set of pipes. Everything just dovetailed. He was a true pro's pro."

Pettit retired from the Blackhawks in 1976 over a dispute about the quality of his broadcast partners.

After walking away from broadcasting, Pettit and his wife, Jane Bradley Pettit, daughter of Harry Lynde Bradley, a Milwaukee-area businessman and philanthropist who founded the Bradley Foundation, returned to Wisconsin full time. In 1976, the couple purchased the American Hockey League's Milwaukee Admirals. They were key players in the construction of the Bradley Center, which served as the home arena to the Admirals, Marquette University's men's basketball team, and the NBA's Milwaukee Bucks, with whom the Pettits held a minority ownership stake, until its closing in 2018. Jane Bradley, along with her husband, donated $90 million to the building's construction. Over the course of her life, Jane donated over $250 million to Milwaukee area causes and community projects.

Pettit was awarded the Foster Hewitt Memorial Award by the Hockey Hall of Fame in 1986.

When the NHL expanded in the early 1990s, the Pettits pursued an NHL franchise. Milwaukee was considered one of the favorites to land a team, but the Pettits pulled out due to overly expensive expansion fees.

Pettit died on November 11, 2003. "The hockey world lost a great friend in Lloyd Pettit," the Blackhawks said in a statement after his passing. "Listening to Lloyd Pettit broadcast a game was like having a front-row seat at the stadium. You felt every hit, blocked every shot, made every save, and were truly involved in the game."

Do yourself a favor and spend a few minutes with Pettit on YouTube. Minutes will turn to hours, and you'll feel as if you're sitting beside him in his perch at the Chicago Stadium.

48

BOB PULFORD

Bob Pulford may never have earned the love of Blackhawks fans. He was the right-hand man of Bill Wirtz for decades and became a representation of what Chicago fans liked least about their franchise. However, if you ask the men who played for him, coached with him, and worked with him, you'll struggle to find a negative word.

Pulford's impact on Blackhawks history cannot be ignored.

His Hall of Fame playing career began, as most hockey careers do, during his childhood. Pulford was raised outside of Toronto and spent his formative years in the Maple Leafs organization. He made his NHL debut during the 1956–57 season and quickly established himself as one of the game's best two-way forwards. He was a hardworking checker, often drawing matchups against the opponent's top players.

"Pulford is one of my private headaches," said Red Wings legend Gordie Howe, "because he has to be classed as one of hockey's greatest fore-checkers. There's a deep knowledge of the game in his fore-checking, hook, poke-check, strength of arms, quickness, the whole bundle of wax."

That knowledge of the game would translate to a long and prosperous post-playing career in the NHL. When he finally hung up the skates after the 1971–72 season, Pulford had played 16 seasons with Toronto and Los Angeles, winning four Stanley Cups with the Leafs. He was also a five-time All-Star, but Pulford's NHL career was just getting started.

He was named the head coach of the Kings the next season, a job he held for five seasons. When he took over in Los Angeles, the Kings hadn't finished higher than fourth in their division in four years. Pulford's first season as coach didn't produce immediate results, but their fortunes improved the next season, when the team finished third with a 33–33–12 record. The next season, in 1974–75, the Kings finished in second place with an excellent 42–17–21 record. Pulford's teams finished in second place the next three seasons.

His success in Los Angeles quickly drew the attention of Wirtz, who convinced Pulford to leave the Kings by offering him the dual role of coach and GM. In his first season in Chicago (1977–78), he led the Blackhawks to a first-place finish after a 20-point increase from the season prior.

Two years later, Pulford relinquished his job as head coach to focus on his GM duties, but he'd be back again and again.

When the Blackhawks struggled, Pulford was often called upon to take over behind the bench, and that usually doesn't happen with winning teams.

Pulford's greatest legacy may be his influence on some of hockey's best and most accomplished coaches and GMs. Sixteen of his former players went on to work in those positions in the NHL, including future Blackhawks GM Dale Tallon and head coach Darryl Sutter.

"You wonder what influence I had on all those players," wondered Pulford. "It had to be something. They all went on and stayed in hockey and some have been very successful."

Tallon, one of the architects of the modern-day Blackhawks dynasty, was in his fourth season as an NHL player when Pulford took over in Chicago.

"He had a reputation of being a disciplinarian, a hard-nosed coach," Tallon said. "He had a real good knowledge of the technical aspects of the game and he was intense. You learned this is what has to be done to be successful. Really be involved; that's basically what we learned from Pully."

"Growing up in western Canada, at that time, you were a huge Toronto fan," Sutter remembered. "I saw him win Stanley Cups on our black-and-white TV, and my dad told me more about Pully than I could ever hope to know. It was funny, when I was with the Hawks and Dad would see me on the road or come to Chicago to see me, he would hang out with Pully."

Other members of Pulford's tree include San Jose Sharks GM Doug Wilson, Montreal Canadiens GM Marc Bergevin, former Penguins coach and NHL analyst Eddie Olczyk, and Anaheim Ducks GM Bob Murray.

"I had [Pulford] so many years as a coach and/or general manager," Murray recalls. "He was a teacher. You have to teach different people different ways, and he was very good at that. He built foundations for your career, things that are always there."

"Pully was the best coach I ever played for," said Olczyk. "Pully was old school, and there was constructive criticism and tough love [but] you always knew exactly where you stood. That's what separated him from other coaches I played for. It made a huge impression on me as a player, as a coach during the time I was in Pittsburgh, and now as a broadcaster."

Pulford served four tours of duty as Blackhawks GM. The first lasted from June of 1977 to June of 1990. He served again from November of 1992 until July of 1997. His third stint ran from December of 1999 until September of 2000. Pulford's last stretch ran from October of 2003 until June of 2005, when he was succeeded by Tallon.

It's important to note that even when Pulford wasn't officially the coach or GM, he was always around, looming over the shoulder of the current coach or threatening to replace the current GM.

As a GM, Pulford's early tenure was very successful. In his first three years with the team, he selected Doug Wilson and Jack O'Callahan in 1977, and Keith Brown in 1979. In 1980, Pulford drafted one of the best classes in Blackhawks history, selecting Denis Savard in the first round, Troy Murray in the third round, and Steve Larmer in the sixth round. The next season, Pulford pulled off the trade that brought Al Secord to Chicago in exchange for defenseman Mike O'Connell.

The Hawks were making the playoffs with regularity, but Pulford's draft and trade successes started to become less frequent. There were a few exceptions, including Jeremy Roenick, Dominik Hasek, and Eddie Olczyk, but there were far too many misses.

Pulford was also the GM in charge of some of the most controversial and infuriating trades in Blackhawks history. As Wirtz's right-hand man, Pulford was (rightfully) the face of unpopular moves, of which there were plenty. Under Pulford's watch, the Blackhawks traded Savard, Larmer, Hasek, Ed Belfour, Roenick, and Chris Chelios. If you ask fans of that era who their most beloved Blackhawks were, you could pretty much copy and paste that list.

One of the most damning statements about Pulford's ability to assess talent late in his career came in a May of 2018 article on The Athletic. Former GM Mike Smith, who ran the Blackhawks from September of 2000 to October of 2003, shared his memories of drafting Stanley Cup hero and All-Star Dustin Byfuglien.

"Not everyone at the Blackhawks liked Dustin," Smith wrote. "Bob Pulford, the senior vice president of hockey, growled by the end of the week that Dustin 'was the second-worst player ever drafted by the Hawks.' Dustin could not be the *worst* pick ever because Pulford had already awarded that distinction to Duncan Keith, who we drafted in 2002. Pulford would turn out to be a real obstacle for Dustin in his quest to reach the NHL."

After Bill Wirtz's passing in 2007, Pulford left his role as senior vice president of the Blackhawks and became a vice president with Wirtz Corporation, a holding company founded by Arthur Wirtz.

To this day, Pulford attends every home game the Blackhawks play at the United Center. His legacy in Chicago is complicated, but as important as any in the team's history.

49

THE VOICE OF THE FANS

There's something about real Blackhawks fans. Even today, after three Stanley Cups during the bandwagon era of the 2010s, there's something counterculture about being a Hawks fan.

When my fandom was blossoming in the mid-1990s, I found myself hungry for more and feeling aggravated, feeling like my team didn't matter. The home games weren't on TV. The Internet wasn't really a thing just yet, at least not in its current form. Even when the teams were competitive, the lack of televised games and the dominance of the Bulls always kept the Hawks in the shadows; on the local news, they were typically relegated to an "...also, the Blackhawks beat the Oilers 3–2 tonight," after minutes of Michael Jordan highlights.

Hawks fans didn't have a voice.

One night, on my way into the United Center for a game, I heard someone yelling, "Programs here! Get the program Bill Wirtz doesn't want you to read!" My ears perked up. You see, in the mid-1990s, I was finding myself, often with punk rock and metal. The concept of "sticking it to the man" was something that very much appealed to me, as full of shit as I was. No one represented "The Man" more than Bill Wirtz. After all, he was the reason for our misery. I made a beeline toward the vendor and purchased my first issue of *Blue Line*.

Blue Line was a publication run by Chicago lawyer Mark Weinberg from 1991 to 1998. I had found my program. It was everything I'd been searching for. Profane cartoons about Wirtz and Bob Pulford, hateful comments about that evening's opponents, foul-mouthed game previews. It was incredible. It was as if the program was written for me alone. The *Chicago Tribune* described *Blue Line* as "...a cross between *Mad* magazine and *Hockey Digest*, with a touch of *Hustler*'s perverse and crude humor."

"I always saw the *Blue Line* as something more than being about fandom," Weinberg says. "I always wondered why there wasn't something good to read about the game."

Weinberg came through. From its satirical humor to its in-depth coverage of the opponent, every adult fan was covered.

Needless to say, the team wasn't in love with the idea.

"The Blackhawks hated the fact that we did this program that made merciless fun of their ownership and their team," Weinberg recalls. "We were the only thing the Blackhawks didn't own at the United Center. They did everything they could do to intimate us away from selling our program on the public sidewalk, including having me arrested three times." Weinberg collected a total of $75,000 from the Blackhawks after his arrests. "The first time, I didn't know enough to get money for the false arrests or the malicious prosecution, but the second time I got $15,000 for it and the third time I got $60,000. For me it was very lucrative when the Blackhawks would sic the United Center security or the cops on me."

In 1998, Weinberg, reading the tea leaves of how bad the Blackhawks were about to be, knew it was time to pull the plug on the publication.

"We were always more popular than profitable," Weinberg says. "When there's 20,000 people at a game, there are maybe 10,000 true hockey fans, but when there are only 15,000 total at a game, you're lucky if there are 5,000 real hockey fans. We did some of the best sports satire around. If everybody who read it bought it, we'd have a business. But you get four or five people who come to a game and they buy one copy and pass it around."

Alas, *Blue Line* was gone. Fortunately for Blackhawks fans, Internet message boards were just taking off. One of my favorite boards, BlackhawkZone.com, was my haven for hockey conversation, and a site that challenged me to look at the game from a different angle. Yes, the angle was typically cynical, but what else should be expected from Blackhawks fans of that era?

My discovery of BlackhawkZone.com coincided with me entering the workforce out of college. I didn't have a home or many expenses at the time, so with my old Lewis University ID, I'd go to every Hawks game on the $8 student discount. All the "BHZ" people, my wife and I included, would sit in Section 329 of the United Center for every game. There, I made lifelong friends with whom I had no other connection than the message board. We'd head to Stanley's Kitchen & Tap on Sedgwick after every game (typically a loss) and see players hanging out there. We were groupies, in a way. The Hawks were our beloved misfit punk band.

Hunt, CP, Wendy, Heather, Frank, and Jim C are all people I remain in touch with (admittedly not as often as I'd prefer) all these years later. Many of us were priced out when the Blackhawks exploded onto the scene in the 2010s, but it was a small price to pay to see our team, the team we suffered for and with for decades, hoist the Stanley Cup three times over the course of five seasons.

Even with message boards on the scene, the lack of a tangible, physical fans program still felt like a huge void to Hawks fans like me.

THE DEAN OF THE BLACKHAWKS BEAT

For many of my formative years as a Blackhawks fan, coverage was difficult to find. It felt like many of the writers assigned to the beat viewed the Hawks as a stepping-stone to a better gig, like covering the Bears, Bulls, Cubs, or White Sox.

The *Daily Herald*'s Tim Sassone was the exception.

Tim covered the game he loved with passion, honesty, and a deep knowledge of hockey from 1988 until his death on March 25, 2014.

"Tim was a true professional," *Daily Herald* sports editor Tom Quinlan said. "He loved hockey. He loved the Blackhawks, but he knew how to do his job as a beat writer in a competitive environment."

"He was the authority on this beat," said the *Chicago Tribune*'s Chris Kuc. "It was a fun dynamic to be in direct competition with somebody and be friends with them at the same time. Tim was really able to balance that very well."

Personally, Sassone was an idol. When I began semi-covering the Blackhawks for 670 The Score in 2008, he was larger than life. It took all my nerve to introduce myself to him—well, if I'm being totally honest, I never actually found the nerve. Tim came up to me first and complimented my coverage. I was nearly speechless.

I never got over that feeling of adoration. Tim was everything I wanted to be.

Rest in peace, Tim Sassone. You are missed every day.

Then, during Game 3 of the 2008 series between the Blackhawks and Sharks, Sam Fels had an idea. He was going to fill that void.

"Basically, I had watched the '07–08 Hawks, Toews and Kane's first year, and felt everything I used to feel about being a Hawks fan," Fels recalls. "It had been so dark and miserable for so long, and suddenly I just thought of it, and I knew that many others were rediscovering their Hawks fandom they had sworn off, and for many it was a big part of being a Hawks fan/game experience."

Fels named his new publication *The Committed Indian*, an homage to then head coach Denis Savard's "Commit to the Indian" speech after a disappointing game in January of 2008. "It felt like the time and place and I could be the guy to do it," Fels says. "Luckily, it worked out."

The first issue of *The Committed Indian* was published on Halloween in 2008, a fitting date given the publication's love of heavy metal and punk music. Unlike Weinberg, Fels never got any pushback from the organization.

"My first ticket rep with the Hawks asked for his own subscription on his personal email so the Hawks wouldn't know. I know some within the organization saw it, but I never heard anything," Fels says. "They never had me arrested though, which is cool. I think we were too small-time for them to pick any fights with us. There was nothing to be gained for them to do so, and they would only give me more publicity and stronger standing if they did."

Fels and his crew printed the program until the 2016 playoffs. These days, the rag lives online only, and is called Faxes from Uncle Dale.

"The eight years I did the actual program were the best of my life, and it's not even really close. I went back and read some of my early programs while writing [my] book, and though the actual writing is awful and the editing even worse, it's amazing to see how much fun I was having," Fels remembers fondly. "It was never work."

Fels' book, *Madison St. Station*, was born from an intention to put a bow on his previous work. "I didn't want to do the program anymore," Fels says, citing the financial and physical demands of a game-day program, "but I wanted to wrap it all up in some way, and that felt the right way to do it. Nick Hornby's *Fever Pitch* is one of my favorite books, so it seemed cool to try and do my own."

I'm not much of a reader myself; my ADD kicks in and I read words with no recollection. But I read Sam's book cover to cover in a matter of days. Fels also wrote the book as a tribute to his late brother Adam, with whom he shared dozens of hockey and life memories.

"I felt like it would be the story for a lot of Hawks fans my age and how these things intersect with our entire lives. I don't know if it became all those things, but I did my best," he said.

50

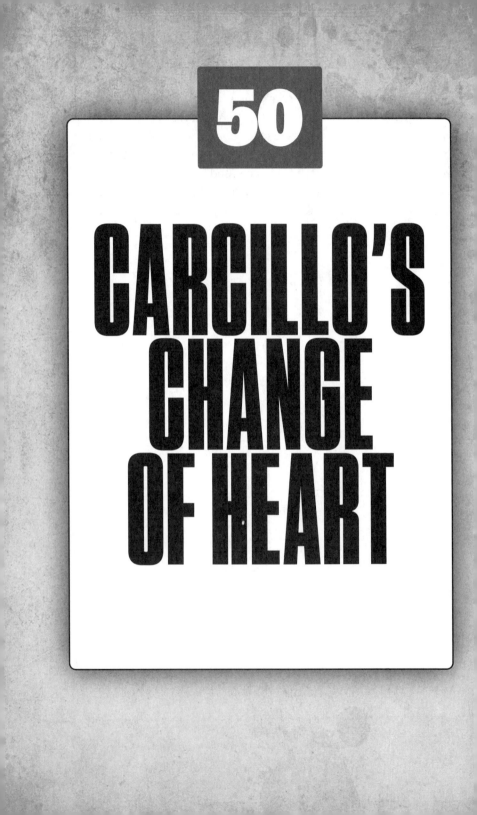

CARCILLO'S CHANGE OF HEART

Daniel Carcillo's career as a Blackhawk was short-lived. In two stints with the team, the rugged winger appeared in 90 games. He scored eight goals, picked up 14 assists, and piled up 147 of his 1,233 career penalty minutes.

"When you come into the league, you want to make a name for yourself," Carcillo said. "Not everyone is a top-six forward, so you have to do other things that people take notice. If one of those things is when someone is taking liberties, you're going to step up and answer the bell and not let them do that. I kind of figured that out early."

Carcillo was an agitator, a pest, a fighter, and a player who often crossed over the line of what was acceptable. During his nine-year career, he was suspended nine times for 32 total games. As Greg Wyshynski pointed out in a 2015 column titled, "Why Does Daniel Carcillo Still Have a Job in the NHL?" Carcillo was suspended once for every 42 games he played.

But everything changed for Carcillo on February 15, 2015. That was the day Carcillo received the news that his former teammate and friend Steve Montador had passed away.

"I'm about to walk into the room to get dressed. My phone is ringing off the hook," Carcillo tweeted years later. "I answer. It's a friend crying on the other line saying, 'Steve's gone. Steve's gone.'"

Montador, who had suffered several concussions over the years, died from complications of extensive chronic traumatic encephalopathy, also known as CTE. In fact, there were at least 15 documented concussions on his NHL file, including four within three months in 2013 while Montador was a member of the Blackhawks.

Exactly seven months after Montador's passing, Carcillo announced his retirement in a column on The Players Tribune.

"Today, I'm retiring from the National Hockey League," Carcillo wrote. "My immediate goal is to help athletes transition to the next phase of their life—whether it's continuing education, finding internships with companies, or networking with other athletes who are dealing with the same issues. My mission is to help guys who are dealing with anxiety, depression, and uncertainty about their future. Not down the line, not next week, but right now."

Carcillo delivered, founding the Chapter 5 Foundation.

The Chapter 5 Foundation serves many purposes for athletes transitioning to life after sports, from dealing with post-concussion syndrome, substance abuse, anxiety, and depression to financial planning, résumé building, and networking. Carcillo points out that not everyone involved in Chapter 5 needs treatment for post-concussion syndrome.

Carcillo has also been a vocal critic of what he calls "the league of denial." "This is the only professional sports league that continues to deny [the link between traumatic brain injuries and CTE]," he said, "and because they deny it, they're killing people."

Is the NHL truly denying the connection? Here's what NHL commissioner Gary Bettman had to say in May of 2019: "I don't believe there has been, based on everything I've been told—and if anybody has information to the contrary, we'd be happy to hear it—other than some anecdotal evidence, there has not been that conclusive link."

Despite the pushback, Carcillo hasn't been deterred in his battle. In June of 2018, Carcillo, along with former Blackhawks defenseman Nick Boynton, filed a lawsuit against the NHL. In the suit, Carcillo and Boynton claimed that they had both suffered several concussions during their NHL careers, but were never educated as to the long-term effects of repeated head trauma. The suit accused the NHL of withholding information from players of their era, and that players could continue practicing and playing despite head injuries.

"I'm doing this on behalf of all former NHL players that are struggling with the difficulties of transitioning from a life in the NHL with brains that have been damaged," Carcillo said in a statement. "Players today are still being denied proper care for concussions. It's time for the NHL to finally acknowledge that serious, permanent damage can be done if head trauma is ignored or neglected."

In November of 2018, the NHL reached a settlement on a separate suit, awarding $18.9 million to 300 players who sued the league.

Carcillo called the settlement a joke, condemning the fact that NHL and NHLPA doctors would be deciding eligibility for the benefits. Carcillo also pointed to the NFL's much bigger settlement, which covers more than 20,000 retired players. Lawyers expect payouts to exceed $1.5 billion over the next six decades. In fact, as of October of 2018, the NFL concussion lawsuit claims panel had approved more than $500 million in awards and paid out $330 million.

Concussions and mental health aren't Carcillo's only causes.

In November of 2018, Carcillo revealed that in 2003, he had been the victim of severe and extreme hazing and abuse while a member of the Sarnia Sting of the OHL. Carcillo described being beaten with a sawed-off goalie paddle on a daily basis, as well as being forced to endure a "shower train," where rookies would take turns being urinated and spit on by veteran players.

"There's no stopping me [sharing these stories]. This sport and that culture has taken a lot from me," said Carcillo.

In the fall of 2019, Calgary Flames head coach Bill Peters was forced to resign from his post after former Blackhawks prospect Akim Aliu accused the coach of using racial slurs in his presence during their time together in Rockford, home of Chicago's AHL affiliate. In the storm of the story, Carcillo spoke to Aliu.

"It's upsetting to hear," Carcillo said in an interview with CBC. "I know Akim. He's had a really, really hard career. He's had a hard road and a lot of trauma and he's been taken advantage of by a lot of people."

"You believe in these coaches because these coaches can help you achieve your dreams," Carcillo said. "They prey on young men's dreams. If you say a word, all of the work and time and energy and sweat and blood is all for naught. So you do whatever they tell you to do and take whatever abuse they throw your way. You shut up."

In the days following Aliu speaking out, several other coaches, including Chicago assistant Marc Crawford, were called out for extreme verbal and physical abuse.

What does Carcillo say to those who believe he's just seeking attention?

"I just want to make sure that people understand these uncomfortable truths. That parents understand what really goes on and that it happens way more often than just me talking about it," he said.

In January of 2020, Carcillo founded Made Plant Health, which grows and manufactures organic, minimally processed CBD capsules.

"I regained my brain health and my brain atrophy in seven months. I am all about minimally processed and equitable access," Carcillo says. "We are specifically targeting brain health."

However you feel about Carcillo and his tactics on the ice, he has certainly affected change. Change is never comfortable. Change is never easy. But in situations like this, change is necessary.

[Sources]

Special thanks to Steve Rosenbloom and Barry Rozner for their guidance and advice during the writing process.

Chapter 1

https://www.hhof.com/htmlSpotlight/spot_oneononep198303.shtml

Mikita, Stan, and Bob Verdi. 2011. *Forever a Blackhawk*. Chicago: Triumph Books.

Chapter 2

http://www.espn.com/espn/eticket/story?page=110421/missingpuck

https://theathletic.com/1211549/2019/09/15/i-had-no-idea-what-was-going-on-oral-history-of-patrick-kanes-2010-stanley-cup-clinching-goal/

Chapter 3

https://www.chicagotribune.com/sports/blackhawks/ct-flashback-bobby-hull-blackhawks-spt-0719-20150718-story.html

Hull, Bobby, and Bob Verdi. 2010. *The Golden Jet*. Chicago: Triumph Books.

Murray, Derik, dir. *Legends of Hockey*. 2001. Opus Pictures.

Chapter 4

http://www.nhl.com/ice/m_news.htm?id=369824

https://www.denverpost.com/2007/10/19/blackhawks-get-2-late-goals-to-beat-avalanche-5-3-after-blowing-3-goal-lead/

https://www.youtube.com/watch?v=ExMOwtBCz_g

Chapter 5

https://www.sportsnet.ca/hockey/nhl/kane-savard/

https://www.youtube.com/watch?v=wQPleDNib9A

Lazerus, Mark. 2017. *If These Walls Could Talk: Chicago Blackhawks: Stories from the Chicago Blackhawks' Ice, Locker Room, and Press Box*. Chicago: Triumph Books.

Spittin' Chiclets. Podcast. "Episode 213."

Chapter 8

https://www.nhl.com/video/nhl100-chris-chelios/t-277350912/c-48790103

https://www.hhof.com/htmlInduct/ind13Chelios.shtml

https://www.chicagotribune.com/news/ct-xpm-1990-07-01-9002250804-story.html

Chapter 10

https://www.nbcsports.com/chicago/video/inside-look-tony-esposito-part-1
https://www.nhl.com/video/esposito-on-iconic-mask/t-277350912/c-52421903
http://www.legendsofhockey.com/Legendsofhockey/Tony%20Esposito/ate-the%20mask.htm
https://www.nhl.com/news/tony-esposito-reveals-stories-behind-legendary-goalie-mask/c-290451266
https://www.youtube.com/watch?v=UajHySJ51JM
https://www.youtube.com/watch?v=geb_91x9CGc

Chapter 12

http://www.fundinguniverse.com/company-histories/wirtz-corporation-history/
Smith, Bryan. 2018. *The Breakaway: The Inside Story of the Wirtz Family Business and the Chicago Blackhawks*. Evanston, IL: Northwestern University Press.
Verdi, Bob. 2000. *Chicago Blackhawks: Seventy-Five Years*. San Diego: Tehabi Books.

Chapter 14

https://www.sportsnet.ca/hockey/nhl/how-freakish-keith-became-an-nhl-workhorse/
https://bleacherreport.com/articles/2494683-freak-of-nature-duncan-keith-defying-human-limits-in-chicagos-2015-playoff-run
https://sports.yahoo.com/blogs/nhl-puck-daddy/duncan-keith--the-blackhawks--unstoppable-freak-231713724.html

Chapter 15

https://twitter.com/aieey_yo/status/979541798568841216?s=20
https://www.nbcchicago.com/blogs/madhouse-enforcer/chicago-blackhawks-detroit-red-wings-game-7-209432781.html

Chapter 17

https://www.letsgohawks.net/2017/03/23/throwback-thursday-belfour-loses-his-mind/
https://www.chicagotribune.com/news/ct-xpm-1993-04-26-9304260254-story.html
https://www.nbcsports.com/chicago/chicago-blackhawks/ed-belfour-reflects-fulfilling-childhood-dream-playing-blackhawks

Chapter 18

https://www.youtube.com/watch?v=t_M1v9SXRLY
https://www.nhl.com/news/glenn-hall-100-greatest-nhl-hockey-players/c-283864802
https://theprovince.com/sports/qa-with-mr-goalie-glenn-hall-the-man-threw-up-all-the-time

Chapter 19

https://www.cbc.ca/sports/hockey/jeremy-roenick-retires-from-nhl-1.818002

https://www.chicagotribune.com/sports/hockey/blackhawks/ct-spt-jeremy-roenick-blackhawks-hall-of-fame-rosenbloom-20180724-story.html

https://www.si.com/vault/1989/05/08/119857/toothsome-sacrifice-after-jeremy-roenick-took-a-stick-to-the-choppers-the-surprising-blackhawks-stuck-it-to-st-louis

https://www.chicagotribune.com/sports/hockey/blackhawks/ct-spt-jeremy-roenick-blackhawks-hall-of-fame-rosenbloom-20180724-story.html

Chapter 20

https://www.nytimes.com/2013/06/11/sports/hockey/how-the-national-anthem-turned-into-a-blackhawks-rallying-cry.html

https://www.chicagotribune.com/news/ct-xpm-2001-09-16-0109160039-story.html

https://en.wikipedia.org/wiki/42nd_National_Hockey_League_All-Star_Game

https://www.nhl.com/blackhawks/news/the-verdict-fans-rallied-behind-the-cause-at-1991-all-star-game/c-550706

Chapter 22

https://www.cbssports.com/nhl/news/the-stanley-cup-wasnt-in-the-building-when-blackhawks-won-in-1938/

https://records.nhl.com/history/playoff-formats

https://www.chipublib.org/blogs/post/1938-blackhawks-win-stanley-cup/

https://www.chicagotribune.com/sports/blackhawks/ct-xpm-2013-06-27-ct-spt-0628-1934-blackhawks-history-special-chicag-20130628-story.html

Chapter 23

https://www.blackhawkalumni.com/page/show/787666-about-the-chicago-blackhawk-alumni-

Chapter 24

https://www.sportingnews.com/us/nhl/news/corey-crawford-injury-update-details-chicago-blackhawks-mvp-nhl-standings-central/ac707t7ixjtb1f6niupscz349

https://bleacherreport.com/articles/2067737-ranking-the-biggest-conn-smythe-trophy-snubs-in-nhl-history#slide5

https://www.nbcchicago.com/blogs/madhouse-enforcer/Was-Patrick-Kane-the-Right-Pick-for-the-Conn-Smythe-Trophy--212878881.html

Chapter 27

https://www.chicagotribune.com/nation-world/chi-chicagodays-1961stanleycup-story-story.html

The Forgotten Champs: The Story of the 1961 Stanley Cup Champion Chicago Blackhawks. 2007. Sundown Entertainment.

Chapter 28

http://blackhawkslegends.blogspot.com/2007/03/al-secord.html
https://www.nbcsports.com/chicago/blackhawks/brawls-and-big-goals-al-secord-brought-both-blackhawks
https://www.youtube.com/results?search_query=al+secord+fights

Chapter 30

https://www.chickensoup.com/book-story/34308/70-my-dad-the-coach
https://www.chicagotribune.com/news/ct-xpm-2007-12-25-0712240942-story.html
https://www.nhl.com/blackhawks/news/the-verdict-reay-was-truly-a-players-coach/c-552871
https://www.chicagotribune.com/news/ct-xpm-2004-09-25-0409250169-story.html
https://www.nhl.com/blackhawks/news/blood-sweat-and-cheers-billy-reay/c-632375

Chapter 31

https://www.stltoday.com/sports/hockey/professional/blackhawks-continue-to-struggle-in-outdoor-games/article_b157aa49-4cd9-5280-8679-41ceca51bb29.html

Chapter 33

https://www.madeinchicagomuseum.com/single-post/w-f-mclaughlin
https://www.hhof.com/LegendsOfHockey/jsp/LegendsMember.jsp?type=Builder&mem=B196303&list=ByName
https://www.nytimes.com/2017/06/11/sports/hockey/frederic-mclaughlin-chicago-blackhawks-american-players.html
Verdi, Bob. 2000. *Chicago Blackhawks: Seventy-Five Years*. San Diego: Tehabi Books.
Wong, John. 2005. *Lords of the Rinks: The Emergence of the National Hockey League, 1875–1936*. Toronto: University of Toronto Press.

Chapter 34

https://www.nhl.com/blackhawks/news/the-verdict-hall-induction-emotional-for-olczyk/c-643520
https://www.chicagotribune.com/suburbs/barrington/sports/ct-bcr-eddie-olczyk-barrington-appearance-tl-1031-20191026-4p2lchfzqnd2ronxe752sasc3e-story.html
https://www.nbcsports.com/chicago/chicago-blackhawks/blackhawks-analyst-eddie-olczyk-diagnosed-cancer
Olczyk, Eddie, and Perry Lefko. 2019. *Eddie Olczyk: Beating the Odds in Hockey and in Life*. Chicago: Triumph Books.

Chapter 36

https://deadspin.com/mike-keenan-the-nhls-last-great-asshole-coach-5958837
https://player.fm/series/spittin-chiclets-1550122/spittin-chiclets-episode-223-featuring-chris-chelios
https://www.chicagotribune.com/news/ct-xpm-1990-12-10-9004130062-story.html
https://www.chicagotribune.com/news/ct-xpm-1990-12-11-9004130102-story.html

Chapter 40
https://www.cbc.ca/sports/hockey/fleury-lands-in-chicago-1.340219
https://www.nashvillepost.com/home/article/20448507/nhl-blackhawks-fracas-at-tootsies-garners-national-coverage

Chapter 41
http://lakingsinsider.com/2013/03/25/frank-pellico-and-the-united-center-allen-organ/
https://www.chicagotribune.com/news/ct-xpm-1994-10-20-9410200204-story.html
https://www.nydailynews.com/sports/hockey/history-behind-goal-horn-nhl-ubiquitous-scoring-sound-article-1.2613820
https://www.chicagotribune.com/sports/ct-cb-united-center-things-to-know-20190817-iwid5sdt7zfspbezk4n2drhbqi-story.html
https://www.chicagotribune.com/news/ct-xpm-1994-09-07-9409070059-story.html
https://wgnradio.com/2015/06/19/baz-fratelli-talks-about-royalties-made-from-chelsea-dagger/
http://sportsmockery.com/2014/11/chelsea-dagger-blackhawks-goal-song/

Chapter 44
http://www.hockey-reference.com/boxscores/199103170CHI.html
https://hawktalkhockey.com/2017/03/16/remembering-the-st-patricks-day-massacre-march-17-1991/
http://blog.hockeyworld.com/taking-it-back-to-the-st-patricks-day-massacre/
https://www.youtube.com/watch?v=Y4aNFjr0GK0

Chapter 45
https://www.latimes.com/archives/la-xpm-1992-05-29-sp-130-story.html
https://www.nhl.com/penguins/news/pens-miraculous-comeback-against-blackhawks/c-642727
https://omny.fm/shows/the-bernstein-and-goff-show/parkins-greenstein-eddie-belfour-interview-hour-3
Chelios, Chris, and Kevin Allen. 2014. *Chris Chelios: Made in America*. Chicago: Triumph Books.
Roenick, Jeremy, and Kevin Allen. 2015. *Shoot First, Pass Later: My Life, No Filter*. Chicago: Triumph Books.
Spittin' Chiclets. Podcast. "Episode 223."

Chapter 46
https://www.nbcsports.com/chicago/chicago-blackhawks/alumni-game-preview-jeremy-roenick-excited-rekindle-rivalry
https://www.chicagotribune.com/news/ct-xpm-1991-04-05-9101310487-story.html
https://www.nbcsports.com/chicago/chicago-blackhawks/roundtable-blackhawks-alumni-remember-rivalry-north-stars
McNeil, Dan, and Ed Sherman. 2009. *The Great Book of Chicago Sports Lists*. Philadelphia: Running Press.

Chapter 48

https://chicagolymag.com/web/2016/06/the-legacy-of-bob-pulford/
https://www.hhof.com/htmlSpotlight/spot_oneononep199103.shtml
https://www.hhof.com/LegendsOfHockey/jsp/LegendsMember.jsp?mem=p199103&type=Player&page=bio&list=

Chapter 49

https://www.chicagotribune.com/news/ct-xpm-1997-11-30-9711300025-story.html
http://orphanradio.podbean.com/mobile/2012/05/16/a-conversation-with-mark-weinberg-publisher-of-the-blue-line-1991-98/

Chapter 50

https://www.cbc.ca/sports/hockey/nhl/daniel-carcillo-hockey-culture-1.5376092
https://www.chicagotribune.com/sports/ct-spt-nhl-concussion-lawsuit-20181112-story.html
https://www.secondcityhockey.com/2018/6/22/17494618/chicago-blackhawks-nick-boynton-daniel-carcillo-lawsuit-nhl-concussion-brain-injuries
https://www.facebook.com/670TheScore/videos/daniel-carcillo-talks-hawks-chapter-5-foundation-w-danny-parkins/10155612659428543/
https://www.chicagotribune.com/sports/blackhawks/ct-steve-montador-concussion-lawsuit-20151208-story.html
https://www.cbc.ca/sports/hockey/nhl/carcillo-hazing-hockey-ohl-1.4920922
https://www.secondcityhockey.com/2015/9/17/9345373/daniel-carcillo-announces-retirement-in-moving-tribute-to-steve-montador
https://www.theplayerstribune.com/en-us/articles/daniel-carcillo-retirement
http://www.chapter5foundation.com/about-us/